Dandelion

Phonics Instructional Manual

Catch-up

PhonicBooks®

DK Learning

Produced for DK by Westchester Education Services

Publisher Sarah Forbes
Managing Editor Katherine Neep
Managing Art Editor Sarah Corcoran
Senior Editor Amelia Jones
Production Controller Isabell Schart
Production Editor Shanker Prasad

First American Edition, 2024
Published in the United States by DK Publishing,
a division of Penguin Random House LLC
1745 Broadway, 20th Floor, New York, NY 10019

24 25 26 27 28 10 9 8 7 6 5 4 3 2 1
001–344994–Oct/2024

Published in Great Britain by
Phonic Books, an imprint of Dorling Kindersley Limited

A catalog record for this book
is available from the Library of Congress.
ISBN 978-0-5938-4854-8

www.dk.com

Printed and bound in China

CONTENTS

INTRODUCTION

WHAT IS PHONIC BOOKS?

Phonic Books specializes in publishing systematic synthetic phonic books for beginner and catch-up readers.

The company was founded in 2006 by Wendy Tweedie, Tami Reis-Frankfort, and Clair Wilson, three special needs teachers passionate about teaching all children to read. Using their expertise, they set about developing phonic reading books for young children and older readers.

Following demand from customers, the range has extended from the initial 10 titles to over 300 today, and is continuing to grow. Our US range of books caters for students in Pre-K and Kindergarten to older readers in Middle School.

With a growing reputation for quality and effectiveness, our books are now used by schools, tutors, and parents in the US and 40 countries around the world.

HOW TO USE THIS MANUAL ?

The Phonics Instructional Manual Catch-up is organized into three main parts. The first part introduces foundational concepts and prevalent teaching strategies in phonics instruction.

In the second part, the focus shifts to the practical elements of the Phonic Books program. It provides an overview of the program, a scope and sequence, guidelines for lesson planning, complementary teaching methods, and strategies for differentiation providing teachers with the necessary tools for effective teaching.

The third section of the manual forms its core: the lesson plans for the Phonic Books program for catch-up readers. The first set of lesson plans, Moon Dogs Set 1, focuses on the alphabet's sounds articulated in CVC words and expands to include double consonants. Progressing to That Dog!, learners are introduced to an expanded set of CVC words, alongside CVCC words, consonant blends, and digraphs. In the next set, the lesson plans explore Vowel-Consonant-e (VCe) spellings, guided by the Moon Dog VCe Spellings series. In the next set of lesson plans, the Moon Dogs Vowel Spellings series, students are introduced to alternative vowel spellings. The final set ends with the Island Adventure series, which delves into further alternative spellings for vowel sounds and features longer texts.

Although the manual primarily centers on these four series, its lesson plans are designed to be adaptable to any series from the Phonic Books catalog. The manual includes a diagnostic assessment tool that pinpoints which phonics skills require attention, and then offers reading suggestions to create a personalized learning journey. Through identifying a student's strengths and areas for improvement, educators and parents can choose the most appropriate series as a starting point. They can then teach or adjust the lesson plans to align with their student's skill level.

Each series introduces a new phonic focus, while reinforcing previously acquired knowledge and high-frequency words. These lesson plans are not only adaptable but also compatible with various US phonics curricula.

Teachers can access curriculum mapping grids on the Phonic Books website to align these lesson plans with their specific curriculum requirements.

A glossary is provided at the back of the book.

ADVICE FOR TEACHERS

Decodable books, such as the Phonic Books series, are important for teaching foundational skills. These controlled texts allow the student to practice their phonetic knowledge and read successfully at each developmental stage. They also encourage students to use the most effective and reliable reading strategies for life (sounding out words).

Many teachers find they need additional resources to support students who are beginner and older readers. For example: students may face challenges with letter sounds, phonemic awareness, retaining phonics lessons, or have gaps in their vocabulary. The Phonic Books series, encompassing both decodable readers and activity books, can be used as a classroom resource in various ways: with a whole class, in reading groups, or in 1:1 reading support.

The Phonic Books website also contains many free teaching resources as well as advice for teachers. The resources include phonics infographics, teaching strategies, word lists, word chains, dictation exercises, phonic code tables, high-frequency word charts, game templates, and progress trackers. The website also includes assessment tools such as reading assessments and assessment cards, alongside advice on how to use the Phonic Books series in different educational settings.

SUPPLEMENTARY RESOURCES

This instructional manual primarily focuses on the Moon Dogs, That Dog!, and Island Adventure series of decodable books and the corresponding activity books. However, Phonic Books has a wealth of parallel books and supplementary materials to help teachers with their phonics instruction. More details are provided in the program overview section on page 19.

FOUNDATIONS OF PHONICS

WHAT IS PHONICS?

Phonics is a method of teaching reading and writing that focuses on the relationship between sounds (**phonemes**) and their spellings (**graphemes**). It involves teaching students to connect sounds in words with letters or groups of letters and to blend these sounds to form recognizable words.

English has a complex writing system. It has 26 letters but roughly 44 sounds (this depends on pronunciation), leading to roughly 160+ different spellings for these 44 sounds. In order to teach them in a methodical way, they have been organized according to the 44 sounds they spell. This organization is called the **Alphabetic Code** or **Phonic Code**. Research has shown that students who are taught these letter–sound correspondences will learn to decode words more successfully. Decoding underpins fluency, and fluency underpins reading comprehension.

Unlike languages with "transparent" writing systems like Italian and Spanish, where letters spell sounds in a simple and consistent way, English has an "opaque" writing system. Its complexity is a result of layers of adopted words from different languages and shifts in pronunciation over many years. Consequently, learning to read in English is more time-consuming, often taking years compared to the few months it might take in more phonetically consistent languages.

Where to start in phonics instruction

All phonics programs start with the sounds of the letters of the alphabet. The Phonic Books program starts with the simple principle of one letter corresponding to one sound. Students initially learn a few letters at a time, building simple words as they progress.

THE ALPHABETIC CODE abc

The **Alphabetic Code** is the framework that shows how the 44 sounds of English are represented by letters and letter combinations.

Key aspects include:

1. 26 letters are used and reused in many different combinations to represent the 44 sounds of speech.
2. A sound can be represented by 1–4 letters.
3. A sound can be spelled in numerous ways.
4. A spelling (or grapheme) can represent different sounds.

Students need to recognize these letter–sound relationships automatically to become fluent readers. Due to the complexity of the code, many phonics programs will first introduce a simple part of it and later the more complex letter–sound correspondences.

CHALLENGES IN THE ALPHABETIC CODE

Navigating the complexities of the Alphabetic Code can be a daunting task, especially for students learning English. The Alphabetic Code is marked by a notable disparity between the sounds (phonemes) and the letters (graphemes) used to represent them. This mismatch leads to various challenges.

English uses the same letters to represent different sounds because of the mismatch between the number of letters and sounds. Because of this disparity, letters are reused to spell the extra sounds. For example, the letters 's' and 'h' together spell a completely new sound: /sh/ as in the word "**sh**ip." This is a **consonant digraph**. That wouldn't be such a problem if our Alphabetic Code were simple and straightforward—but it isn't!

Sounds spelled by 1–4 letters

Sounds in English can be spelled by 1–4 letters. In the word "cat," each letter spells one sound. In the word "chip," the consonant digraph 'ch' spells the sound /ch/. Here two letters spell one sound. In the word "night," the vowel team 'igh' spells one sound /ie/. Finally, in the word "dough," the four-letter spelling 'ough' spells just one sound, /oe/.

Multiple spellings for one sound

A further complication is that a sound can be spelled in different ways. For example, the sound /ae/ can be spelled in numerous ways: r**ai**n, m**ay**, c**a**m**e**, th**ey**, w**eigh**, v**ei**l, gr**ea**t, etc. Students need to learn these alternatives so that when they see them within words, they know how to sound them out. And when they learn to encode (spell), students will need to remember which alternative fits in which word.

One spelling, multiple sounds

Not only are there different ways to spell these sounds, but once learned, students find that some spellings can be pronounced in different ways. For example, the spelling 'ea' spells the sound /e/ in "h**ea**d," /ee/ in "m**ea**t," and /ae/ in "gr**ea**t."

These are difficult concepts to teach, and students need a structured system to learn them. This is why it is so important that reading instruction is taught in a systematic and structured way. When taught well, the Alphabetic Code is unlocked and students learn to decode and encode any word.

UNLOCKING THE ALPHABETIC CODE

Demonstrating the mechanics

We begin by illustrating the basic mechanics of the English language: reading from left to right, and understanding how individual letters and their combinations represent distinct sounds in speech.

Teaching the code

We then teach the Alphabetic Code, focusing on specific letter–sound correspondences in the English language.

Neglecting to teach the Alphabetic Code risks depriving students of the key to learning to read and the vast opportunities for learning and exploration it offers.

THE ALPHABETIC CODE

Consonant sound spellings

/j/

j	**j**et
g	**g**entle
ge	bar**ge**
dge	ju**dge**

/n/

n	**n**o
nn	pla**nn**ing
kn	**kn**ow
gn	**gn**at
pn	**pn**eumonia

/z/

z	**z**ip
zz	bu**zz**
s	i**s**
se	choo**se**
ze	snoo**ze**
x	**x**ylophone

/r/

r	**r**at
wr	**wr**ite
rr	ca**rr**y
rh	**rh**ino

/h/

h	**h**ot
wh	**wh**ole

/qu/ (/k/ + /w/)

qu	**qu**een

/t/

t	**t**in
tt	ge**tt**ing
ed	jump**ed**
bt	de**bt**
pt	**pt**erodactyl
te	grani**te**

/x/ (/k/ + /s/)

x	fo**x**
cc	a**cc**ept

/y/

y	**y**es

/ng/

ng	si**ng**
n	pi**n**k

/s/

s	**s**ip
ss	gra**ss**
se	hou**se**
c	**c**ent
ce	voi**ce**
st	ca**st**le

/v/

v	**v**ery
ve	ha**ve**

/ch/

ch	**ch**ip
tch	ma**tch**

/b/

b	**b**ig
bb	ra**bb**it

/th/ (voiced)

th	**th**at

/th/ (unvoiced)

th	**th**in

/f/

f	**f**at
ff	sta**ff**
ph	**ph**one
gh	lau**gh**
ffe	gira**ffe**

/w/

w	**w**ig
wh	**wh**en

/g/

g	ra**g**
gg	ju**gg**le
gh	**gh**ost
gu	**gu**est

/d/

d	**d**id
ed	grabb**ed**
dd	mu**dd**le

/l/

l	**l**ip
ll	fu**ll**
le	app**le**
el	trav**el**
il	pup**il**
al	fin**al**

/sh/

sh	**sh**op
ch	ma**ch**ine
s	**s**ugar

/p/

p	ho**p**
pp	ha**pp**y

/m/

m	**m**an
mm	su**mm**er
mb	la**mb**
mn	Autu**mn**

/k/

k	**k**ite
c	**c**at
ck	du**ck**
ch	**ch**ord

/zh/

s	lei**s**ure
ge	presti**ge**
z	sei**z**ure

THE ALPHABETIC CODE

Vowel sound spellings

/oe/

o	m**o**st
o–e	n**o**t**e**
oe	t**oe**
oa	b**oa**t
ow	gr**ow**
ough	th**ough**
ou	s**ou**l
ew	s**ew**

/i/

i	**i**n
y	m**y**th

/o/

o	n**o**t
a	w**a**s

/ie/

i	w**i**ld
ie	p**ie**
i–e	l**i**k**e**
igh	n**igh**t
y	dr**y**
eigh	h**eigh**t

/ee/

e	m**e**
ee	m**ee**t
ea	s**ea**t
e–e	**e**v**e**
ie	ch**ie**f
y	funn**y**
ey	k**ey**
ei	rec**ei**ve
i	var**i**ation
eo	p**eo**ple

/ae/

a	t**a**ble
ai	r**ai**n
a–e	g**a**m**e**
ea	gr**ea**t
ay	s**ay**
ey	th**ey**
ei	v**ei**n
aigh	str**aigh**t
eigh	**eigh**t

/or/

or	f**or**
our	y**our**
ore	m**ore**
oor	d**oor**
oar	b**oar**d
ar	w**ar**m

'aw'

aw	l**aw**n
awe	**awe**some
a	b**a**ll
al	w**al**k
au	**Au**gust
ough	f**ough**t
augh	d**augh**ter

/e/

e	b**e**d
ea	br**ea**d
ai	s**ai**d
ie	fr**ie**nd
eo	l**eo**pard

/er/

er	p**er**k
ur	t**ur**n
ir	g**ir**l
or	w**or**ld
ear	l**ear**n
ar	coll**ar**
yr	zeph**yr**

/oo/

oo	c**oo**k
oul	c**oul**d
u	p**u**t
o	w**o**man

/a/

a	c**a**t

/ear/

ear	n**ear**
eer	d**eer**
ere	h**ere**

/u/

u	t**u**b
ou	t**ou**ch
o–e	s**o**m**e**
a	**a**bout
o	M**o**nday
oo	bl**oo**d

/ar/

ar	c**ar**

/ow/

ow	c**ow**
ou	**ou**t
ough	dr**ough**t

/oi/

oi	j**oi**n
oy	b**oy**

/ue/

u–e	m**u**l**e**
u	p**u**pil
ew	f**ew**
ue	c**ue**

/air/

air	ch**air**
are	d**are**
ear	b**ear**
eir	th**eir**
ere	wh**ere**
ayor	m**ayor**
ayer	pr**ayer**
ae	**ae**rosol

/oo/

oo	b**oo**t
ue	bl**ue**
ew	gr**ew**
u	s**u**per
ui	s**ui**t
u–e	fl**u**t**e**
ou	s**ou**p
oe	sh**oe**
o	d**o**
ough	thr**ough**

PHONICS CONCEPTS

What is a phoneme?

A **phoneme** is the smallest unit of sound in a word. For example: the word "cat" has three phonemes: /k/ /a/ /t/.

Why do we need phonemes?

Phonemes are essential in learning to read and write because they are the building blocks of words, enabling us to segment and blend sounds to form words. Understanding phonemes helps in the development of literacy skills.

The English Alphabetic Code is based on the 44 phonemes in the English language. The letters of the alphabet represent those sounds with 160+ letter combinations.

When we teach reading, we need to show how the Alphabetic Code works: that the *letters* on the page *spell sounds in words*.

What is a grapheme?

A **grapheme** is a written representation or *spelling* of a sound (phoneme) in a word. A grapheme can be spelled by 1–4 letters.

In a **1-letter grapheme**, each sound is spelled by one letter:

c	a	t
↓	↓	↓
/k/	/a/	/t/

In a **2-letter grapheme**, a sound is spelled by two letters:

sh	o	p
↓	↓	↓
/sh/	/o/	/p/

In a **3-letter grapheme**, a sound is spelled by three letters:

n	igh	t
↓	↓	↓
/n/	/ie/	/t/

In a **4-letter grapheme**, a sound is spelled by four letters:

d	ough
↓	↓
/d/	/oe/

What is a digraph?

A **digraph** is when two letters represent one sound in a word (phoneme).

di	graph
↓	↓
two (from Greek)	to write letters (from Greek)

Therefore, a digraph means two written letters.

A **consonant digraph** is when two letters represent a consonant sound. For example: the letters 's' and 'h' spell the sound /sh/ in the word "ship."

A **vowel team** is when two or more letters represent a vowel sound. For example: the letters 'a' and 'i' spell the sound /ae/ in the word "rain."

What are consonant blends?

Consonant blends are also called **consonant clusters**. These are two or more adjacent consonants in a word that spell two separate sounds. For example, in the word "stop" the letters 's' and 't' spell the sounds /s/ and /t/.

stop

What are Vowel–Consonant–e (VCe) spellings?

A **Vowel–Consonant–e (VCe) spelling** is when the spelling for the vowel sounds /ae/, /ee/, /ie/, /oe/, and /ue/ is split by a consonant:

/ae/	a–e	→	gate
/ee/	e–e	→	eve
/ie/	i–e	→	fine
/oe/	o–e	→	hope
/ue/	u–e	→	cute

What is a schwa?

A schwa is a weak vowel sound in an unstressed syllable.

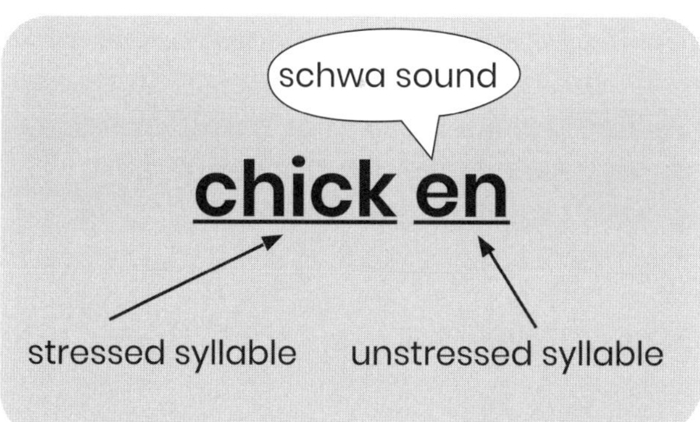

An example of a schwa is 'e' because it is a weak vowel sound in an unstressed syllable. It gets swallowed up when we pronounce the word "chicken," becoming "chickin" or "chick'n." We need to teach students to use their "spelling voice" in order to spell the word correctly and not as they hear it.

LANGUAGE UNITS AND PRINCIPLES

Words to morphemes

There are different ways of looking at a word.

A **word** is a distinct meaningful unit of speech or writing.

Letters are characters used for representing sounds in speech.

Syllables are mouthfuls of words.

Phonemes are speech sounds in words.

Graphemes are spellings of sounds in words.

Morphemes are units of meaning in words.

Distinguishing phonology, phonological awareness, and phonics

Phonology is an area of linguistics that deals with speech sound systems and sound patterns of spoken language.

Phonological awareness is the ability to break down words into smaller parts: syllables (mag net), alliteration (Bobby beetle bounced), onset and rime (m at), and phonemic awareness (m a t).

Phonemic awareness is the ability to identify and manipulate individual sounds in words (to blend, segment, and manipulate sounds).

Phonics is the teaching of:

- letter/sound correspondences for reading and spelling: c a t = /k/ /a/ /t/
- blending of individual letters/sounds for reading: m a t
- segmenting of individual sounds/letters for spelling: m a t

The Alphabetic Principle

The **Alphabetic Principle** is a fundamental concept in phonics instruction.

According to this principle, written letters or graphemes correspond to specific sounds (phonemes) of a spoken language. These sounds come together to form words.

This is crucial for learning to read, as it allows students to decode written text into spoken language.

Mapping words vs learning words by sight

There are two key word recognition strategies in reading: **mapping words** and **learning words by sight**.

Learning a word by shape (sight) is inefficient and clogs up precious memory.

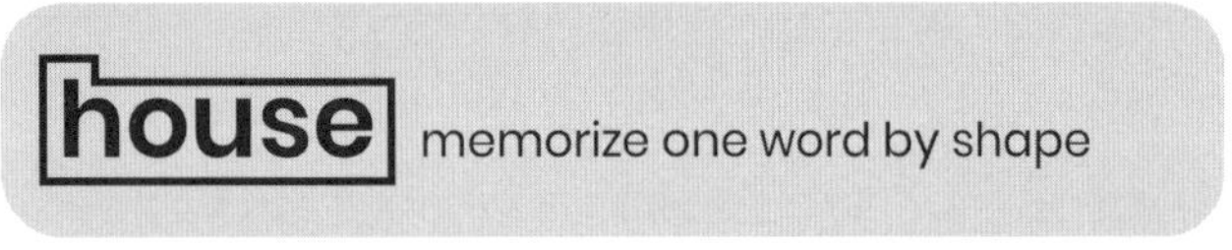

Learning to map words helps readers to generalize and continue to "self-teach" new words.

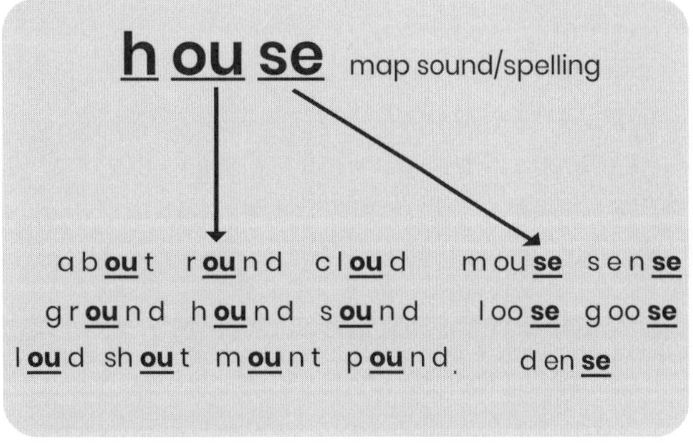

HIGH-FREQUENCY WORDS

High-frequency words are words that appear very frequently in stories and other written texts, such as "or" and "the." It is important for students to learn how to recognize these words quickly and effortlessly.

Many high-frequency words do not follow regular phonetic patterns or are not decodable until students have learned more advanced phonics patterns. This irregularity can make them challenging for students to decode them using phonics rules alone. Therefore, it is important for students to learn these words using different recognition strategies. In some other phonics programs, these words might be referred to as "tricky words," "sight words," or "heart words."

Teaching high-frequency words helps students read more smoothly and focus their decoding efforts on less common and more complex words. Mastery of high-frequency words significantly enhances reading fluency and comprehension, allowing students to become more confident readers.

High-frequency words: teaching by sound, not shape

Teaching high-frequency words by sound rather than shape offers a more effective approach to phonics instruction.

When learning high-frequency words through this method, students not only memorize these words more efficiently, but they also gain skills that are transferable to new, unfamiliar words.

This approach enhances the ability of students to decode and understand a wider range of vocabulary, supporting their overall reading fluency and comprehension.

How to teach students to spell high-frequency words

When we teach high-frequency words as whole words, we are encouraging students to remember them by shape. This method contradicts the phonics approach that explains that all words can be decoded—but some have complex spellings! Unfortunately, many of the common words beginner readers encounter are such words.

So how do we combine phonics with teaching difficult high-frequency words? Build on the knowledge the reader already has and explicitly teach the tricky part.

Here is an example of how to teach the word "car," which contains the phoneme /ar/ that is introduced in Dandelion Readers Level 1 Book 12 in the Phonic Books program.

1. Segment the word into its phonemes (sounds).

car

/c/ /ar/

2. Map the word showing its grapheme (spellings of the phonemes).

c̣ ar

3. Identify the tricky spellings in the word and show familiar words with these spellings.

c̣ ar

4. Ask the student to say the words as they write the word.

'c' 'ar' → car

DECODING AND ENCODING

It is important for teachers to distinguish between the concepts of **decoding** and **encoding**. Decoding involves translating symbols or letters into sounds and words.

Encoding, on the other hand, is the reverse process, where words and sounds are translated into symbols or letters.

For students to understand this reversible code, it's important that decoding and encoding are taught together. This approach helps students understand that "mat" can be segmented into the sounds /m/ /a/ /t/ and spelled out, just as these sounds can be blended together to form the word "mat." By teaching reading and spelling together in the same lesson, teachers can provide a more comprehensive and effective lesson.

The following figure overleaf illustrates how the two essential skills of decoding and encoding work in tandem to form a complete understanding of reading and spelling.

Decoding

(translating symbols/letters to sounds and words)

is the reverse of ⟷

Encoding

(translating words/sounds into symbols/letters)

For students to understand this reversible code, decoding and encoding should be taught together!

mat /m/ /a/ /t/ "mat"

Sound out the words and blend them together into a word.

mat /m/ /a/ /t/ *"mat"*

Sound out the words and blend them together into a word.

Teach reading and spelling in the same lesson!

SYNTHETIC PHONICS VS ANALYTIC PHONICS

In **synthetic phonics** instruction, the reader is taught to sound out individual sounds in a word and blend these sounds together to form the word. This method emphasizes the *synthesis* (blending) of individual sounds into a word. For example, the word "frog" is learned by sounding out each phoneme, /f/ /r/ /o/ /g/, and then blending these sounds to say "frog."

Conversely, **analytic phonics** focuses on teaching readers to break the word up into parts. This begins with an *analysis* of the whole word, which is broken into onset and rime, e.g. 'fr' + 'og' → "frog."

The conclusion based on research, notably Watson and Johnson (2004) and the Rose Report (2006), is that synthetic phonics is the most effective way to teach all children to read.

Analytic phonics often includes using known words as analogies. For example: if you know that "cat" ends with 'at' then you know that "mat" must also end with 'at.'

Systematic Synthetic Phonics

Systematic Synthetic Phonics (SSP) is a method that focuses on the systematic instruction of phonics. In this approach, students are taught to recognize graphemes and their corresponding phonemes. SSP involves a sequenced order of teaching where children first learn simple letter–sound correspondences (like 's' for /s/) and then progress to more complex sound patterns (like 'igh' for /ie/). The method emphasizes the blending or synthesizing of these sounds to read words.

SSP is a highly structured approach that ensures that no phonics elements are left out and each new skill builds upon previously learned skills. This approach is widely considered effective for phonics instruction and is used in many educational systems.

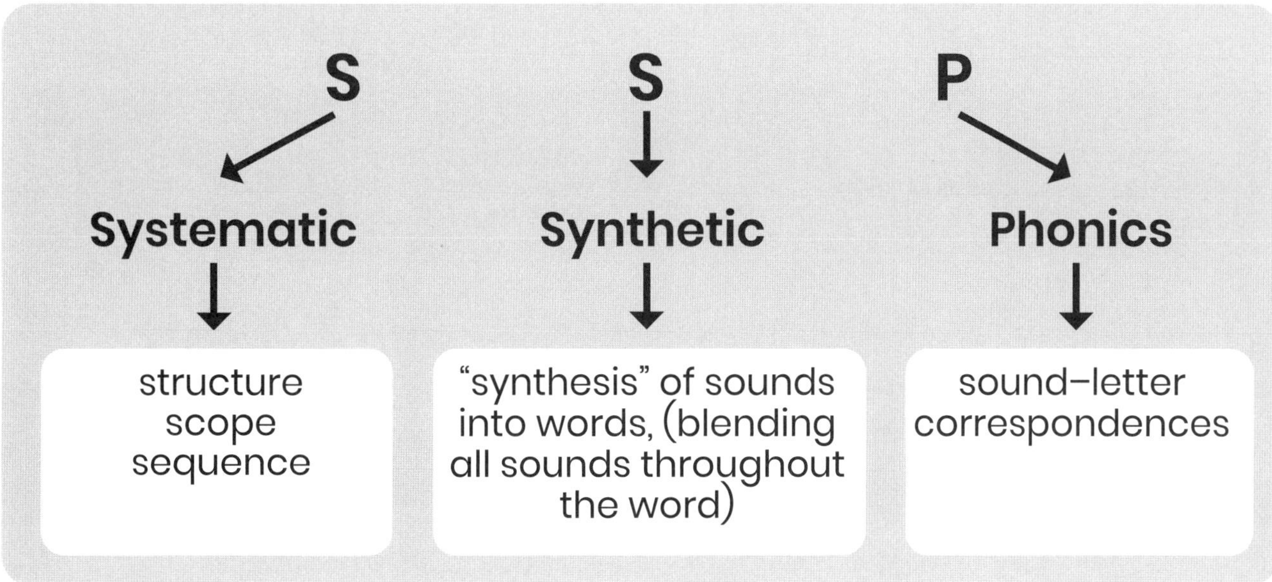

Systematic phonics in reading instruction

Teaching reading through systematic phonics is important because of the complexity of the English Alphabetic Code. To navigate this complexity, teachers should employ a scaffolded pedagogical framework:

- simple to complex: starting with the most basic elements and gradually introducing more challenging concepts
- stair-step progression
- systematic scope and sequence
- practice and consolidation along the way
- cumulative teaching

This methodical approach ensures that learners have a solid foundation, enabling them to confidently tackle the complexities of reading.

PHONEMIC AWARENESS AND READING STRATEGIES

Phonemic awareness: why it matters

Phonemic awareness is a pivotal skill for beginner readers that will play an important role in their journey towards literacy. Research has shown that phonics and phonemic awareness grow in tandem, and the most effective reading instruction teaches phonemic awareness with phonics.

The Simple View of Reading

The Simple View of Reading is a model that demonstrates the view that reading has two basic components: word recognition and language comprehension. This model offers a clear and effective framework for reading instruction.

The use of decodable books, the interaction between teachers, parents, and students, and the transition from learning to read to reading to learn are crucial elements of the Simple View of Reading approach. They shape how students progress towards independent reading across various texts and subjects.

Oral language × decoding = reading comprehension

Oral language

1a What to teach
Language and knowledge enrichment through reading fiction and nonfiction texts to beginner readers

Decoding

1b What to teach
The Alphabetic Code, phonemic awareness, decoding (blending), and encoding (segmenting)

Learn to read

2a Who reads what
Teachers and parents read "authentic texts" to students to enrich oral language, background knowledge, and story grammar.

2b Who reads what?
Beginner readers apply the phonics they have learned in decodable books until they can read any grade text and "authentic texts."

Read to learn

3 Who reads what?
Learners can read all books across the curriculum.

3-cueing vs decoding

The benefits of **3-cueing** versus **decoding strategies** is the subject of ongoing debate in literacy education. While 3-cueing focuses on using context and visual cues to identify words, decoding emphasizes the systematic breaking down of words into their phonetic components.

Decoding is increasingly recognized for its effectiveness in developing strong, foundational reading skills. This approach is grounded in systematic phonics and equips learners with the tools to tackle new and complex words independently. Conversely, 3-cueing relies on guessing that can lead the reader away from the text.

INSTRUCTIONAL MATERIALS

The role of decodable books in reading instruction

Practical application

Decodable books serve as practical tools where students apply their phonics knowledge in a controlled text. They offer students an opportunity to practice the phonic knowledge and skills they have learned. When students are taught mathematics, they are given exercises to practice what they have been taught, in order to internalize the new learning and to develop automaticity. Decodable texts perform a similar role in reading instruction.

Strategy and success

Based on the Science of Reading, decodable books focus on the decoding of graphemes and blending them into words, which steers students away from guessing. The controlled vocabulary is tailored to the phonic skills of the students, providing immediate reading success and boosting their confidence.

Focusing on a target phoneme (sound) or grapheme (spelling)

Decodable books target specific phoneme–grapheme correspondences, allowing students to practice reading with a focus on newly taught sounds and spellings. As students progress, the complexity of words in these books increases, and they start to look similar to more traditional reading books.

Motivation and independence

The sense of achievement students gain from successfully reading these books increases their motivation to continue learning to read, embodying the sentiment, “I can do this!”

Detractors of decodable books confuse the purpose of these books. They are not created to compete with wonderful children’s literature, but are used for only a short time, as “training wheels” to help children develop good decoding skills. As students’ proficiency in decoding grows, these supports can be removed, enabling them to take off and explore more complex reading materials. This means they can move on to and enjoy independent reading of rich and varied children’s literature.

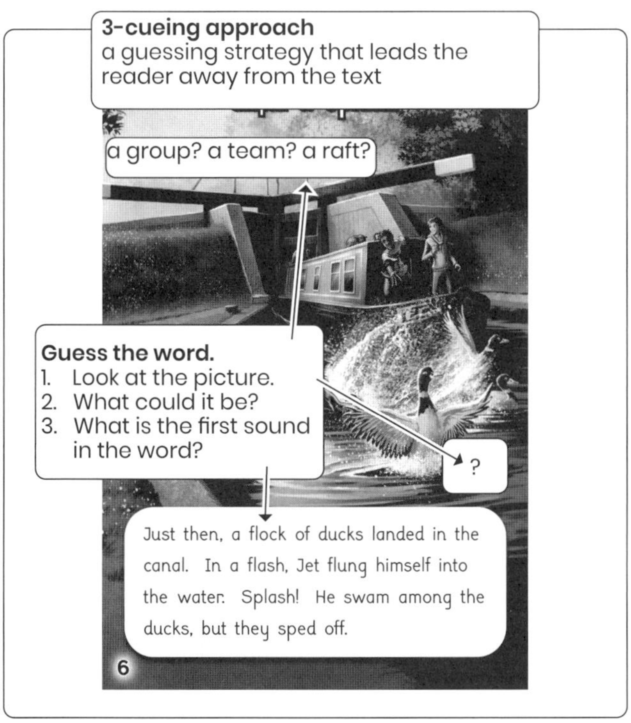

THE PHONIC BOOKS PROGRAM

METHODOLOGY

The principles underlying our books are based on current thinking in the **Science of Reading**. We believe that all students can learn to read, and the best way to achieve this is by teaching them how the English writing system works by following a systematic approach. Written English is based on an alphabetic code that students need to unlock. Teaching students to recognize these graphemes and how to sound them and blend them into words is the route to reading success.

Our books and resources develop the five pillars of learning to read:

1. phonemic awareness
2. phonics
3. vocabulary
4. fluency
5. comprehension

At a later stage, students need to learn about morphemes (units of meaning) to enhance their vocabulary and comprehension.

Our books follow a systematic phonics approach. Starting by introducing only a few letters and sounds at a time, the reader can experience success from the very beginning. Our program teaches the following reading skills using explicit systematic phonics.

BLENDING AND SEGMENTING

Students learning to read with explicit systematic phonics are encouraged to sound out letters in words and push the sounds together into words. This is called **blending**. Each letter is sounded out separately and blended from left to right, throughout the word. This is the most reliable strategy to read a new word.

It's helpful for beginner readers to blend using "continuant" consonant sounds (e.g., /m/, /n/, /l/, /r/, and /s/) because these sounds are easier to prolong and blend together smoothly.

Students learn that spelling is the reverse activity of blending. When spelling, they learn to isolate each sound in the word and represent it with a spelling. This is called **segmenting**.

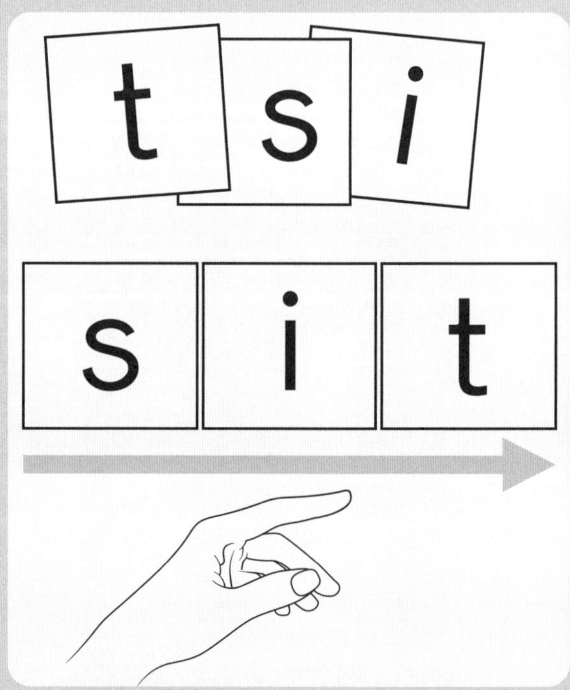

PHONEME MANIPULATION

Students learn to identify and isolate phonemes in words and to manipulate them by deleting, adding or swapping sounds in the words. This skill helps the reader to self-correct when making errors in reading.

Once students have been taught letter–sound correspondences, they can practice this new knowledge within controlled **decodable texts**. This means that students can sound out words that they can't yet read. Decodable texts encourage students to use "blending" sounds into words as the first strategy when reading, using the phonics they have been taught.

Learning a new skill takes a lot of practice so our books for beginner readers include games to practice reading words in the book. Our readers often include a **reading practice page** to ensure a successful reading experience of the text in the book.

All our books have cumulative progression which allows for previous learning to be included as the reader progresses. This ensures what has been learned is included and practiced along the way.

Students learn new **vocabulary** through reading and our books offer an opportunity for this. As they learn to decode a growing number of words, new words are introduced which will help them develop their language skills.

The **activity books** are a supplementary resource to support students who need extra practice at each level. Although our books can be used independently, we recommend using the activity books alongside to enhance and consolidate learning. Some activities, such as blending, segmenting, and phoneme manipulation precede the books, whereas others are directly linked to the books in the corresponding series and are designed to develop reading fluency, spelling, writing, and comprehension skills.

PROGRAM OVERVIEW

In line with explicit systematic phonics and the Science of Reading, our Catch-up readers support older students needing foundational reading reinforcement. Perfect for Tier 2 and Tier 3 intervention, these books are ideal for summer reading programs. Students are assessed to determine their knowledge and skills, and based on this, a set of Catch-up readers is recommended.

The Catch-up readers cover sounds of the alphabet, consonant blends and digraphs, vowel sounds, alternative vowel and consonant spellings, VCe spellings, and suffixes, prefixes and root words. Each series builds progressively from basic to advanced skills.

Complementary activity books provide extensive practice in reading, spelling, and comprehension, helping students decode effectively and retain what they read. This systematic approach ensures students master the necessary skills to become proficient readers, boosting their confidence and reading success.

Moon Dogs Set 1

This set is a fully decodable phonic series for students at the very early stages of reading.

Each book introduces only a few letter/sounds at a time, which allows for independent reading from the beginning. The set provides practice while offering different stories, with each unit introducing new letters/sounds and revising previously taught phonic letters/sounds and high-frequency words.

Comprehension questions and a Jumping Jack game are included at the back of each book, offering a fun way to practice the new phonic skills and knowledge introduced at each stage.

Moon Dogs Extras Set 1

These books are designed to complement the Moon Dogs Set 1 Series, providing additional practice for the sounds of the alphabet at CVC (Consonant–Vowel– Consonant) level.

They follow the same cumulative scope and sequence as the original Moon Dogs Set 1 Series, meaning they progress in the same way and cover the same content.

The Extras Series includes 24 different readers that aim to reinforce the learning by introducing only a few letters/sounds at a time, similar to the original series, but with different stories.

Moon Dogs Set 2

This set builds upon the foundation laid in Moon Dogs Set 1 (and Moon Dogs Extra Set 1). It provides additional practice of CVC words before introducing consonant blends and digraphs.

Each book introduces new letter–sound combinations gradually. The progression is CVC, VCC and CVCC, CCVC, CCVCC, ch, sh, th and ng, and ck and qu.

Games and comprehension questions are included for engagement and to ensure understanding.

Moon Dogs Extras Set 2

This is a parallel set of readers to Moon Dogs Set 2. These 16 additional readers follow the same cumulative scope and sequence as the original Moon Dogs Set 2 Series.

Moon Dogs Set 3 Vowel Spellings

This set explores first vowel spellings, presenting two alternative vowel spellings (such as 'ai' and 'ay') for a single sound in each book. These books are slightly longer in length, spanning 100–130 words and offer progressive reading experiences.

Each book features a vocabulary page to address challenging words, along with dedicated reading practice pages. As with previous Moon Dogs books, each reader includes a Jumping Jack game and comprehension questions.

Moon Dogs VCe Spellings

The Moon Dogs VCe Series is a series of decodable books that specifically targets the silent 'e' spellings in the English language. This series introduces the key VCe (Vowel-Consonant-e) spellings, a–e, e–e, i–e, o–e, and u–e, through various engaging and illustrated stories.

The first five books introduce one VCe spelling pattern at a time, ensuring that students can gradually master these spelling conventions. The sixth book in the series covers all spellings introduced in the previous readers.

Magic Belt, That Dog!, Mel on Mars, and Get Out of the Game

These 12 fantasy and adventure stories are suitable for students ages 8 through to 14 who would benefit from a beginning phonics program. The Magic Belt, That Dog!, Mel on Mars, and Get Out of the Game series start at CVC/CVCC level text, then build up reading skills in a step-by-step phonics progression, allowing practice and consolidation at each level. To promote interest, the series feature one continuous story when read in sequence with the conclusion in the final book.

Alba, Totem, and Pet Sitters

The 12 books in these sets offer step-by-step progression within exciting beautifully illustrated, age-appropriate stories.

The series cover the essential phonics foundations a catch-up student will need, starting at CVC/CVCC level.

The series introduces new phonic skills, including alternative vowel spellings, at a faster pace than previous series.

The Alba, Totem and Pet Sitters series follow the exact same phonics progression.

Dragon Eggs

The Dragon Eggs series is a set of 10 books designed to develop reading fluency. Focusing on early teaching of alternative spellings for vowel sounds, these books are simple and engaging, with repetitive text to reinforce learning.
This series provides ample opportunities to teach and reinforce these foundational skills, ensuring young readers build a strong phonics base.
The Dragon Eggs series prepares readers to progress to the Talisman 1, Rescue, and Island Adventure series, which also cover alternative spellings for vowel sounds but with more complex stories and faster progression.

Talisman 1, Rescue, and Island Adventure

These three sets of 10 books cover alternative spellings for vowel sounds: /ai/, /ee/, /oe/, /er/, /ow/, /oi/, /oo/, /ue/, /ie/, /aw/, /air/, and /ar/.

The four series follow a similar phonics progression, providing many opportunities to teach and practice alternative vowel spellings.

Talisman 2

The Talisman 2 series continues the fantasy/adventure stories of the Talisman 1 series, and overlaps the alternative vowel and consonant spellings and Latin suffixes of the Titan's Gauntlets and Hidden in Paris series, including additional variant spellings.

The series offers increasingly challenging texts for young readers making progress in reading the complex spellings of English.

Each book has 16 full-color pages to stimulate and engage older readers.

Titan's Gauntlets and Hidden in Paris

Titan's Gauntlets and Hidden in Paris are sets of 10 imaginative stories with fantastic illustrations. They introduce further alternative vowel and consonant spellings and common Latin suffixes.

Titan's Gauntlets follows on from the Talisman series and offers increasingly challenging texts for students who are coming to grips with the complex spellings of English. Twenty full-color pages in each book will stimulate and engage the older reader.

Amber Guardians

Action packed from start to finish, these 10 exciting stories are carefully written with a high text-to-illustration ratio. These longer stories (32 pages) build reading stamina and motivate older readers.

Designed to bridge the gap between decodable and mainstream books, these stories are a stepping stone toward having the confidence to understanding meaning purely from text.

Activity books

Each series has an accompanying activity book. These books are integral to the reading program, as they include teaching and practice activities to support the learner.

Some of the activities precede reading the books, whereas others should be completed after reading them.

PROGRAM FEATURES

The Phonic Books Catch-up Readers program is designed to engage 8- to 14-year-old readers by offering a range of features tailored to support reading success and build confidence in students.

- **Engaging content:** the program includes engaging and imaginative stories featuring appealing characters that captivate young readers. The text is designed to be engaging, ensuring that readers remain engaged and motivated.
- **Accessible design:** the books use a dyslexia-friendly font and present text on suitable backgrounds, making them more accessible and easier to read.
- **Structured progression:** a highly structured sequence carefully guides the student from simple to more complex phonics concepts.
- **Cumulative learning:** the books follow a cumulative progression, ensuring that previously learned phonics skills are revisited and reinforced.
- **High-frequency words:** the program gradually introduces high-frequency words.
- **Decodable texts:** the program uses controlled decodable texts that allow students to apply their phonic knowledge to reading texts.
- **Vocabulary development:** as students' decoding skills improve, new words are introduced to help develop their language skills.
- **Interactive games and activities:** the program also offers a variety of games and activities, such as fishing games, snap cards, and dice games, to make learning more interactive and enjoyable, while helping to consolidate learning.
- **Activity books:** accompanying activity books are available to reinforce the skills learned in the books. These books are designed to support reading fluency, spelling, writing, and comprehension skills.
- **Free printable resources:** a range of free printable reading and spelling sources are available on the Phonic Books website.

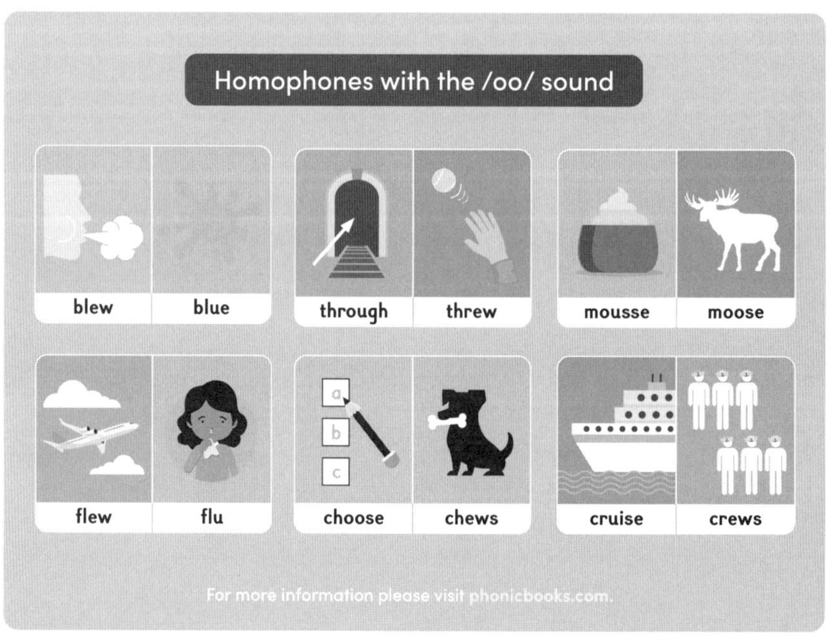

The Phonics Book website offers a wealth of free teaching resources, such as this one on homophones.

SCOPE AND SEQUENCE

The scope and sequence provided below offers a detailed overview of our Phonic Books Catch-up Readers program. It outlines each stage of the curriculum and the corresponding parallel series that focus on the same phonic skills, which can be used for additional practice.

Phonic Books sets and series		Book	Phonic focus	Word structure
			Books for Catch-up Readers	
Moon Dogs	Set 1 and Set 1 Extras	Book 1	s, a, t, i, m	CVC
		Book 2	n, o, p	CVC
		Book 3	b, c, g, h	CVC
		Book 4	d, e, f, v	CVC
		Book 5	k, l, r, u	CVC
		Book 6	j, w, z	CVC
		Book 7	x, y, ff, ll, ss, zz	CVC
		Book 8	All initial sounds CVC	CVC
	Set 2 and Set 2 Extras	Book 1		CVC
		Book 2		VCC CVCC
		Book 3		CCVC
		Book 4		CCVCC
		Book 5	ch	
		Book 6	sh	
		Book 7	th, ng	
		Book 8	ck, qu	
	Set 3 Vowel Spellings	Book 1	ai, ay	
		Book 2	ee, ea	
		Book 3	oa, ow	
		Book 4	ur, ir	
		Book 5	e, ea	
		Book 6	ow, ou	
		Book 7	oo, ue	
		Book 8	igh, i	
		Book 9	oo, oul	
		Book 10	a, aw	
		Book 11	oy, oi	
		Book 12	ar	
		Book 13	air, are	
		Book 14	ear, eer	
	VCe Spellings	Book 1	a–e	
		Book 2	e–e	
		Book 3	i–e	
		Book 4	o–e	
		Book 5	u–e	
		Book 6	All VCe spellings	

<table>
<tr><th colspan="4" rowspan="2">Phonic Books sets and series</th><th>Book</th><th>Phonic focus</th><th>Word structure</th></tr>
<tr><th colspan="3">Books for Catch-up Readers</th></tr>
<tr><td rowspan="12">Magic Belt</td><td rowspan="12">That Dog!</td><td rowspan="12">Mel on Mars</td><td rowspan="12">Get Out of the Game</td><td>Book 1</td><td></td><td>CVC, CVCC</td></tr>
<tr><td>Book 2</td><td></td><td>CVCC</td></tr>
<tr><td>Book 3</td><td></td><td>CVCC</td></tr>
<tr><td>Book 4</td><td>-ed</td><td>CVCC</td></tr>
<tr><td>Book 5</td><td></td><td>CCVCC</td></tr>
<tr><td>Book 6</td><td>ch, tch</td><td></td></tr>
<tr><td>Book 7</td><td>sh</td><td></td></tr>
<tr><td>Book 8</td><td>th</td><td></td></tr>
<tr><td>Book 9</td><td>ck, qu</td><td></td></tr>
<tr><td>Book 10</td><td>ng</td><td></td></tr>
<tr><td>Book 11</td><td>wh, -ing</td><td></td></tr>
<tr><td>Book 12</td><td>le</td><td></td></tr>
<tr><td rowspan="12">Alba</td><td rowspan="12">Totem</td><td rowspan="12">Pet Sitters</td><td rowspan="12"></td><td>Book 1</td><td></td><td>CVC, CVCC</td></tr>
<tr><td>Book 2</td><td></td><td>CCVC</td></tr>
<tr><td>Book 3</td><td></td><td>CCVCC</td></tr>
<tr><td>Book 4</td><td>sh, ch, tch, th</td><td></td></tr>
<tr><td>Book 5</td><td>ck, ng, qu, wh, le, -ed</td><td></td></tr>
<tr><td>Book 6</td><td>ay, ai, a, a-e</td><td></td></tr>
<tr><td>Book 7</td><td>ee, ea, y, e, ey</td><td></td></tr>
<tr><td>Book 8</td><td>o, ow, oa, o-e</td><td></td></tr>
<tr><td>Book 9</td><td>er, ir, ur</td><td></td></tr>
<tr><td>Book 10</td><td>ow, ou</td><td></td></tr>
<tr><td>Book 11</td><td>igh, y, i, i-e</td><td></td></tr>
<tr><td>Book 12</td><td>oo, u, u-e, ew</td><td></td></tr>
<tr><td colspan="4" rowspan="10">Dragon Eggs</td><td>Book 1</td><td>ay, ai, a, a-e, ea, ey</td><td></td></tr>
<tr><td>Book 2</td><td>ee, ea, y, e, ie, e-e, ei</td><td></td></tr>
<tr><td>Book 3</td><td>ow, oa, o, oe, o-e</td><td></td></tr>
<tr><td>Book 4</td><td>er, ir, ur, or, ear</td><td></td></tr>
<tr><td>Book 5</td><td>ow, ou and oi, oy</td><td></td></tr>
<tr><td>Book 6</td><td>oo, ue, u-e, ew, ou, u</td><td></td></tr>
<tr><td>Book 7</td><td>igh, ie, i-e, i, y</td><td></td></tr>
<tr><td>Book 8</td><td>aw, awe, a, au, al, ough</td><td></td></tr>
<tr><td>Book 9</td><td>air, are, ear, ere, eir</td><td></td></tr>
<tr><td>Book 10</td><td>ar</td><td></td></tr>
</table>

Phonic Books sets and series			Book	Phonic focus
			Books for Catch-up Readers	
Talisman 1	Island Adventure	Rescue	Book 1	ay, ai, a, a–e, ea, ey
			Book 2	ee, ea, y, e, ie, e–e, ei
			Book 3	ow, oa, oe, o–e, or
			Book 4	er, ir, ur, or, ear
			Book 5	ow, ou and oi, oy
			Book 6	oo, ue, u-e, ew, ou, u
			Book 7	igh, ie, i–e, i, y
			Book 8	a, aw, awe, au, al, ough
			Book 9	air, are, ear, ere, eir
			Book 10	ar
Titan's Gauntlets	Hidden in Paris		Book 1	u, ue, u–e
			Book 2	u, o, ou
			Book 3	s, ss, se, c, ce
			Book 4	l, ll, le, al
			Book 5	j, g, ge
			Book 6	f, ff, ph
			Book 7	-ture
			Book 8	-tion
			Book 9	-cial, -tial
			Book 10	-sion
Talisman 2			Book 1	u–e, ue, ew, u
			Book 2	u, o, ou, o, a, ou, au
			Book 3	s, ss, c, ce, se, sc, st
			Book 4	l, ll, le, il, al, ol, el
			Book 5	j, g, ge, dge, dj
			Book 6	f, ff, gh, ph
			Book 7	-ture
			Book 8	-tion, -ssion, -tian, -sion, -cian
			Book 9	-cial, -tial, -tious, -cious, -ious
			Book 10	-sion

Phonic Books sets and series	Book	Phonic focus
	Books for Catch-up Readers	
Amber Guardians	Book 1	-s, -es, -ed, -ing
	Book 2	-ful, -less, -ness, -er, -est, -ly, -en, -ish, -y, -able, -ible
	Book 3	un-, in-, im-, ir-, il-, dis-, mis-
	Book 4	re-, pre-
	Book 5	uni-, tri-, quad-
	Book 6	super-
	Book 7	magna-, mini-, micro-
	Book 8	cap, man, spec, viv
	Book 9	mem
	Book 10	ject, tract, struct, labor, fact, form

GETTING STARTED

Start by reviewing the diagnostic assessment tool outlined in the next section. This tool is essential for evaluating your students' current knowledge, understanding what they have already learned, and identifying the areas where they still need to develop. Conducting a thorough diagnostic assessment will enable you to tailor your teaching approach more effectively. Based on the assessment results, the tool will recommend a set of readers and an accompanying activity book tailored to your students' specific needs.

Next, examine the scheme of work charts provided in the following section. These charts offer an easy-to-navigate overview of the sample lesson plans provided in this manual. They guide you through their progression, detailing the sequence in which phonic skills are introduced and developed by each set of readers. They cover the phonic focus for each lesson plan, high-frequency words, vocabulary lists, resources, and parallel series. This information will help you understand how the program is structured and how each component contributes to the overall learning objectives.

The manual includes specific lesson plans for the Moon Dogs Set 1, That Dog!, Moon Dogs VCe Spellings, Moon Dogs Vowel Spellings, and Island Adventure series. These lesson plans serve as discrete examples to illustrate how the program can be implemented in the classroom or at home. Although the manual provides detailed plans for these series, the principles and methods outlined can be adapted for other parallel series and more advanced series not covered in this manual. This flexibility ensures that you can tailor the program to fit the unique needs of your students and their varying levels of proficiency.

Proceed to the lesson structure and teaching methods section for detailed information and guidance on these lesson plans. This section explains the program's lesson framework, including the sequence and pattern of activities designed for effective teaching. Each lesson plan is divided into five distinct lessons, with explanations of their structure and purpose.

Following this, the teaching methods section describes how to teach the core lesson activities effectively. It uses examples from the activity books to demonstrate how to integrate the resources into the lessons.

Additionally, the differentiation section on page 62 provides strategies for tailoring lessons to meet diverse student needs. It offers detailed guidance on using activity book resources to create customizable lessons that cater to all students, including support for the lowest-attaining 20% of students, those with special educational needs, and students for whom English is a second language.

Finally, regular student assessment is crucial for enhancing both learning and teaching. The lesson plans incorporate formative assessments through various activities and games, allowing you to monitor student progress and adjust your teaching strategies accordingly.

After thoroughly reviewing these sections, you will be well-prepared to proceed with the main lesson plans of the program, which begin on page 67. By following this structured approach, you can ensure a comprehensive and effective implementation of the Phonic Books program in your classroom.

Diagnostic Assessment

Catch-up Series

When a student begins a reading program, it is important to assess where the student is at, what knowledge and skills they have acquired and what they need to learn. It is also useful to observe their reading strategies. This will inform the teacher where to start and what to focus on. This is particularly important for students who are struggling with reading. This assessment will help to determine from which point the teacher should start teaching. The "Recommendations" sheet will match suitable decodable books (from the Phonic Books range) to the reading level of the student.

How to use this Diagnostic Assessment

1. Cut out the reading cards below. The student should read them in sequential order. The teacher's sheet is for the teacher to record the student's responses.
2. Ask the student to start with sounding out the letters at the beginning of the assessment. Note if the pronunciation of the sounds is "precise" (no "uh" after the consonants). Is the student using letter names instead of sounds?
3. Explain to the student that the words in lists 2–5 are nonsense words which help to assess decoding skills.
4. If the student starts to struggle, complete that section for diagnostic purposes. The teacher will need to use their judgement as to whether to start at this point or to start from the previous section in order to build up the confidence of the learner.
5. Record what the student has said (not just a check or cross). This will inform the teacher about the student's reading strategies.
6. Use the "Recommendations" sheet to see where to start and which books to use with your student.

Student's reading cards

Card 1

s a t i m n o p b c

g h d e f v k l r u

j w z x y ff ll ss zz

Card 2

sof jum rel ked vug ziff

Card 3

kand seft ump roft benk lant

Card 4

trop frem prab glim druff
snop glim druff snop

Card 5

stend plimp slupt
pronk flant stroft

Card 6

chip shed thin quest
that rock wing

Card 7

brittle which crackle thanking
glinted swinging when rested

Card 8

plain tweet stoat burst
instead frown stool might hood
stork coil chart clear

Card 9

stay belong so person tread
sound grew wild could bald
annoy grass stare steer table
cream slow shirt again glue cry
push clash half there here

Card 10

tape toe Pete messy world
flute tie fault laugh pear break
stone learn dine talk heart their

Name: **Date:**

Diagnostic Reading Assessment: Teacher's Sheet

1	s a t i m n o p b c g h d e f v k l r u j w z x y ff ll ss zz
2	sof jum rel ked vug ziff
3	kand seft ump roft benk lant
4	trop frem prab glim druff snop
5	stend plimp slupt pronk flant strof
6	chip shed thin quest that rock wing
7	brittle which crackle thanking glinted swinging when rested
8	plain tweet stoat burst instead frown stool might hood stork coil chart clear
9	stay belong so person tread sound grew wild could bald annoy grass stare steer table cream slow shirt again glue cry push claw half there here
10	tape toe Pete messy world flute tie fault laugh pear break stone learn dine talk heart their

Recommendations

	Diagnostic reading sheet	Knowledge/skill that needs addressing	Recommendations for older readers
1	s a t i m n o p b c g h d e f v k l r u j w z x y ff ll ss zz	Sounds/letter correspondences	Moon Dogs Set 1 / Activities
2	sof jum rel ked vug ziff	CVC level words and non-words	Moon Dogs Set 2 / Activities and CVC reading activities in Totem 1 and Alba Activities
3	kand seft ump roft benk lant	Blending real and non-words at VCC and CVCC level	Moon Dogs Set 2 or Magic Belt / That Dog! Book 1, or Totem / Alba Book 1 and Activities
4	trop frem prab glim druff snop	Blending real and no- words at CCVC level	Moon Dogs Set 2 / Activities or start at Magic Belt / That Dog! Book 4 and Totem and Alba Book 2 and Activities
5	stend plimp slupt pronk flant stroft	Blending real and non-words at CCVCC and CCCVC level	Moon Dogs Set 2 or start at Magic Belt / That Dog! Book 5 and Totem / Alba Book 3 and activity books
6	chip shed thin quest that rock wing	ch, sh, th, ck, and ng	Moon Dogs Set 2, Book 5 or start at Magic Belt / That Dog! Books 6–10 and Totem / Alba Book 4 and Activities
7	brittle which crackle thanking glinted swinging when rested	tch and ve Two-syllable words ending in -ed, -ing, and le	Start at Magic Belt / That Dog! Books 11–12 and Totem / Alba, Book 5 and Activities
8	plain tweet stoat burst instead frown stool might hood stork coil chart clear	Spellings: ai, ee, oa, ur, ea, ow, oo, igh, l/oo/k, or, oi, ar, air, and ear	Start at Moon Dogs Vowel Spellings, then Totem / Alba Book 6 and Activities
9	stay belong so person tread sound grew wild could bald annoy grass stare steer table cream slow shirt again glue cry push claw half there here	Alternative spellings of target vowel sounds (see above)	Start at Moon Dogs VCe Spellings, then Totem / Alba Books 6–12 and Activities
10	tape toe Pete messy world flute tie fault laugh pear break stone learn dine talk heart their	More alternative spellings of target vowel sounds (see above list 8).	Start at Talisman 1 / Rescue / Island Adventure, Books 1–10 and Activities

SCHEMES OF WORK

Moon Dogs Set 1

Parallel series: *Moon Dogs Extras Set 1*

Lesson plan	Objectives	Resources
s, a, t, i, m	In this first lesson plan, students will learn to accurately read new words by applying the phonic sounds /s/, /a/, /t/, /i/, and /m/. They will focus on blending these sounds to form and recognize simple CVC words.	Moon Dogs Set 1, Book 1: Is it Matt? Moon Dogs Set 1 Activities
n, o, p	In subsequent lesson plans, students will consolidate previously learned sounds and learn new sounds. In this lesson plan, students will: • review /s/, /a/, /t/, /i/, and /m/ • read new words using the sounds /n/, /o/, and /p/	Moon Dogs Set 1, Book 2: Tam has a Nap Moon Dogs Set 1 Activities
b, c, g, h	Students will: • review /s/, /a/, /t/, /i/, /m/, /n/, /o/, and /p/ • read new words using the sounds /b/, /c/, /g/, and /h/	Moon Dogs Set 1, Book 3: Sim and the Bat Moon Dogs Set 1 Activities
d, e, f, v	Students will: • review /s/, /a/, /t/, /i/, /m/, /n/, /o/, /p/, /b/, /c/, /g/, and /h/ • read new words using the sounds /d/, /e/, /f/, and /v/	Moon Dogs Set 1, Book 4: Ned, the Cat Moon Dogs Set 1 Activities
k, l, r, u	Students will: • review /s/, /a/, /t/, /i/, /m/, /n/, /o/, /p/, /b/, /c/, /g/, /h/, /d/, /e/, /f/, and /v/ • read new words using the sounds /k/, /l/, /r/, and /u/	Moon Dogs Set 1, Book 5: Kip's Bad Leg Moon Dogs Set 1 Activities
j, w, z	Students will: • review /s/, /a/, /t/, /i/, /m/, /n/, /o/, /p/, /b/, /c/, /g/, /h/, /d/, /e/, /f/, /v/, /k/, /l/, /r/, and /u/ • read new words using the sounds /j/, /w/, and /z/	Moon Dogs Set 1, Book 6: Kip's Bad Leg Moon Dogs Set 1 Activities
x, y, ff, ll, ss, zz	Students will: • review /s/, /a/, /t/, /i/, /m/, /n/, /o/, /p/, /b/, /c/, /g/, /h/, /d/, /e/, /f/, /v/, /k/, /l/, /r/, /u/, /w/, and /z/ • read new words using the sounds /x/, /y/, /ff/, /ll/, /ss/, and /zz/	Moon Dogs Set 1, Book 7: The Big Hill Moon Dogs Set 1 Activities
All initial sounds CVC	Students will review all previously learned sounds to form simple CVC words.	Moon Dogs Set 1, Book 8: The Big Hill Moon Dogs Set 1 Activities

That Dog!

Parallel series: *Magic Belt, Mel on Mars, and Get Out of the Game*

Lesson objectives: *In these lesson plans, students will learn and practice CVC to CCVCC words, consonant blends and digraphs, wh, final le, and suffixes -ed and -ing*

Lesson plan	Reading practice words	Resources
CVC CVCC	can, get, box, fun, top, hum, had, yes, and, end, it's, hops, sulk, limp, dent, lots, jump, next, went, ramp, dump	That Dog! Book 1: The Ramp That Dog! Activities
CVCC	runs, lost, pant, jump, pats, sits, begs, hand, gulp, fond, fact, lets, hint, nuts, tells, lift, soft, damp, lamp	That Dog! Book 2: The Lost Dog That Dog! Activities
CCVC	mend, help, best, just, left, rest, yelp, yaps, sobs, hugs, tells, limp, lift, kept, pond, silk, soft, desk, mist, wind	That Dog! Book 3: No Dogs! That Dog! Activities
CCVC and -ed	CVCC: still, from, gran, stop, stun, fret, drop, step, spot, fled -ed: jumped, lifted, pressed, patted, dressed, handed, stunned, spotted, tipped, dropped	That Dog! Book 4: Drop It! That Dog! Activities
CCVCC	print, skunk, drink, snaps, frank, stops, sniffs, brink, smells, stand, trips, drags, plods, spins, spots, twist, slips, grabs, stink, steps	That Dog! Book 5: Ben Gets Strict That Dog! Activities
ch and tch	ch: chin, champ, chat, much, lunch, branch, stench, bench, crunch, rich tch: patch, hatch, pitch, fetch, catch, match, snatch, stitch, switch, scratch	That Dog! Book 6: Catch Me! That Dog! Activities

Lesson plan	Reading practice words	Resources
sh	fish, hush, wish, gash, dish, flash, flesh, crash, brush, splash, shed, shut, shop, ship, shall, shell, shift, shrub, shrug, shrimp	That Dog! Book 7: Fishing That Dog! Activities
th	voiced: that, the, then, this, the, with unvoiced: thin, think, thank, theft, thump, moth, sixth, tenth, width, depth	That Dog! Book 8: Cherished Things That Dog! Activities
ck and qu	ck: back, duck, check, pick, stick, Mick, rock, luck, black, smack qu: quick, quack, quest, quiff, quill, quit, quench, quilt, squid, squint	That Dog! Book 9: Good and Bad Luck That Dog! Activities
ng	long, along, king, thing, sang, lungs, clung, sprang, swung, length, pang, flung, among, strong, dung, strength, wing, gong, hang, bring	That Dog! Book 10: The Long, Thin Boat That Dog! Activities
wh and -ing	wh: when, which, what, whip, whack, whisk, whelk, whizz, whim -ing: acting, digging, yelling, ringing, running, nodding, fretting, dragging, jumping, wagging	That Dog! Book 11: Shopping for Props That Dog! Activities
le	little, middle, muzzle, battle, puzzle, cuddle, paddle, shuffle, niggle, dazzle, struggle, handle, hurtle, mumble, tumble, grumble, scramble, winkle, crackle, horrible, terrible	That Dog! Book 12: Dog in Trouble That Dog! Activities

Moon Dogs VCe Spellings

Lesson plan	Objectives	Reading practice words	Resources
a–e	Students will learn and practice the 'a–e' spelling for the sound /ae/ (e.g. "**late**"). In this and subsequent lesson plans, reading practice pages and games help to consolidate learning, reading practice pages and games help to consolidate learning.	came, mate, pale, bale, made, game, cake, pale, state, brake, rake, shave, skate, crate	Moon Dogs VCe Spellings Book 1: The Shape Game Moon Dogs VCe Spellings Activities
e–e	Students will learn and practice the 'e–e' spelling for the sound /ee/ (e.g. "**theme**").	eve, Pete, these, delete, compete, athlete, discrete, theme, concrete, complete, evening, extreme	Moon Dogs VCe Spellings Book 2: These Things Moon Dogs VCe Spellings Activities
i–e	Students will learn and practice the 'i–e' spelling for the sound /ie/ (e.g. "**fine**").	dine, kite, ride, hive, lime, bike, wine, time, drive, swipe, smile, pride, spine, glide	Moon Dogs VCe Spellings Book 3: Bike Ride Moon Dogs VCe Spellings Activities
o–e	Students will learn and practice the 'o–e' spelling for the sound /oe/ (e.g. "**rope**").	nose, rope, rode, note, joke, bone, mole, hope, stove, glove, stole, spoke, stone, drove	Moon Dogs VCe Spellings Book 4: A Good Nose Moon Dogs VCe Spellings Activities
u–e	Students will learn and practice that the VCe spelling 'u–e' can represent two sounds: /oo/ as in "**rude**" and /ue/ as in "**cute**."	/oo/: rule, rude, flute, June, Luke, brute, plume, tune /ue/: use, cute, mule, cube, muse, fume, mute, acut	Moon Dogs VCe Spellings Book 5: A Useful Bag Moon Dogs VCe Spellings Activities
a–e, e–e, i–e, o–e, and u–e	Students will consolidate their understanding of VCe patterns by practicing these previously learned patterns in different words	cake, same, pale, blame, stale, flame, fine, hive, wife, spine, slime, prize, note, hope, joke, bone, broke, stone, rude, rule, flute, use, cute, tube, Eve, Pete, these, compete, complete	Moon Dogs VCe Spellings Book 6: A Place to Hide Moon Dogs VCe Spellings Activities

Moon Dogs Vowel Spellings

Lesson objectives: *In these lesson plans, students will learn and practice two alternative spellings for each vowel sound*

Lesson plan	Reading practice words	Resources
ai, ay	/ai/: rain, mail, wait, train, snail, faint, brain, paint, chain, sprain /ay/: day, say, way, away, play, may, stay, tray, today, spray	Moon Dogs Vowel Spellings Book 1: Wet Day in Spain
ee, ea	/ee/: see, tree, three, need, beef, meet, sleep, green, creep, steep /ea/: eat, sea, tea, read, team, meat, real, cheap, treat, dream	Moon Dogs Vowel Spellings Book 2: Lost in the Street
oa, ow	/oa/: goal, boat, goat, road, coat, foam, moan, toast, float, groan /ow/: low, row, bow, show, know, grow, flow, crow, snow	Moon Dogs Vowel Spellings Book 3: The Boat Trip
ur, ir	/ur/: fur, hurt, curl, turn, burp, lurch, burse, burned, church, Thursday /ir/: sir, girl, first, bird, firm, third, stir, skirt, birthday, thirst	Moon Dogs Vowel Spellings Book 4: Birthday Lunch
e, ea	/e/: get, then, them, well, went, end, send, next, self, spend /ea/: read, head, bread, dread, meant, sweat, health, spread, ready, instead	Moon Dogs Vowel Spellings Book 5: Matt's Bad Head
ow, ou	/ow/: now, how, cow, down, town, frown, clown, growl, drown, brown /ou/: out, our, loud, shout, house, mouse, round, found, about, around	Moon Dogs Vowel Spellings Book 6: Mouse in the House
oo, ue	/oo/: too, food, soon, cool, moon, room, root, boot, gloom, school /ue/: Sue, blue, true, glue, clue, due, Tuesday, avenue, bluebell, subdue	Moon Dogs Vowel Spellings Book 7: A Gloomy Room

Lesson plan	Reading practice words	Resources
igh, i	/igh/: high, night, right, tight, fight, light, might, bright, fright, sight /i/: I, I'm, find, kind, child, mind, wild, grind, blind, final	Moon Dogs Vowel Spellings Book 8: A Wild NIght
oo, oul	/oo/: look, wood, good, foot, took, hood, book, cook, stood, brook /oul/: could, couldn't, would, wouldn't, should, shouldn't	Moon Dogs Vowel Spellings Book 9: A Jog in the Woods
a, aw	/a/: all, ball, called, fallen, water, tall, small, also, bald, halter /aw/: aw, saw, jaw, claw, draw, straw, lawn, yawn, awful, prawn	Moon Dogs Vowel Spellings Book 10: An Awful Day
oy, oi	/oy/: boy, toy, joy, Roy, soya, royal, loyal, enjoy, annoy, destroy /oi/: oil, boil, coin, foil, join, noise, choice, spoil, toilet, voice	Moon Dogs Vowel Spellings Book 11: Out of Oil
ar	art, car, barn, farm, hard, part, park, start, March, garden	Moon Dogs Vowel Spellings Book 12: Beach Party
air, are	/air/: air, hair, fair, pair, Clair, chair, dairy, fairy, unfair, repair /are/: care, bare, hare, rare, fare, dare, mare, share, stare, glare	Moon Dogs Vowel Spellings Book 13: A Scary Haircut
ear, eer	/ear/: dear, gear, near, hear, fear, rear, tear, beard, clear, appear /eer/: deer, peer, jeer, veer, sneer, steer, cheer, career, cheerful, meerkat	Moon Dogs Vowel Spellings Book 14: Steer Clear

Island Adventure

Parallel series: *Talisman 1, Rescue*

Lesson objectives: *In these lesson plans, students will learn and practice alternative spellings for the vowel sounds ae, oe, er, ow/oi, oo, ie, or, air, and ar.*

Lesson plan	Reading practice words	Resources
ay, ai, a, a–e, ea, ey	day, pay, clay, stay, tray, delay; crazy, lazy, raven; great, steak, break; they, prey; rain, pain, chain, fail, aim, stain, complain, explain; fake, blaze, amaze, save, hate, snake, chase	Island Adventure Book 1: Saving the Day Island Adventure Activities
ee, ea, y, e, ie, e–e, ei	free, deep, feel, bleed, steep, creep, breeze, agree; each, weak, lead, leave, steam, dream, scream, easy, sea; he, she, we, began, belong, relax; sunny, chilly, angry; seize, ceiling, receive, protein; Pete, delete, stampede; chief, grieve, shriek, shield	Island Adventure Book 2: Sea Change Island Adventure Activities
ow, oa, o, o–e, o	ow, know, show, flow, snow, narrow, elbow, below; boat, coal, float, moan, groan, shoal, roast; no, go, most, bold, hero, zero, joking, broken; foe, toes; hole, rope, home, close, slope, stone, lonely, probe	Island Adventure Book 3: Coast to Coast Island Adventure Activities
er, ir, ur, or, ear	her, serve, nerve, stern, over, finger, singer; sir, girl, bird, first, stir, twirl, whirl; hurt, curl, turn, burn, lurch, disturb; word, world, worth, work, worm	Island Adventure Book 4: A World Away Island Adventure Activities
ow, ou, and oi, oy	cow, owl, now, howl, brown, power, scowl; out, our, mouth, pouch, bound, ground, about; boy, toy, destroy, annoy, enjoy; oil, boil, coin, voice, spoil	Island Adventure Book 5: Sounds and Shad-ows Island Adventure Activities

Lesson plan	Reading practice words	Resources
oo, ue, u–e, ew, ou, u	too, soon, cool, swoop, scoop, foolish; clue, blue, true, cruel, gruesome; rude, rule, brute, include, conclude; chew, grew, drew, flew, threw; you, soup, youth, group; truth, july, super	Island Adventure Book 6: A Shrewd Route Island Adventure Activities
igh, ie, i–e, i, y	light, might, tight, right, flight fright; die, tie, cried, tried; time, life, pipe, hide, glide, smile, stripe; find, wild, climb, spider, giant, behind; my, by, try, fly, dying	Island Adventure Book 7: An Amazing Find Island Adventure Activities
a, aw, awe, au, al, ough	all, call, small, almost; saw, claw, straw, draw, awful; aw, awesome; maul, haunt, august, assault; walk, talk; fought, thought	Island Adventure Book 8: Awesome Morning Island Adventure Activities
air, are, ear, ere, eir	air, fair, chair, stair, despair; bare, dare, share, glare, spare; bear, pear, tear, wear, swear; there, where; their	Island Adventure Book 9: Don't Be Scared Island Adventure Activities
ar	lart, car, card, farm, star, shark, alarm, mark, yard, dark, sharp, hard, shards, afar, arches, guard, large, barbed, darted	Island Adventure Book 10: Arty Party Island Adventure Activities

LESSON PLAN STRUCTURE

Each lesson plan is divided into five distinct steps, focusing on:

1. Preparation
2. Application for reading
3. Application for spelling
4. Comprehension and consolidation
5. Tracking progress

A typical lesson plan follows the structured format below, though not every lesson will follow this exact structure. Lessons or activities should be offered daily, when possible, and last not more than 15 minutes for younger students.

Step 1: Intention and preparation

In this first step, the teacher begins by outlining the primary objectives: learning new sounds, reinforcing previously learned sounds, or introducing new spellings or word structures. Additionally, a couple of minutes should be spent introducing the story that will be central to the lesson plan.

When demonstrating a new sound or word structure, word-building activities can be highly effective in making the lesson engaging and interactive. In these activities, students listen to the sounds in each word and then build the words using sound cards or magnetic letters. Picture cards can also be used for younger students. The objective is for students to construct words that match the pictures by using the sounds they have learned. It's important for students to focus on the sounds first, and then identify the letters that represent these sounds, reinforcing the connection between phonemic awareness and written language.

This lesson also focuses on segmenting and blending sounds in words. A multisensory approach is effective for teaching this skill. Using gestures, such as d using a swishing motion with your finger for blending, can aid learning.
This phase serves as a transition to spelling activities, which help link phonics skills with reading and writing.

This step typically concludes with a word chain activity. This activity is designed to reinforce the concepts taught in the lesson while also being fun and interactive.

Step 2: Application for reading

In the second lesson, students apply their phonic skills by reading a decodable text. They are encouraged to sound out the words and blend them together. The teacher can also reread the sentence after the students to help them comprehend the text. Ensure that any new vocabulary is discussed and explained.

The Phonic Books lesson plans in this instructional manual suggest that reading the story should take the form of a directed reading by the teacher. However, a number of options for teachers reading the book are also recommended:

- The teacher reads the book and students follow.
- Students engage in choral reading.
- Students engage in individual whisper reading while the teacher circulates and listens to each student.

- Students participate in paired reading, taking turns reading to one another—either by reading and rereading the books or by taking turns to read alternate pages.

It is important to emphasize that students must have an opportunity to read to the teacher individually so that they engage actively with the text and the teacher can offer error correction. This is also the time when the teacher can assess their decoding skills and their phonic knowledge.

For extension, as students progress through the program and learn to read more fluently, the teachers can support students to read with expression and prosody.
For example, adjusting their pitch, pace, and emphasis. This helps students to improve their reading fluency, improve their understanding of texts, and make reading more enjoyable. In later stages in the program, the activity book introduces a **Reading fluency** exercise. Here, students are presented with an extract from the story or text and are instructed to read it twice. The first reading emphasizes fluency and accuracy. The second reading focuses on expressive reading, helping to bring the text to life.

Step 3: Application for spelling

In this step, students practice writing the graphemes they have learned in the previous lessons. The teacher should encourage the students to say the sounds as they write them and to blend the sounds in each word together. Following this, the lesson progresses to writing entire words. Students can engage in various activities designed to reinforce this skill. For instance, they might participate in exercises like or instance, they might participate in exercises like the **Writing captions** activity, which asks students to dictate captions from the previous Reading captions activity. Moreover, the **Fill in all the missing sounds** activity challenges students to identify and write the missing sounds in words. Additionally, some activity books include **Sentence dictation** activities. During these activities, students should be encouraged to sound out each word as they spell it. This practice not only enhances their spelling skills but also reinforces their understanding of how individual sounds come together to form words within the context of a sentence.

Step 4: Comprehension and consolidation

In this step, the teacher revisits the story, reading it aloud to help students consolidate their understanding. Following the reading, students engage in a variety of comprehension activities. For example, the **Reading captions** activity in Moon Dogs Set 1 Activities tests reading accuracy as students match descriptions about the book to the correct pictures. Moreover, the **Retell the story** activity found in the That Dog! Activities book contains pictures and words on a photocopiable page. Students retell the story or create their own story using the pictures and word cards provided. Additionally, the Island Adventure Activities book includes an **Is it true?** activity in which a passage from the reader is provided with a passage containing false information, and the student is tasked with circling any false information that has been planted in the story. Further comprehension exercises are also available in the activity books, offering a range of options for further reading practice or support.

Step 5: Tracking progress

In this final step, the focus shifts to monitoring and assessing the progress students have made with the new phonic skills and sounds they have learned. To facilitate this, teachers can draw from a range of activities for formative assessments, through their performance in games such as the **4-in-a-row game** or **Stepping stones game**. The Moon Dogs VCe Spellings Activities and Island Adventure Activies also include a **Spelling assessment** page for each book, which can be used to assess students' ability to spell the spellings and sounds they have learned.

Additional activities to supplement lessons

Additional activities can be found in the activity books and online teaching resources. These can be used to widen literacy development, but they also offer the flexibility to create differentiated lessons to meet the diverse needs of students. They can be used to address gaps in understanding, enhance punctuation and comprehension skills, or provide extension for more advanced students. Here are some examples.

Reading and spelling: Students are given a list of target words on the left for them to check off the when they have read them correctly. Students then turn over the sheet and the teacher dictates the words to the student. The student then spells the words by segmenting and sounding out the sounds as they write them on the lines. The student then checks off the words they have spelled correctly.

Reading accuracy: Students are provided with a list of a few words for each picture. They have to circle the word that matches the correct picture.

Timed reading: This activity involves students reading a series of words as quickly as they can, recording their times in three attempts. This repetitive practice can help to improve a student's reading pace and fluency.

Reading practice cards: Words are provided on cards for reading practice. These cards provide examples of words containing sounds the students have just learned. These pages can be photocopied for use in a matching game format or to introduce new vocabulary, offering a more structured approach to reading practice.

Splitting two-syllable words: Later in the program, students are introduced to two-syllable words. In this activity, students practice splitting words into syllables, writing each syllable, then reassembling them while vocalizing each syllable. This improves phonemic awareness and students' understanding of word structure.

Playing with sounds: Students build nonsense words using the cards provided. This is a useful activity for older students as they are required to listen to sounds in words they have not seen before and therefore cannot rely on their visual memory. This develops their ability to segment sounds in words.

Vocabulary: This activity includes new vocabulary introduced in the focal text. It encourages the student to think about the meaning of the new words and to use them in the context of a complete sentence.

Picture the scene: Students are given a written description and then have to draw a picture based on the description.

Comprehension: Students are provided with a list of comprehension questions to be discussed after reading the text. They will help develop speaking and listening skills, comprehension and vocabulary.

Spot it!: Students provided with a picture from the text. They circle "yes" or "no" to descriptions of what the picture shows.

Sequence the story: Students are given descriptions of the text that are jumbled up in the wrong order of sequence. Students cut out and stick the sentences in the correct order.

Write the story in your own words: Students retell the story in their own words—first orally and then by writing it down in the space provided.

What happens next? Students are provided with a passage of text. They read the text again and underline their favorite part. They then draw an illustration in the box to match their favorite part.

Make a page for a comic: Students read the text and draw pictures to match the text in the boxes.

Punctuation: This activity involves giving students an extract from a story with missing capital letters and periods. Students identify the correct placement and quantity of these punctuation marks. This exercise is useful for reinforcing punctuation rules and writing skills.

Dice game: This game is for two players. Each player needs a batch of counters of one color. The players take turns to throw the die. They read a word in the column that corresponds to the number on the die and place their counter on that word or letter. The first to have three of their counters in a row in any direction is the winner.

Parallel books

Lesson plans in this book are provided for Moon Dogs Set 1, That Dog!, Moon Dogs VCe Spellings, Moon Dogs Vowel Spellings, and Island Adventure. However, Phonic Books has parallel books for the series that can be used to teach the same lessons. These alternative or supplementary resources are clearly indicated in the lesson plans, specifying which parallel books align with each lesson. This provides teachers with the flexibility to vary their teaching materials and cater to different preferences. In the subsequent section on teaching methods, there is a more in-depth exploration of how to effectively implement these techniques. It includes specific references to the activity books and offers practical guidance on how to integrate these resources into a multisensory teaching approach.

TEACHING METHODS

This section expands on the teaching methods mentioned in the preceding section on lesson plan structure, connecting them to the program's activity books. It provides practical tips for integrating these methods and resources into your lessons. The figure below shows an example of an activity from one of the activity books.

The top of each page clearly indicates the specific book and the phonic skills being targeted.

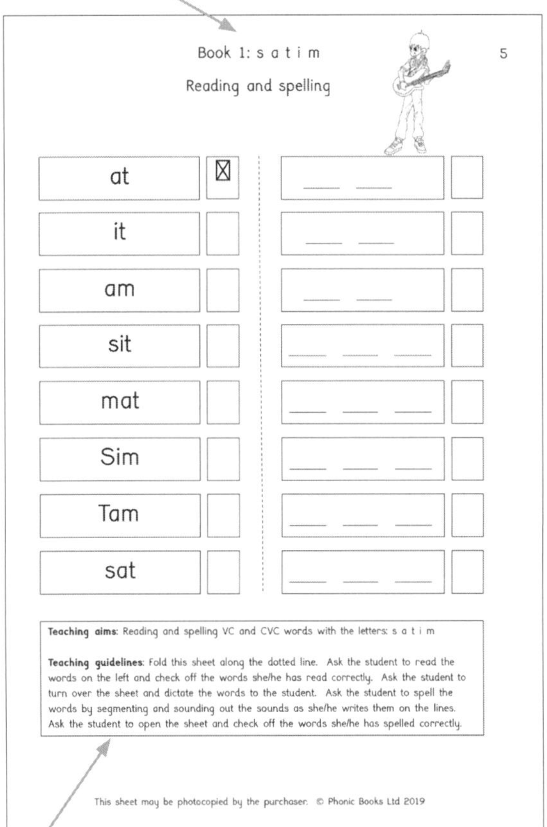
Book 1: s a t i m 5

Reading and spelling

at	☒	___ ___	
it		___ ___	
am		___ ___	
sit		___ ___ ___	
mat		___ ___ ___	
Sim		___ ___ ___	
Tam		___ ___ ___	
sat		___ ___ ___	

Teaching aims: Reading and spelling VC and CVC words with the letters: s a t i m

Teaching guidelines: Fold this sheet along the dotted line. Ask the student to read the words on the left and check off the words she/he has read correctly. Ask the student to turn over the sheet and dictate the words to the student. Ask the student to spell the words by segmenting and sounding out the sounds as she/he writes them on the lines. Ask the student to open the sheet and check off the words she/he has spelled correctly.

This sheet may be photocopied by the purchaser. © Phonic Books Ltd 2019

Teacher instructions at the bottom of the page offer step-by-step directions for teaching the activities.

Activities can be photocopied, allowing for widespread use for multiple students.

Introducing new letter sounds

In the Phonic Books program, multiple letter sounds are introduced in each lesson. This provides students with an immediate foundation for word creation. In the second and subsequent lesson plans, previously learned sounds should be reviewed in short bursts of revision.

An important part of this process is demonstrating the correct pronunciation of each sound, e.g. modeling the consonant sounds without the 'uh' sound: /m/ and not /muh/. Learning to pronounce the sounds precisely will help beginner readers to blend them into recognizable words.

After modeling the sound, encourage students to carefully watch and replicate the sound.

Employing a multisensory approach in teaching new letter sounds can improve the effectiveness of the learning process. Using **Sound cards** or **Word-building cards** from the activity books can be useful for modeling these new sounds.

Word-building cards

s a

t i m

Teaching guidelines:
Photocopy this page onto card. Cut out the letter and picture cards. Teach the letter sounds. Teach precise pronunciation, e.g. 'm' not 'muh'. Students may wish to draw pictures on the reverse of the letter cards to help them remember the sounds, i.e. sun for 's'.

Use these letter and picture cards for the word-building activity on the following page.

This sheet may be photocopied by the purchaser. © Phonic Books Ltd 2019

How to teach word building

Word building is the most effective activity to teach segmenting, blending, and spelling. Word building teaches segmenting with letters. **Segmenting** is the ability to separate sounds in words. The smallest sounds are called phonemes. We use segmenting when we sound out a new word, for example /k/ /a/ /t/ → "cat." We say the sounds separately and then we push them together to make a word.

We also use segmenting when we spell. When spelling the word "cat," we need to segment the word into the sounds /k/ /a/ /t/ and then spell those sounds with letters. Many programs introduce segmenting as an oral activity. For example, students listen to the sounds in words and then count them or place counters to represent the sounds.

While these activities may develop segmenting, they are not the most effective way to learn this skill. It is important to recognize that when we speak, we don't say all the sounds precisely. Many sounds get gobbled up, or clipped, and others change depending on where they are in the word.

Research has shown that teaching segmenting is more effective when introduced with letters. Oral segmenting is only a stepping stones that has no benefit on its own.

How to teach segmenting with letters

The most effective way of teaching segmenting is through a word-building activity. The teacher asks the student to build a word. This entails listening to the sounds in the word, placing the letters into the correct sequence, then sounding out the word and reading it. This should also be combined with writing the word as this links reading and spelling.

Step 1: Lines scaffold the word

Draw the number of lines on a whiteboard that correspond to the number of sounds in the word. In this example, draw three lines for the word "mat." Place the cards needed to build the word jumbled up above the lines.

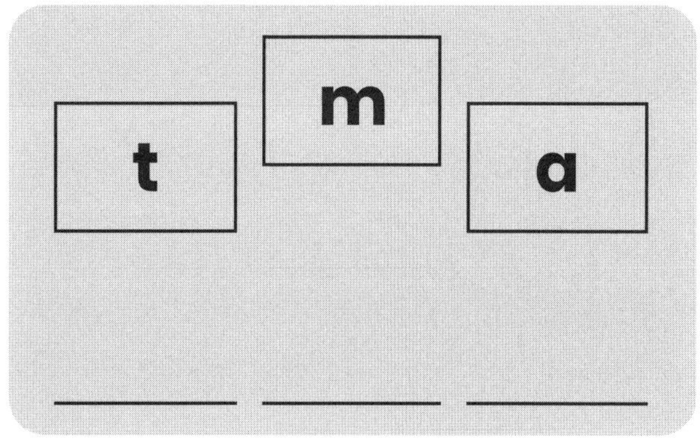

Step 2: Build the word

Tell the student that you are going to build the word "mat." Point to the first line and ask the student to listen to the first sound as you say the word slowly. Move your finger along the lines in sync with the sounds in the word.

When the student says /m/, ask them to bring down the letter for /m/ onto the first line. Repeat this process with the remaining letter/sounds in the word.

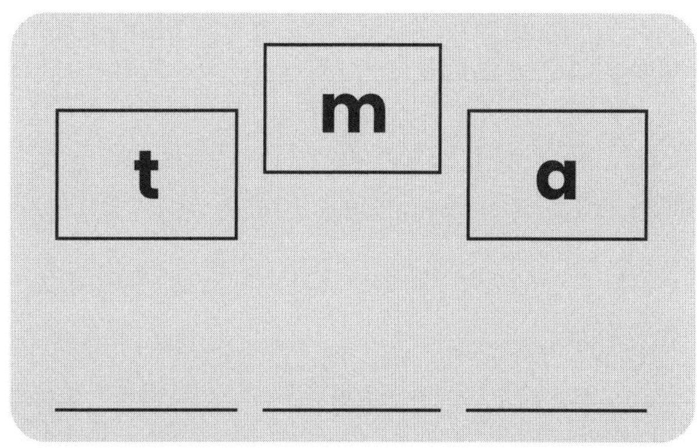

Step 3: Sound out and blend into the word

Now that the student has built the word, ask them to sound out the word and blend the sounds together into a word: /m/ /a/ /t/ → "mat."

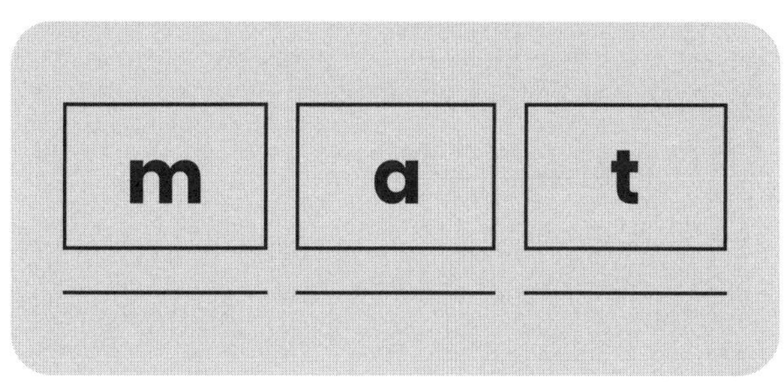

Step 4: Spell the word

Ask the student to spell the word under the lines and to say the sounds as they write each letter.

Finally, the student sounds out the word they have written and reads it.

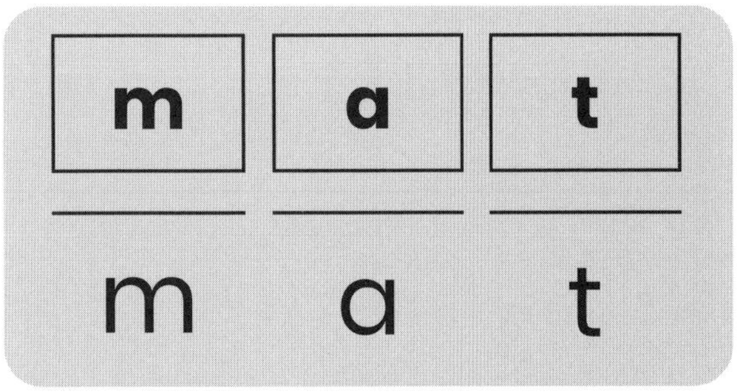

As you can see, word-building activities that use letters give the student a visual representation for the sounds in words. We show them the sequence of the sounds and how they are represented by letters. This is a direct and effective way of teaching segmenting and blending. It also demonstrates the link between reading and spelling in a clear way.

Word-building activities are a core feature of the activity books in the program. In the early stages, this activity takes the form of letters and picture cards, like in this example from Moon Dogs Set 1.

Book 1: s a t i m 3

Word-building cards

s a t i m

Teaching guidelines:
Photocopy this page onto card. Cut out the letter and picture cards. Teach the letter sounds. Teach precise pronunciation, e.g. 'm' not 'muh'. Students may wish to draw pictures on the reverse of the letter cards to help them remember the sounds, i.e. sun for 's'.

Use these letter and picture cards for the word-building activity on the following page.

This sheet may be photocopied by the purchaser. © Phonic Books Ltd 2019

As the program progresses, a more advanced word-building activity is introduced, as demonstrated in the example from That Dog!

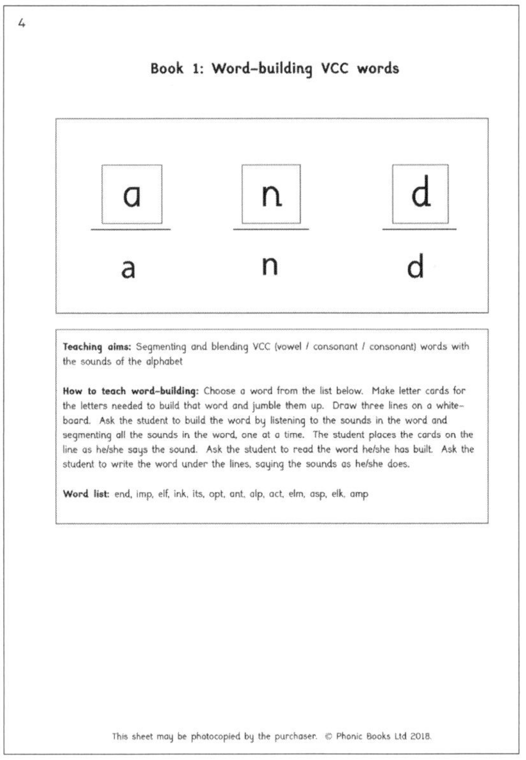

4

Book 1: Word-building VCC words

a n d

a n d

Teaching aims: Segmenting and blending VCC (vowel / consonant / consonant) words with the sounds of the alphabet

How to teach word-building: Choose a word from the list below. Make letter cards for the letters needed to build that word and jumble them up. Draw three lines on a white-board. Ask the student to build the word by listening to the sounds in the word and segmenting all the sounds in the word, one at a time. The student places the cards on the line as he/she says the sound. Ask the student to read the word he/she has built. Ask the student to write the word under the lines, saying the sounds as he/she does.

Word list: end, imp, elf, ink, its, opt, ant, alp, act, elm, asp, elk, amp

This sheet may be photocopied by the purchaser. © Phonic Books Ltd 2018.

This activity involves using a whiteboard or paper with lines drawn underneath each sound. Small card pieces are used to construct words. The activity starts by the teacher selecting a word from a specified list, then jumbling its letters at the top of the whiteboard. The student then builds the word by articulating and identifying the sounds, arranging the cards from left to right. Each sound is emphasized as the corresponding card is placed. Afterwards, the student writes the word below the lines, saying each sound during the writing process.

Three blending methods

Blending is a pivotal skill in learning to read, where students combine individual sounds (phonemes) to form whole words. Here are three distinct methods designed to enhance a student's ability to decode and blend words. Each method offers a unique approach to breaking down words into sounds and merging them to form complete words.

Method 1: Decode and blend

"Say the sounds and read the word."

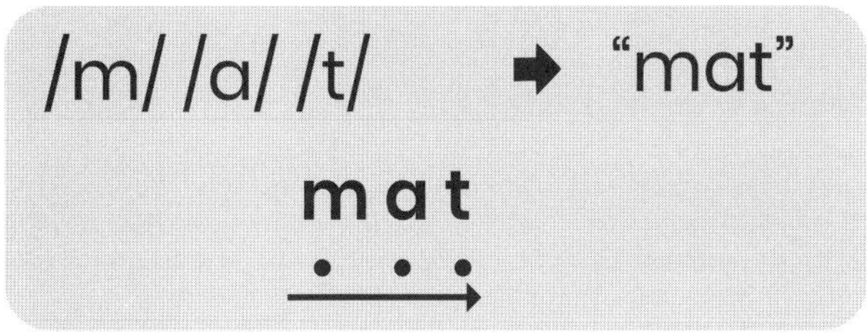

The student points to and says the sounds in the word one at a time, pointing to each sound. Then they move their finger under the whole word, blending all the sounds into the word. This first method has a greater load on working memory relative to the next two methods.

Method 2: Stretch and blend

"Stretch the sounds and push them together to read the word."

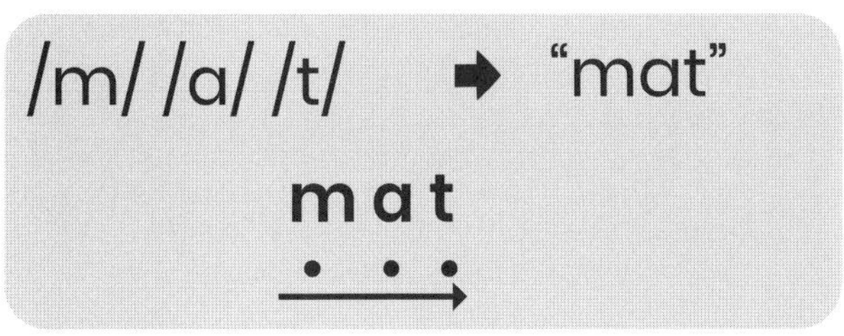

The teacher points to the first letter/sound, asking the student to say the sound and stretch it until their finger reaches the next sound in the word. The teacher moves their finger under the whole word, as the student blends all the sounds in the word.

Method 3: Blend and add

"Blend the first two sounds, then add the next sound."

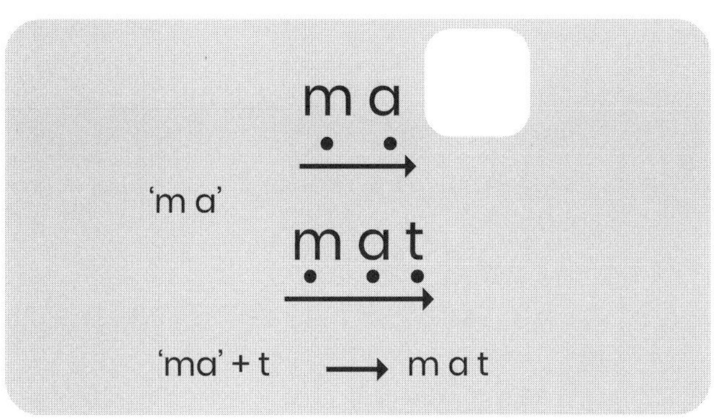

The teacher conceals the third letter/sound. Next, the teacher moves their finger under the first two sounds and asks the learner to blend just two sounds, e.g. 'm' + 'a' = 'ma.' Then the teacher repeats 'ma.' The teacher reveals the last letter/sound and asks the student to add 't.' Finally, the teacher points under the whole word as the student reads "mat."

Methods 2 and 3 have a lesser load on working memory relative to the first method.

How to write a word chain

A **word chain** is a list of words used to develop phonemic awareness skills: blending, segmenting, and phoneme manipulation. These are the underlying skills needed for reading. Word-chain activities are the most effective way to develop these skills.

In a word-chain activity, the teacher will ask the student to build a word (with letter cards or letters) and read it. The student is then asked to make a change to the word; for example, "Change the word 'pot' to 'pit'." The student will need to identify where the change in the word has occurred and then change, remove, or add the letter needed to read the new word.

What does a word chain look like?

This is an example of a word chain:

Letters: s, a, t, i, m, n, o, p

Word chain: nip—nap—tap—top—mop—map—sap—sip—tip

Many programs include word-chain activities, but it is useful to know how to write one. This skill allows the teacher to design a word-chain activity that can address a specific difficulty a student may have. For example, the student may confuse the sound and spelling of /ch/ and /sh/. A word chain to address this difficulty would look like this:

Letters: m, u, sh, ch, n, b, f, i, p, a, r, c
Word chain: mush—much—munch—bunch—bun—shun—shin—fin—finch—inch—pinch—pin—bin—ban—bash—brash—brush—crush—crash

The two examples above use real words, and this is suitable for young students. For older students, you can also use nonsense word chains. A typical example would look like this:

Letters: b, l, i, n, a, o, t, u
Word chain: blin—blan—lan—lon—lont—lunt—lut—blut

Here are some guidelines for creating a word chain:

1. Use one syllable words.
2. Use spellings from the simple code. It can get very confusing if vowel teams are included as many of them can be pronounced in different ways.
3. The word chain can include changing sounds, removing sounds, and adding sounds.
4. Make only one change at a time.

How to teach reading

One of the primary goals in teaching phonics is to equip students with the skills necessary to decode and comprehend text effectively. When students are reading, encourage them to sound out each word phonetically and then blend these sounds to form words. This lays the groundwork for developing fluent reading skills, as it enables students to approach unfamiliar words with confidence. Slow, labored reading can interfere with comprehension. When a student reads very slowly, reread each sentence after them to maintain comprehension of the text.

Once students are comfortable with sounding out and blending words, a next step could be to read a book from a previous lesson for a second time or multiple times to enhance fluency. This repetition helps to consolidate students' decoding skills. As students revisit the text, they begin to transition from mechanical decoding to reading with greater fluency.

This can be progressed to teaching them to vary their pitch, pace, and emphasis according to the words and punctuation in the text. Reading with expression not only makes the reading experience more fun but also aids in comprehension, as it brings the text to life and highlights its meaning.

How to correct reading errors

One of the most important elements of learning is receiving error feedback. With every error feedback, the student can adjust their knowledge or skill and can fine-tune them and make their reading increasingly accurate. Making and correcting errors is a great learning opportunity!

Reading with our students is a fantastic opportunity for error feedback. But before we can address the error, we need to know what kind of error the reader is making. Here are a few tips:

1. Error feedback should be a positive experience in which the student can succeed. So, after the feedback has taken place, the student should be able

to use the new information and read a word or sentence successfully.

2. It is very helpful to use a pointer or a pencil to show the student where the error occurred in the word. The error can even occur between letters on the page, so accurate pointing is essential.
3. When the student has read the word correctly, it is helpful to reread the whole sentence so that they can reread the correct word in the context of the text.

What kinds of reading errors do students make?

Lack of Alphabetic Code knowledge

Many students make reading errors because they have insufficient knowledge of the Alphabetic Code. For example, when a student reads the word "goat" as /g/ /o/ /a/ /t/, we can see that they don't know that the grapheme 'oa' spells the sound /oe/.

So, how can feedback be given? Point to both letters and say: "These two letters represent one sound: /oe/. Sound out the word with /oe/ here (pointing to the letters 'oa')." The student then blends the sounds together: /g/ /oe/ /t/ → "goat."

Not matching sounds to graphemes (letter/s)

Students may add or omit sounds when they read. To develop reading accuracy, they will need to match the graphemes to the sounds in the word. Here are typical examples of reading errors.

Adding sounds: When a student reads the word "back" as "black," we can see that they are adding the sound /l/. To give feedback, point to the word and say: "You read "black" but there is no /l/ here (pointing to the place the 'l' would be in the word "black"). Sound out the word." The student should then sound the word correctly: /b/ /a/ /k/ → "back."

Omitting sounds: When a student reads the word "frog" as "fog," we can see that they are omitting a sound in the word. To give feedback, point to the letter 'r' and say: "There is a /r/ here. Sound out the word with the /r/ here (pointing to the letter 'r')." The student then sounds out the word pointing to the letters /f/ /r/ /o/ /g/ → "frog."

Reversing a word

When a student reads "was" for "saw," we can see that they have flipped the word. So, how can feedback be given? Ask the student to sound out the word. /s/ /aw/. Remind the student that 'aw' spells /aw/. Ask the student to blend the sounds into a word: /s/ /aw/ → "saw."

Developing vocabulary

Systematic synthetic phonics focuses on the mechanics of learning to read: developing the skills to sound out, blend to read, and segment to spell. It is a structured, progressive program towards reading fluency. However, alongside that process, it's critical to develop the broader reading skills: prosody, pace, comprehension, and vocabulary. Phonics success is based on careful, steady progression, so that students are only exposed to words in their books which contain the sounds and high-frequency words they know. Yet, every reading experience is an opportunity to develop a student's wider vocabulary, through questioning and discussion. For example: Later in the Catch-up series program, the readers will include a vocabulary list that highlights difficult words and expressions found within the story. This list will be accompanied by definitions to help readers better understand and engage with the text, encouraging the student to think about what they have read.

Additionally, the That Dog! and Island Adventure activities books include a vocabulary activity for each chapter, which tests their understanding of new vocabulary. The students have to match two parts of sentences so that they make sense.

Talking about the words students decode: exploring meaning, looking at patterns, and discussing synonyms and antonyms will not only help secure comprehension and reading for meaning, but will also grow and develop a student's more general language knowledge. For example, while reading the word "swift," students can explore synonyms like "quick" and "fast," and antonyms such as "slow." Discussing these words not only enhances vocabulary but also clarifies the concept of speed as it applies to different contexts, thereby enhancing students' understanding of linguistic relationships.

Oracy is one of the key elements of vocabulary development; therefore, alongside the phonics skills, high-quality discussion around texts furthers the learning opportunities and outcomes.

There are lots of different ways to structure the discussion and get the most out of every page in a reading book—at any level.

For instance, in Book 4: Ned, the Cat (Moon Dogs Set 1), the following prompts could be used around page 1, "Dan has a pet cat, Ned." in order to extend the language around the book.

- What words rhyme with "cat"? (bat, mat, sat, rat)
- What is Ned doing? (climbing on top of Dan)
- What is the setting? (the living room)
- What else is in the picture? (Ned (the pet cat), sofa)

Then, on page 2:

- What is Dan feeding to Ned? (a cod)
- What other fishes do you know? (salmon, tuna, goldfish, clownfish, etc)
- How do you think Ned feels? (happy, excited, pleased)

Likewise, at a phonetically more challenging level there are still plenty of discursive opportunities, for example in *Saving the Day* (Island Adventure, Book 1) the following prompts could be used around the content on pages 2 and 3:

- Which words on the two pages end with the suffix -ed? (jumped, filled, hopped, tipped, grabbed, grinned)
- How do you think Jack is feeling? (happy, excited, relieved)
- What were Jack and Gran waiting for? (They were waiting to get a great shot (photograph) of the puffins.)

How to teach reading comprehension

For students to become fluent readers, they need to be able to understand what they are reading. Students should be encouraged to discuss what happens in the stories and to give spoken answers to comprehension questions. This improves students' understanding of language, develops their wider vocabulary and increases their interest in learning to read.

The activity books contain various types of activities to enable students to put their comprehension skills into practice. For example, That Dog! Activities includes **Retell the story** activities where students retell the story or create their own story using the pictures and word cards provided on the page.

Other comprehension activities include the **Comprehension** activity where students are given a list of discussion questions to answer after reading the focal text. This activity will help students to develop speaking and listening skills, comprehension, and vocabulary.

Additionally, there is a **Spot it!** activity where students are presented with a picture from the story and a list of statements, which they have to circle the words "yes" or "no" depending on what they can see in the picture.

In the **Sequence the story** activity, students are given a set of jumbled sentences, which they then read and sequence in the correct order to match the story.

The **Fill in the missing words** activity provides students with a passage to read. They then fill in the gaps with missing words. The students should be encouraged to sound out the words as they write them on the lines.

Other examples include the **Make a book** activity where students read the text and then draw a picture to match the text on each page, and the **Is it true?** activity where students are given a passage and they have to identify the falsehoods planted in the story.

Book 1: Comprehension

Questions for Discussion

Chapter 1

1. What can Ben see from the top of the ramp? (page 1)
2. Ben wants to fix something in the dump. What is it? (page 2)

Chapter 2

1. Why does the dog yelp? (page 4)
2. Why does the man bring the dog to the dump? (pages 4 and 5)

Chapter 3

1. Why do you think Ben falls from his bike? (page 7)
2. How does the dog react when Ben falls from his bike? (page 8)

Chapter 4

1. Why do you think Ben is cross with himself? (page 9)
2. 'Ben is fond of dogs, but his mom is not.' What does that mean? (page 10)
3. What do you think will happen next? (page 12)

Teaching guidelines:
These questions can be discussed after reading the text. They will help develop speaking and listening skills, comprehension and vocabulary.

Book 3 51

Is it true?

Jack and Gran set off for the mainland in a speedboat. The sea is rough and choppy. A climber calls to them from a sea stack. He has dropped his hat and can't reach it. Jack jumps from the boat to help him. The man is very grateful and is able to finish his climb. They reach the mainland. Gran collects up an old camper van. A massive rock rolls down the hill and crashes into them. Jack is excited to see it has carvings on it. He thinks it looks like a football!

There are **5** things in the story above that are not true. Can you spot them?

Ask the student to read the text carefully and circle any false information that has been planted in the story.

How to teach letter formation

Following reading and comprehension activities, the next step is to teach students how to practice writing the graphemes they have learned.

First, learning how to grip a pencil correctly is an important step for developing neat handwriting. The pencil should rest comfortably between the thumb and index finger, supported by the middle finger, with the other two fingers curled inwards. With their hands resting on the table, students should learn to move the pencil forward using their hand muscles. Regular practice in letter formation and careful monitoring of each student's technique during dictation exercises are key to cultivating long-term neat handwriting and preventing the development of poor habits.

When teaching letter formation, it is recommended to use lined paper that will demonstrate the proportions of ascender and descender letters. This way the students can practice forming letters correctly from the get go.

Teachers play a vital role in this learning process. They can demonstrate letter formation effectively by writing on the whiteboard or visually tracing the letters' movements in the air.

The activity books include writing, spelling, and dictation exercises, such as **Writing captions**, where students are dictated captions by the teacher for them to write on the page. To reinforce their learning, students should be encouraged to vocalize the sounds as they write, and then blend these sounds together while forming each word.

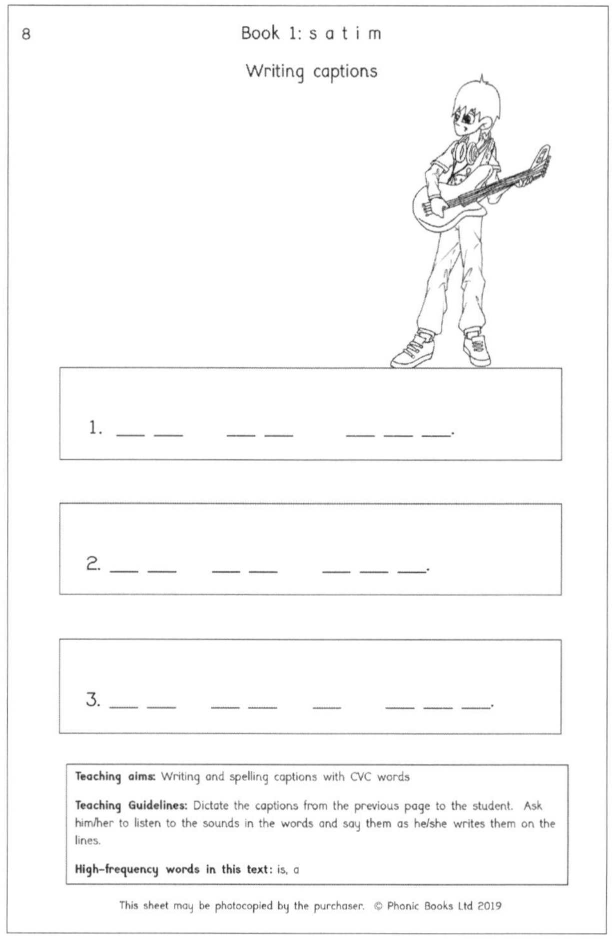
8

Book 1: s a t i m

Writing captions

1. __ __ __ __ __ __ __.

2. __ __ __ __ __ __ __.

3. __ __ __ __ __ __ __ __.

Teaching aims: Writing and spelling captions with CVC words

Teaching Guidelines: Dictate the captions from the previous page to the student. Ask him/her to listen to the sounds in the words and say them as he/she writes them on the lines.

High-frequency words in this text: is, a

This sheet may be photocopied by the purchaser. © Phonic Books Ltd 2019

How to do a dictation activity

Dictation is a great way to consolidate the bonds between reading and spelling. It is a controlled exercise where students can succeed because the teacher includes words with spellings the students have already learned. Unlike a story writing activity where the students will attempt to spell words they may not be able to encode yet, dictation provides a "safe" activity where all students can succeed.

Dictation can be done at word level or sentence level. Writing and spelling words is hugely taxing on working memory. The student must hear and understand the word or sentence. Then, they must hold it in working memory while retrieving a letter/s (grapheme) for each sound in each word. Some students may forget the word or part of the sentence. For this reason, it is important to follow a clear routine for dictation.

Dictation activities can serve as useful records of learning and identifying difficulties that students are experiencing. It can be done on small individual whiteboards or in notebooks.

The teacher can photograph or keep these and identify any students who need further support.

Many students will still have difficulties forming letters correctly. The purpose of a dictation activity is to see how students use their phonics knowledge to encode words. If the words are illegible, letter formation should be addressed. If not, find another opportunity to work on letter formation.

Single word dictation

Choose a list of words that the students have been learning. Make sure they have had sufficient practice reading and spelling these words. Say the word first; next, put it within the context of a sentence; and then repeat the word. This way the students can understand the word before they write it down. Pause after each word to check that all the students have finished writing.

The teacher can say, for example:

"I am going to dictate some words and I would like you to write them down.
dog. The dog barked. dog.
bag. Gran has a bag. bag.
gap. There is a gap in the road. gap."
etc.

Sentence dictation

Writing a sentence is more taxing on working memory than remembering one word at a time and spelling it. Some students will find it difficult to hold the complete sentence in working memory. It is good practice to break any long sentences into parts to enable all students to keep up. After all, we are not checking working memory but how students represent the words with graphemes they have learned.

The teacher will need to decide if they provide their students with high-frequency words that have more complex spellings, for example "the." These words can be written on the board to remind the students how to spell them.

The teacher will also need to decide whether they will include capital letters and periods in this activity. This depends on whether this has been taught previously.

Dictated sentences will need to be decodable—this means that all the words, except a few necessary high-frequency words, will be within the knowledge of the students. The teacher can write these sentences or take them from a decodable book the students have read. For beginner readers, just one or two sentences will be sufficient for this activity.

The teacher can say:
"I am going to dictate a sentence.
I would like you to listen to it and then say it.
Then, write it down.
Sim has a cap on."

The teacher repeats:
"Sim has a cap on. Now you say it."
Students repeat:
"Sim has a cap on."
Students write the sentence.

How to teach high-frequency words

High-frequency words are frequently used words that can potentially present a challenge to students: they cannot easily read or write them through decoding, such as blending and listening for sounds. This difficulty arises because these words often contain letter–sound combinations that the students have not yet learned.

The program gradually introduces high-frequency words to expand the students' vocabulary. The scheme of work charts, found on page 28, list all the high-frequency words introduced in each book covered by the lesson plans in this manual. Furthermore, each Reader conveniently lists the high-frequency words featured in its story at the beginning of the book, providing an easy reference for both students and teachers.

The chart on pages 47–48 provides the first 300 high-frequency words taught in the program.

Simple spellings

vc
am
an
at
if
in
it
on
up
us

/ck/
ba**ck**
bla**ck**
du**ck**

V
a

vcc
and
end
its

cvc /a/
bat
can
cat
ran
dad
had
man
sat

cvcc
best
fast
help
just
jump
land
left
last
list
milk
must
nest
next
went

cvc /e/
bed
get
let
men
bell
red
set
ten
well
yes

ccvc
from
still
spot
stop
gran
step

cvc /i/
big
did
him
sit
six
miss

/th/ (voiced)
that
the
them
then
this
wi**th**

/th/ (unvoiced)
think

cvc /o/
box
dog
got
hot
mom
not

/w/
when
which

/sh/
fi**sh**
wi**sh**

/ch/
mu**ch**
su**ch**

cvc /u/
but
cut
fun
run

/z/
a**s**
i**s**
ha**s**
hi**s**

/ng/
alo**ng**
bri**ng**
ki**ng**
lo**ng**
so**ng**
thi**ng**

/v/
gi**ve**
ha**ve**
li**ve**
o**f**

THE FIRST 300 HIGH-FREQUENCY WORDS

Complex spellings

/ae/

c**a**k**e**
c**a**m**e**
g**a**v**e**
l**a**t**e**
m**a**d**e**
m**a**k**e**
n**a**m**e**
t**a**k**e**
d**ay**
m**ay**
pl**ay**
s**ay**
w**ay**
alw**ay**s
aw**ay**
gr**ea**t
eight
th**ey**

/e/

ag**ai**n
s**ai**d
h**ea**d
r**ea**d
br**ea**d
any
m**a**ny
fr**ie**nds

/oe/

g**o**
g**o**ing
n**o**
s**o**
b**o**th
c**o**ld
d**o**n't
old
h**o**ld
t**o**ld
m**o**st
only
open
b**oa**t
c**oa**t
h**o**m**e**
th**o**s**e**
gr**ow**
kn**ow**
own
sh**ow**
th**ough**

/ie/

I
ch**i**ld
f**i**nd
k**i**nd
f**i**v**e**
l**i**k**e**
l**i**n**e**
t**i**m**e**
wh**i**t**e**
wr**i**t**e**
b**y**
m**y**
fl**y**
tr**y**
wh**y**
h**igh**
n**igh**t
r**igh**t

/i/

been

/ee/

b**e**
h**e**
m**e**
sh**e**
w**e**
even
th**e**s**e**
f**ee**l
f**ee**t
gr**ee**n
k**ee**p
n**ee**d
s**ee**
sl**ee**p
tr**ee**
thr**ee**
each
eat
l**ea**ve
t**ea**
pl**ea**se
r**ea**d
bab**y**
carr**y**
ever**y**
reall**y**
ver**y**
k**ey**

/or/

or
d**oor**
fl**oor**
c**or**n
f**or**
h**or**se
m**or**ning
bef**ore**
m**ore**
sh**or**t

/oi/

b**oy**
t**oy**

/ow/

ab**ou**t
ar**ou**nd
f**ou**nd
h**ou**se
m**ou**se
out
our
r**ou**nd
gr**ou**nd
d**ow**n
c**ow**
h**ow**
n**ow**
t**ow**n

Uncommon spellings

one
once
two
people
everyone

/er/

h**er**
aft**er**
bett**er**
ev**er**
fath**er**
lett**er**
nev**er**
ov**er**
pap**er**
riv**er**
und**er**
wat**er**
w**ere**
b**ir**ds
f**ir**st
g**ir**l
pict**ure**
w**or**k

/oo/

m**oo**n
d**o**
t**o**
int**o**
wh**o**
t**o**gether
c**oo**l
f**oo**d
sch**oo**l
s**oo**n
t**oo**
gr**ou**p
n**ew**

Multisyllable words

American
children
different
little
magic
rabbit
suddenly

/aw/

all
f**a**ll
b**a**ll
c**a**ll
sm**a**ll
w**a**lk
t**a**lk
s**aw**

/ar/

are
c**ar**
d**ar**k
f**ar**
f**ar**m
h**ar**d
g**ar**den
p**ar**k
st**ar**t

/air/

air
b**ear**
th**eir**
th**ere**
wh**ere**

/u/

m**o**ther
d**oe**s
c**o**me
s**o**me
w**a**s

/o/

wh**a**t
w**a**nt
w**a**tch

/oo/

l**oo**k
b**oo**k
g**oo**d
l**oo**k
t**oo**k
w**oo**d
p**u**t
c**ou**ld
w**ou**ld

/ue/

us**e**

How to teach multi-syllabic words

Learning two-syllable words is an important step in learning to read. We often assume that students can transfer their decoding and encoding skills from one-syllable words to words with more than one syllable, but many students struggle with this transition.

To read and spell words with more than one syllable, students need to be able to segment (chunk) longer words into syllables. At this point we begin to work on two levels of phonological processing—the larger, syllable level and at the same time the smaller phoneme level. Some students may find this confusing.

A good place to start is to get students attuned to syllables. It is helpful to explain that a syllable is a mouthful of a word, and that the chin drops between syllables. Children can practice listening to syllables by playing fun clapping games, e.g., clapping the syllables in their names, or the names of animals (elephant, hippopotamus). Once students are attuned into hearing syllables in words, we can begin with building words with more than one syllable.

How to build words with more than one syllable

Preparation: use a whiteboard and the sound cards needed to build the word. Place the sound cards jumbled up on the board.

1. Start with a compound word e.g., "laptop."
2. Draw two lines on the board (one for each syllable) and ask the students to chunk the word "laptop" into syllables. Make sure that the students pronounce the syllables clearly: "lap" "top."

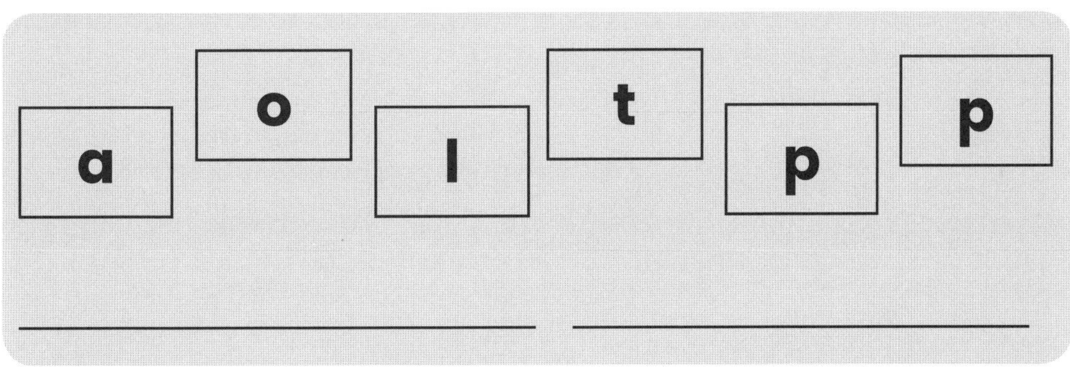

3. Ask the students to tell you the first syllable in the word "laptop" and point to the first line, moving your finger under the whole word as you say it.
4. Students reply "lap."
5. Ask a student to build the syllable "lap" on the first line, pointing to the first line.

6. Ask the students what the second syllable is in the word "laptop," moving your finger under the whole word as you do.
7. Students reply "top." Ask the students to build the syllable "top" on the second line.

l	a	p		t	o	p
___	___	___		___	___	___

8. Now ask all the students to read the word moving your finger as they read each syllable: "lap" "top."
9. Ask the students if they can read the word faster: "laptop."
10. Finally, ask the students to spell the word "laptop" and say each syllable as they spell the word.

laptop

Once the students are confident building, reading, and spelling compound words, the teacher can repeat this word-building activity with two-syllable words, using graphemes the students have learned.

Syllable chunking

Once the students have learned how to build and spell two-syllable words, it is important for them to practice chunking two-syllable words.

Once students have learned how to build and spell two-syllable words, it is important for them to practice chunking multisyllabic words into syllables. This will help them read longer words. When reading a two-syllable word, ask the student where the end of a "mouthful" of the syllable is. A syllable will often have a vowel. Ask the students to note how the jaw drops with every syllable. Students should mark the syllable split with a vertical line. The activities books and Phonic Books website offer many opportunities to do this.

How to teach alternative spellings for vowel and consonant sounds

One of the difficult aspects of the Alphabetic Code is that sounds can be spelled in different ways. For example, the sound /ae/ can be spelled 'ai' (rain), 'ay' (day), 'a–e' (came), 'ea' (great), and 'a' (baby), and these are only the common spellings! As students learn more and more of the code, we want them to build a mental framework that incorporates this concept of multiple spellings. We want our students to understand that sounds can be represented in different ways and to recognize these spelling patterns when they read. Later, they will need to learn which spelling fits in which word. How can we teach this?

Word sorting

The best way to demonstrate how a sound can be spelled in different ways is through sorting activities. After teaching the students about the graphemes 'ai' and 'ay' for example (ideally through word building), the students should be given words to sort according to spelling. This activity enables the students to compare and contrast words. It will often reveal typical spelling patterns, for example, that the spelling 'ay' comes at the end of a base word while 'ai' will usually appear in the middle of the word.

How many alternatives?

The teacher must decide how many alternatives to include when the students carry out this sorting activity. This will depend on the program being followed. It is important not to present these spellings in an isolated way as the students will not make the connection between them. If this activity is part of an intervention program, it is helpful to introduce the different spellings in a gradual way. Always include previous learning so that the concept of "one sound—different spellings" is built on what the students already know.

Word wall in the classroom

A great way to reinforce the different spellings for a sound is to display them in the classroom. This display will remind students of the different ways to spell a sound. New words can be added to the display as they are encountered. This display will then become a useful spelling tool. For example, if a student spells the word "came" as "cam," the teacher can direct them to the display and say, "Use the a–e spelling in this word."

The language we use

We can reinforce the concept that a sound can be spelled in different ways by the language we use. When a student encounters an additional way to spell the sound, we say, "Yes, this is another way to spell the sound /ae/." This dispels the notion that there is only one way to spell the sound /ae/ and develops a flexible approach to a complex code. Students learn that when they spell a sound there are a number of options, and they will need to choose the correct option when they spell a word.

How (and why) we need to teach the schwa sound

Did you know that the schwa is the most common sound in the English language? This is because there is a schwa sound in most multisyllabic words. Additionally, did you know that the schwa can be pronounced in more than one way?

What is a schwa sound?

In most English accents, multisyllabic words are pronounced with at least one stressed syllable. A schwa sound is a "weak" or "lazy" vowel sound in an unstressed syllable. For example, take the word "mountain." The stress is on the first syllable: "<u>moun</u>-tain." The sound of the vowel in the second (unstressed) syllable is a schwa sound: "<u>moun</u>-t**ai**n." This schwa sound is gobbled up and can sound like a clipped /u/ or /i/. A schwa sound is never present in a stressed syllable.

Why do we need to teach the schwa sound?

Once students can decode two-syllable words, they can read them with the stress patterns they know from their speech. For example, when a student has learned to decode the word "mountain," they will instinctively pronounce the word with the stress on the first syllable. They will do this because they already have the word in their lexicon. If the word is new to the student, it is important to teach them how to pronounce it with the correct syllable stress.

The schwa is a spelling issue—not a reading issue. When students spell a multisyllabic word, they will listen to the sounds in the word and all too often they will spell the "lazy" schwa sound incorrectly because they hear the clipped /u/ or /i/ sound. They may even omit the sound altogether. For example, students may spell the word "mount**ai**n" as "mount**u**n," "mount**i**n," "mount**e**n," or even "mountn."

How do we teach students to spell the schwa sound correctly?

Step 1

Model the word and ask the student to say the word with the correct syllable stress.

Step 2

Ask the students to split the word into syllables and identify the stressed syllable.

moun-tain

Step 3

Ask the students to find the schwa sound in the "weak" syllable.

moun-t**ai**n

Step 4

At this point the teacher can introduce the "spelling voice." Students are encouraged to sound out the schwa as it is spelled. For example: when spelling the word "mountain," the teacher will show the students how to say an exaggerated /ai/ sound as they spell the second syllable. They say the sounds /m/ /ou/ /n/—/t/ /**ae**/ /n/. The /ae/ sound is exaggerated to remind the student how to spell the word. Now the student can underline the spelling of the schwa sound. Other words with the same spelling pattern and stress can be tackled at the same time, for example "fountain," "captain," and "certain."

mountain

How to teach vocabulary when reading a decodable book

Decodable books often include target words that students may not know. There are many reasons why students may not know words in a text:

- The word may be unusual.
- The students may have limited language as English language learners.
- The students may have a language disability.
- The students may have had limited opportunities to read books at home.

Learning new vocabulary is beneficial for all students. It helps them develop their expressive and receptive language. This will also develop their comprehension as they become readers.

When we teach new vocabulary, we want our students to learn how a word sounds and how it is spelled. We want them to make connections to words they already know, so the new vocabulary is stored securely in long-term memory and can be retrieved when needed.

Here is how we recommend teaching students new words encountered in a decodable book. The example here is the word "murky" from Book 7: An Amazing Find from the Island Adventure series.

1. Demonstrate how letters map onto the sounds in the word.

murky	or	m	**ur**	k	y

2. Say the word clearly. Ask the students to repeat the word. All too often students are not confident in pronouncing new words. /m/ /ur/ /k/ /y/ → "murky." This is particularly important when the word has more than one syllable as students need to know which syllable to stress.
3. Define the word. For example, "The word 'murky' means somewhere dark and gloomy, often in mist."

4. Give an example from the decodable book. Ask questions, such as, "Why does Ash make Jack go into the cave first?" Students can answer in their own words. ("Ash makes Jack go in first because she jokes that it might be full of wild tigers.")
5. Ask the students to give another example of when a place might be "murky." ("A swamp can be murky because it is full of dark, muddy water.")
6. Ask the students to compare with synonyms. "Is 'foggy a stronger word than 'murky?" Discuss the differences in meaning and usage.
7. Write the word "murky" on the whiteboard and revisit it throughout the week. Discuss how it relates to the passage and encourage students to use them in their own sentences.

How to read a nonfiction decodable book

While the main lesson plans in this instructional manual predominantly focus on the Moon Dogs, That Dog!, and Island Adventure series, which are centred around fiction, this section delves into nonfiction decoding.

Nonfiction decodable books are wonderful reading resources. They combine two essential parts of reading: word recognition (decoding) and world knowledge (language comprehension and subject vocabulary).

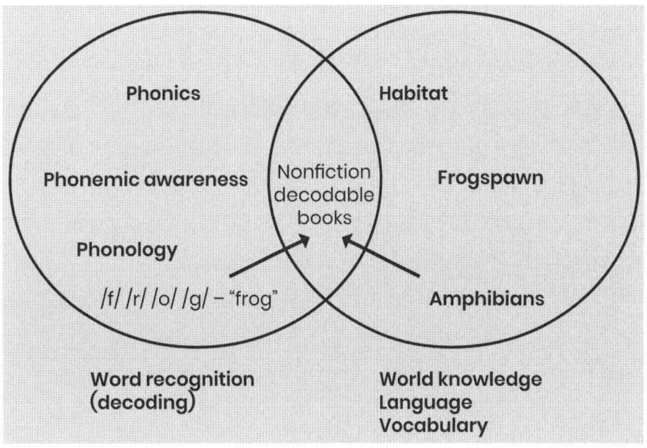

Educators now recognize that world knowledge has an important part to play in reading comprehension. Students who lack world knowledge can't make sense of a text that presumes they have general knowledge. For example, a sentence that describes a character as a "fossil" will have little meaning to a student who has not learned about what fossils are and how they are created.

The Island Adventure Activities book includes non-fiction passages. In this activity students are required to read the text carefully and circle relevant information. Then they are tasked to use this information to produce a piece of writing, such as a flyer or postcard.

Before reading a decodable non-fiction text, teachers can start by asking the students what they know about the topic. This way new learning is built on what the students already understand and know. Next, they can then ask questions to ensure that the students have understood the subject and vocabulary. They then read the text and facilitate a discussion. Finally, teachers can link the text the students have decoded to the subject knowledge already learned.

FLUENCY AND PROSODY

Fluency in reading encompasses the ability to read text accurately and quickly but also with proper expression, known as prosody. Each of these elements are integral for constructing meaning. Fluency and comprehension are interlinked; disfluent reading can significantly hinder comprehension, while difficulty with comprehension can in turn impede fluency. Therefore, the development of a reading pace that supports comprehension, alongside accurate and expressive reading of all words—including high-frequency words—is a fundamental aspect of learning to read.

If students are not able to read fluently, it is a useful indicator of where revision and consolidation are required. Specific grapheme–phoneme correspondences or high-frequency words can be targeted and upskilled to increase a student's confidence. Once students are reading evenly and quickly, with no overt blending, and correctly differentiating between the individual words, it is useful to re-read the text with prosody in mind (reading rhythmically, with intonation and expression).

The basics of sound grapheme–phoneme correspondence knowledge and secure blending skills need to be in place before fluency and prosody can be achieved, but working on these simultaneously, with each text read multiple times, will ensure a more rounded, successful reading experience with much better comprehension outcomes.

When students are focusing on the mechanics of decoding, they are far less likely to grasp meaning from the text than when they read quicker, with no audible blending and with a tone that reflects the content. Reading success and enjoyment is dependent on decoding competence *and* fluent, expressive pace, but it's easy for the latter to get forgotten in the race to achieve decoding proficiency.

A large part of reading accurately and with expression is about understanding punctuation and what impact it has on the text. Encouraging students from the very start of their reading journey to "read" commas and full stops, to change their tone at the beginning and end of a sentence, for parentheses, for speech, and to draw breath at the right points is critical for effective prosody.

In texts as early as Book 3: Sam and the Bat (Moon Dogs Set 1), the language features signify the tone. For example: the repetition of "Sim has a..." influences the intonation and encourages a particular rhythm. By page 6, "Sim can hit it!" might be read slightly louder, with more emphasis and enthusiasm, perhaps with a smile to mirror the character's excitement and satisfcation at hitting the ball.

It can be useful to model reading the text in different ways, with and without expression, in order to highlight the contrast and demonstrate how much meaning can be grasped by the *way* words are read, not just by the words themselves. Understanding how to interpret literary techniques, such as repetition (for example, as an indication of emphasis) will enhance what students get out of text, but it will also help develop what they put into their own texts, with meaningful, sophisticated writing skills.

As the text complexity develops, so does the opportunity for prosody, for example in Book 7: An Amazing Find (Island Adventure).

The use of the ellipsis on page 1 signifies a pause for dramatic effect. This is a good opportunity to draw breath, or even to hold breath momentarily: "Apples for breakfast..." The reader is held in suspense. When the outcome is revealed: "with a side dish of apples" the punchline is revealed and the use of an exclamation mark adds to the staccato effect.

There is a significant amount of direct speech, where the expression is provided: "'Just apples? I wish it was slices of nice, hot apple pie with cream!' groaned Ash."

Students should practice reading this in a sighing or disappointed tone to indicate the character's unhappiness. The exclamation mark after "cream" emphasizes the character's longing.

As the emotional descriptions change, so too should the tone and expression of the reader, so when characters move from being "disappointed" (page 1) to being "excited" (page 3) the use of exclamation marks and the description of direct speech being yelled requires a different voice.

For example: "'Look at the paper!' Ash cried out. 'It has writing on it!'" suggests a loud, quick tone—but in excitement, rather than disappointment as previously.

DIFFERENTIATION

Because of the nature of phonics teaching (the fast, systematic pace), the ideal is to keep the class or cohort together, progressing together. However, this relies on the pace of students' learning needs being similar, which isn't always the case, and there are many reasons why some students will struggle with different aspects of phonics learning. Maintaining a clear picture of how individuals are coping with the new skills as they are taught, means that needs can be identified the moment they become apparent, ensuring that no student gets left behind. Those needs can then be met through a range of activities (delivered in a variety of formats) to bolster and fill any skill gaps, so that students can keep up with their peers and continue their learning with the rest of the group.

It's important to recognize the level of need in terms of whether students are some way off expectations, or just below them, so that the right support can be provided. In the most part, those not meeting expectations would benefit from small-group work to target and consolidate shared skill challenges before they become significant issues. However, the students who are significantly behind expectations (e.g. within the lowest-achieving 20%) are likely to benefit from more specialized, bespoke, individual intervention delivered one-to-one.

The Phonic Books program has a huge volume of resources to accompany every reading book to practice and consolidate learning at each point in the journey. Therefore, when a couple or small group of students are identified as struggling with the same concept, such as a specific grapheme–phoneme correspondence or particular high-frequency words, small-group work using or adapting the activities provided enables a useful, collaborative environment to reinforce learning and upskill the area of challenge.

For example, if students are struggling with any of the grapheme–phoneme correspondences or with blending specifics, during their reading of Moon Dogs Set 1 Book 1: Is It Matt?, there is a wealth of material to support that:

- Depending on which grapheme–phoneme correspondences are proving a struggle, the **Word-building cards** in the accompanying activity book could be revisited. To avoid these being used in the same way as the main lesson and feeling repetitive or predictable, there are lots of creative ways that they can be manipulated (see the next section).
- Re-playing some of the games, e.g. the (**Jumping Jack** game from the readers, or the **Dice game** from the accompanying activity book) provides the opportunity for repeated practice.

It is also possible that students will be secure in the sounds but have trouble making meaning from the text. This is often due to the cognitive load of decoding. For these obstacles, a different focus would be beneficial, again using the material provided. For example: students could work one-to-one, in pairs, or in small groups to retell or recap the story, using the pictures, words, and sentence matching (in the activity book). The ability to accurately and coherently sequence events is critical in early reading comprehension.

As students progress through the program, and the phonics becomes more complex, the volume, range, and variety of accompanying activities increases, providing plenty of differentiation opportunities. For example, in That Dog! Book 12: Dog in Trouble, if students find the sound for the 'le' spelling challenging, the following material could be utilised in various different formats:

- The grapheme cards from the accompanying activity books, and the

Reading practice pages within the readers, would provide an opportunity for revision and reinforcement. Again, the next section provides some creative ideas for differentiation at this level.

- Revisiting the games, for example the **4-in-a-row**, **Stepping stones**, and memory games, also provides useful and fun opportunities for consolidation.

If the stumbling block is around comprehension at a higher level, some vocabulary work would be useful to ensure students understand the words they're decoding. Activities that support this include:

- Looking at real and nonsense le words (from the activity book) is beneficial particularly if students are asked for definitions as they go.
- Matching sentences to pictures (from the activity book) supports sequencing and plot recapping; these activities can all be executed orally, in writing or in a more dynamic, physical capacity such as through role play or mime.
- Using these resources, as well as any of the images from the readers can also help drill down further into the text depth, if discussion is promoted; supporting students to explore how characters feel and think enables much more robust comprehension to be reached.

It is useful to have a flexible approach to differentiation, and to be aware that students are likely to move in and out of different small groups and sometimes not need additional support at all. The idea is that the groups flex and change according to the needs of the class, to ensure continual, steady progress for all students.

English as an additional or foreign language

For students joining the cohort late, and those with English as an additional language, the key is on-entry assessment to see how much phonic knowledge has already been acquired. This means that students start at the right point in the program, whatever their prior experience. Because of the methodical, rigorous nature of systematic synthetic phonics teaching, the pedagogy is very inclusive. However, it's important to be aware of existing concepts of language for those with English as an additional language, which may make grasping the fundamentals (specifically the grapheme–phoneme correspondences) more challenging than for native English-speaking kindergarten students. Having said that, students with English as an additional language are likely to catch up quickly with their peers, and so need fast-paced, short-term differentiated tuition, and then not need on-going additional support, at least not on a phonic level. It's more likely that the stumbling blocks for students with English as an additional language will be around comprehension, for which any of the strategies identified here can be applied. Additionally, it's worth considering extra pronunciation support (to also be available at home for parental use).

Strategies for phonics differentiation

Any of these creative ideas can be adapted according to specific grapheme–phoneme correspondences and/or high-frequency words. They all work to practice and consolidate the key phonic skills, as well as build confidence and familiarity more generally.

Grapheme–phoneme correspondence recognition

- Hold the sound cards behind your back and draw them out one at a time for students to practice sounding out. You can do this quicker and quicker as they become more confident, mixing up the order and increasing the pace. This works with high-frequency words, too.
- Stick the sound cards around the classroom (or playground) and ask students to hop to one sound, skip to one and jump to another as you call them out.
- Find a selection of items in the classroom that start with the sounds on the grapheme cards, and ask students to sort the items into different groups according

to what sound they start with.

- Choose a sound from the cards and encourage students to go on a treasure hunt around the classroom to find as many things as they can that begin with that sound.

High-frequency words

- Play a card-matching game. Can the student find the matching card, for example, for the word "is"?

Blending

- Stick the sound cards on individual building blocks and encourage students to put the blocks together to "build" simple words. Say each sound together and then help students to blend them together to read the words out loud. Next, try separating the blocks again to segment the word back into its individual sounds.
- See the recommendations for how to teach blending (pages 48–49). Methods 2 and 3 can be particularly effective for students who are struggling. For Method 2 (Stretch and Blend), for example the word "mat," use a car or moving toy to stretch the sounds until the car moves to the next sound: /mmmmmaaaaat/. For Method 3 (Add and Blend), hide the last letter in the word. Using a toy car, ask the student to blend the first two sounds and move the car underneath the two first letters: 'ma.' Then add the third letter, and move the toy car under the three letters:
'ma' + 't' = 'mat.'
- Place all the sound cards on the table, and see how many different words students can build. They need to write the words they have built down.

ASSESSMENT

Continuous assessment

To ensure students are confident with the new sounds they have learned in each lesson plan, it's important to track their progress using quick, formative assessments.

For example, Moon Dogs VCe Spellings Activities book contains **Bookmarks**, which feature words printed on them that incorporate the phonic skills covered in the lessons. Teachers can check students are comfortable using these words before moving on to the next stage in the books.

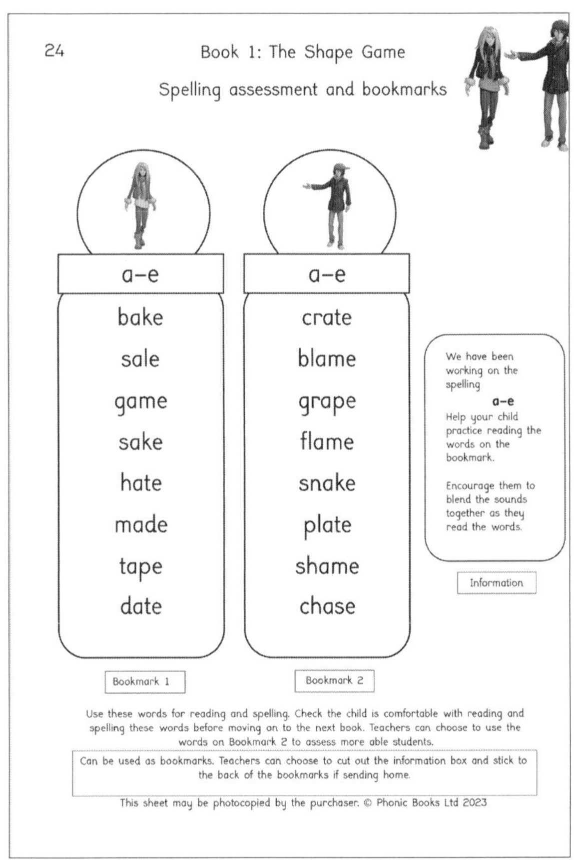

24

Book 1: The Shape Game

Spelling assessment and bookmarks

Bookmark 1	Bookmark 2
a–e	a–e
bake	crate
sale	blame
game	grape
sake	flame
hate	snake
made	plate
tape	shame
date	chase

Information:
We have been working on the spelling
a–e
Help your child practice reading the words on the bookmark.

Encourage them to blend the sounds together as they read the words.

Use these words for reading and spelling. Check the child is comfortable with reading and spelling these words before moving on to the next book. Teachers can choose to use the words on Bookmark 2 to assess more able students.

Can be used as bookmarks. Teachers can choose to cut out the information box and stick to the back of the bookmarks if sending home.

This sheet may be photocopied by the purchaser. © Phonic Books Ltd 2023

Spelling assessments involve dictation exercises where a word is first said in isolation, then used within a sentence, and finally repeated. This method ensures clarity in hearing and understanding the word. For example, the word "Fainted" might be presented as, "Fainted. The boy fainted when he saw the mouse. Fainted." This approach also encourages phonetic spelling, helping to develop writing skills.

24

Book 1

Spelling assessment for words with 'ae' spellings

1.

ai	ay	a	a-e	ea
rain	day	baby	name	break
faint	play	table	late	steak
brain	spray	bacon	shame	great

2.

ai	ay	a	a-e	ea
sprain	payment	David	gatecrash	breaking
fainted	today	May	blameless	steakhouse
explain	haystack	making		

These lists can be used as a spelling assessment at the end of each book. The teacher can add words from list 2 for students who are ready for that stage. When dictating a word, first say the word on its own. Next, say a sentence with the word in it (to put the word in the context of a sentence) and then repeat the word. This ensures that the student has heard the word correctly, e.g. "Fainted. The boy fainted when he saw the mouse. Fainted."

Games within the activity books can also serve as a useful assessment tool. They provide immediate feedback, which is crucial for learning. Students understand quickly what they did right or wrong and learn from it, promoting faster and more effective learning.

LESSON PLANS: Moon Dogs Set 1

s, a, t, i, m

STEP 1
Preparation

15 mins

Learning goal (2 mins)

- Explain the lesson goal. For example: “Today, we are going to be learning the new sounds /s/ /a/ /t/ /i/ /m/ and starting to read and make words such as ‘sit’ and ‘mat.’”
- Show the book Moon Dogs Set 1 Book 1: Is It Matt?
- You will be completing some activities from Moon Dogs Set 1 Activities.

Preparation (13 mins)

- Introduce the new focus sounds: /s/ /a/ /t/ /i/ /m/ using letter cards (Activities, page 3)
- Model how to say each sound correctly and “purely” and ask students to copy.
- Have students watch you as they pronounce /s/.
- Read this list of words: “Sam,” “sat,” and “sit.”
- Repeat this process with /a/ /t/ /i/ and /m/.

Word building and blending

- First demonstrate how to build a word. Use only three sound cards, e.g. for the word “sit.”
- Draw three lines on the whiteboard, and tell the students that you are going to show them how to build the word “sit.”
- As you say the word slowly, move your finger under the lines.
- Ask the students to listen to the first sound in the word “sit”—point to the first line. Emphasize the first sound as you say the whole word. The students respond—/s/.
- Then ask the students which letter spells the sound /s/. The students point to the letter (or you can tell them). Bring the letter down to the first line.
- Repeat with the second and last sounds in the word. Now ask the students to sound all three sounds and blend them into a word, moving your finger under the word: /s/ /i/ /t/ → “sit.”

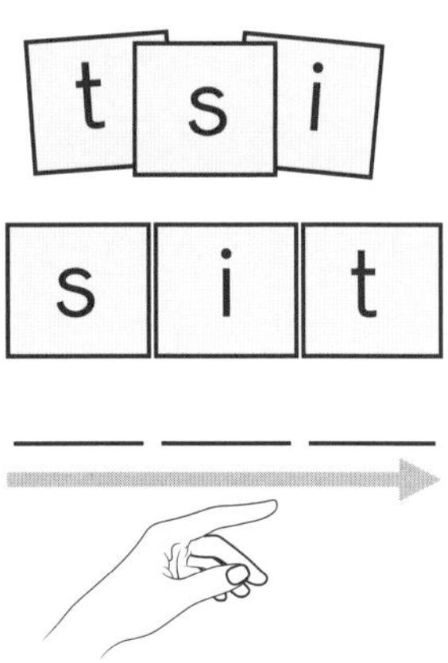

LESSON RESOURCES

Extension activities

1 Word reading

- Write the words you have created on the whiteboard. Then ask students to blend and read the words.
- Show how to say each sound individually and then blend them together to read the word. Model blending by using a swishing motion with your finger for blending.

2 Oral segmenting

- Say a word aloud (e.g. “sit”) and ask students to a count the sounds in the word (3). Write the number of lines you need for all the sounds. Now ask students to listen to the sounds in the word and write a letter for every sound in the word as you spell the word.

3 Word chain

- Using sound cards or magnetic letters, demonstrate how to build the word “it.” Explain to the students that you will be making one change to the word. They must be “sound detectives” and notice if you have added a sound, taken away a sound, or swapped a sound.
- Say that you are going to change the word “it” (moving your finger under the word) to “at.” Ask the students to listen carefully to where the change has occurred. Move your finger under the words as you say it slowly. Once the change has been identified, invite a student to swap the letter card or letter. Ask all the students to sound out the word and read the new word, e.g. /a/ /t/ → “at.”
- Introduce the new sounds gradually.
- Direct students through the following word-chain sequence: it—at—am—Sam—sat—sit—it

4 Jumping Jack game

- Play the **Jumping Jack game** in Book 1: Is It Matt? (page 7) to familiarize students with the vocabulary in the book.

STEP 2
Application for reading
25 mins

Before reading (3 mins)

- Revisit the vocabulary taught in Step 1 (e.g. "mat"). Clearly say the word: /m/ /a/ /t/.
- Then provide a simple definition, for example, "A mat is fabric we put on the floor."
- Ask questions such as "What is a mat?" and "Where can we put a mat?"
- Then write the word on the whiteboard and refer back to it throughout the week for reinforcement.

High-frequency words (2 mins)

- Pre-teach these high-frequency words: "I," "is," and "a."
- Explain that these are high-frequency words that have tricky spellings the students will learn later. Read each high-frequency word aloud. Write the words on the board, showing the separate graphemes in each word.

Application (10 mins)

- The chosen text for this reading activity is Book 1: Is it Matt? Briefly introduce the book to spark interest.
- Lead students through a directed reading of Book 1: Is it Matt?. Encourage students to sound out each word carefully and then blend the sounds together to form the word.
- Provide support by modeling the blending.
- Encourage students to sound out each word and then blend to read.

Reading fluency (10 mins)

- Following the initial reading, revisit Book 1: Is it Matt? with a focus on fluency.
- Reading the book again allows students to practice their newly acquired skills, this time with an emphasis on reading more smoothly and confidently.
- Create an interactive reading environment by inviting students to take turns reading aloud. Encourage them to point to each word as they read.
- As students read more fluently, support them to read with more expression and prosody, changing their pitch, pace, and emphasis according to the words and punctuation.

STEP 3
Application for spelling
20 mins

Segmenting and spelling (20 min)

- Invite students to complete the **Reading captions** activity (Activities, page 7). When reading high-frequency words, point to the grapheme the students do not yet know and sound it out for student, e.g. with the word "the," sound out /th/ and the schwa sound /uh/.
- Ask students to complete the following: **Writing captions** activity (Activities, page 8).
- Dictate the captions from the **Reading captions** activity in the previous page in the Activities book. Have students listen to the sounds in the words and say them aloud as they write them on the lines provided. This activity helps students connect spoken language with written text, enhancing their understanding of letter–sound correspondence.
- After students complete the activity, model the formation of each letter that was written during the activity on the whiteboard. Focus on the starting point, stroke direction, and completion of each letter to ensure proper handwriting techniques. Demonstrating proper letter formation is crucial for developing legible handwriting and building foundational writing skills.

Extension activities

- Ask students to complete the **Reading and spelling** activity (Activities, page 5).
- Fold the sheet along the dotted line. Instruct the student to read the words on the left side and check off the ones they read correctly. Then, turn the sheet over and dictate the words to the student. Ask them to spell the words by segmenting and sounding out each word as they write them on the lines. Finally, have the student open the sheet and check off the words they spelled correctly. This process reinforces phonetic skills and promotes self-assessment.
- For students who finish early or need additional practice spelling, provide extra activity sheets with different captions. Dictate these new captions to the students, allowing them to practice spelling and writing on the lines provided.

STEP 4
Comprehension and consolidation
15 mins

Book reading (5 mins)

- Reread Book 1: Is it Matt?
- Revisiting the book helps to reinforce familiarity with the text and supports phonetic recognition and comprehension.

Sequencing (5 mins)

- For this activity, the students will retell the story using in a small group.
- Divide students into pairs or small groups.
- Provide each group with a set of blank cards and pens.
- Ask each group to recall key events from the story or illustrate them on the cards.
- Once the cards are created, students will work together to arrange them in the correct sequence.
- Invite each group to retell the story using their arranged cards, encouraging them to use their own words to narrate the story.

Comprehension (5 mins)

- To check students' understanding of the story, conduct a group discussion.
- Ask the two comprehension questions at the back of the story ("Why do you think Tam drops her phone on page 2?" and "Are Tam, Sim, and Matt in a running club?")
- Divide the class into small groups and ask each group to answer a question in turn.
- Encourage groups to explain their reasoning.
- Conclude with a brief discussion summarizing the key points of the story and reinforcing vocabulary.

Extension activities

- Ask students to complete the **Reading accuracy** activity (Activities, page 6). Students read the words in each box and circle the word that matches the picture.
- Ask students to complete the **Playing with sounds in real and nonsense CVC words** activity (page 9). Once a student has built a word, ask them to read it. Repeat the activity until the student has returned to the original word "mat."

STEP 5
Tracking progress

- Complete either the **4-in-a-row game** and **Stepping stones game** (Activities, pages 10–11).
- Depending on how the class performs with the games, optionally revisit some of the activities to reinforce any specific skill gaps.

4-in-a-row game

- This game is for two players: Play with two sets of colored counters. Players take turns to read a word or letter and put a counter on it.
- Encourage players to give the sound for the letter rather than the letter name
- The winner is the first to get four of their counters in a row in any direction.
- The winner places a counter on a pizza box.
- The game is played four times until all the pizza boxes are covered.

Stepping stones game

- This game is suitable for 1–4 players and requires counters and a die.
- Students place their counters at the start of the stepping stones path. They then take turns rolling the die. They move their counter according to the number rolled.
- Upon landing on a stepping stone, the student reads the word or letter sound on that stone aloud.
- If a student lands on a stone with a directional arrow, they follow the arrow forward or backward.
- The first student to reach the end of the stepping stones path wins.
- Provide positive feedback and encouragement throughout the game.
- For those needing more support, help them to blend the letter sound or word with assistance.

PARALLEL BOOKS

In addition to Book 1: Is it Matt?, the following books also cover the focus sounds (/s/ /a/ /t/ /i/ /m/) and can be used for more practice of decoding, for book bags to take home.

Moon Dogs Set 1 Extras

Book 1a: Tam and Matt

Book 1b: Sit, Matt

Book 1c: Sam

n, o, p

STEP 1
Preparation

20 mins

Reviewing sounds (3 mins)

- Using sound cards, review some of the previously learned sounds: /s/ /a/ /t/ /i/ /m/. For example, model blending "mat," reading it sound by sound and then the whole word. /m/ /a/ /t/ → "mat."

Learning goal (2 mins)

- Explain to the students that you will be teaching them to read and spell new words using the new sounds /n/ /o/ /p/ and the sounds they have previously learned.
- Introduce the book Moon Dogs Set 1 Book 2: Tam has a Nap.
- You will be completing some activities from Moon Dogs Set 1 Activities.

Preparation (15 mins)

- Model the new focus sounds: /n/ /o/ /p/

Word building and blending

- First demonstrate how to build a word. Use only three sound cards, e.g. for "nap."
- Draw three lines on the whiteboard, and tell the students that you are going to show them how to build the word "nap."
- As you say the word slowly, move your finger under the lines.
- Ask the students to listen to the first sound in the word "nap"—point to the first line. Emphasize the first sound as you say the whole word. The students respond—/n/.
- Then ask the students which letter spells the sound /n/. The students point to the letter (or you can tell them). Bring the letter down to the first line.
- Repeat with the second and last sounds in the word. Now ask the students to sound all three sounds and blend them into a word, moving your finger under the word: /n/ /a/ /p/ → "nap."

LESSON RESOURCES

Extension activities

1 Word reading

- Write the words you have created on the whiteboard. Then ask students to blend and read the words.
- Show how to say each sound individually and then blend them together to read the word. Model blending by pointing using a swishing motion with your finger.

2 Oral segmenting

- Say a word aloud (e.g. "pot") and ask students to count the sounds in the word (3). Write the number of lines you need for all the sounds. Now ask students to listen to the sounds in the word and write a letter for every sound in the word as you spell the word.

3 Word chain

- Using sound cards or magnetic letters, demonstrate how to build the word "pip." Explain to the students that you will be making one change to the word. They must be "sound detectives" and notice if you have added a sound, taken away a sound, or swapped a sound.
- Say that you are going to change the word "pip" (moving your finger under the word) to "pit." Ask the students to listen carefully to where the change has occurred. Move your finger under the words as you say it slowly. Once the change has been identified, invite a student to swap the sound card or letter. Ask all the students to sound out the word and read the new word, e.g. /p/ /i/ /t/ → "pit."
- Introduce the new sounds gradually. This allows students to incorporate the letters and sounds they have learned so far.
- Direct students through the following word-chain sequence: pip—pit—pin—pan—tan—tap—tip—pip

4 Reading game

- Play the **Jumping Jack** game in Book 2: Tam has a Nap (page 7) to familiarize students with the vocabulary in the book.

STEP 2
Application for reading
25 mins

Before reading (3 mins)

- Revisit the vocabulary taught in Step 1 (e.g. "pot"). Clearly say the word: /p/ /o/ /t/.
- Then provide a simple definition, for example, "A pot is a deep pan used for cooking."
- Ask questions such as "What can we put in a pot?"
- Then write the word on the whiteboard and refer back to it throughout the week for reinforcement.
- You could also draw a picture of a pot on the whiteboard or show an actual picture.

High-frequency words (2 mins)

- Pre-teach these high-frequency words: "is," "the," "has," and "a."
- Explain that these are high-frequency words that have tricky spellings the students will learn later. Read each high-frequency word aloud. Write the words on the board, showing the separate graphemes in each word.

Application (10 mins)

- The chosen text for this reading activity is Book 2: Tam has a Nap. Briefly introduce the book to spark interest.
- Lead students through a directed reading of Book 2: Tam has a Nap. Encourage students to sound out each word carefully and then blend the sounds together to form the word.
- Provide support by modeling the blending.
- Encourage students to sound out each word and then blend to read.

Reading fluency (10 mins)

- Following the initial reading, revisit Book 2: Tam has a Nap with a focus on fluency.
- Reading the book again allows students to practice their newly acquired skills, this time with an emphasis on reading more smoothly and confidently.
- Create an interactive reading environment by inviting students to take turns reading aloud. Encourage them to point to each word as they read.
- As students read more fluently, support them to read with more expression and prosody, changing their pitch, pace, and emphasis according to the words and punctuation.

STEP 3
Application for spelling
20 mins

Segmenting and spelling (20 min)

- Invite students to complete the **Reading captions** activity (Activities, page 18). When reading high-frequency words, point to the grapheme the students do not yet know and sound it out for student, e.g. with the word "the," sound out /th/' and the schwa sound /uh/.
- Ask students to complete the following: **Writing captions** activity (Activities, page 19).
- Dictate the captions from the **Reading captions** activity in the previous page in the Activities book. Have students listen to the sounds in the words and say them aloud as they write them on the lines provided. This activity helps students connect spoken language with written text, enhancing their understanding of letter–sound correspondence.
- After students complete the activity, model the formation of each letter that was written during the activity on the whiteboard.
- Focus on the starting point, stroke direction, and completion of each letter to ensure proper handwriting techniques.
- Demonstrating proper letter formation is crucial for developing legible handwriting and building foundational writing skills.

Extension activities

- Ask students to complete the **Reading and spelling** activity (Activities, page 15).
- Fold the sheet along the dotted line. Instruct the student to read the words on the left side and check off the ones they read correctly.
- Then, turn the sheet over and dictate the words to the student.
- Ask them to spell the words by segmenting and sounding out each word as they write them on the lines. Finally, have the student open the sheet and check off the words they spelled correctly.
- This process reinforces phonetic skills and promotes self-assessment.
- For students who finish early or need additional practice spelling, provide extra activity sheets with different captions.
- Dictate these new captions to the students, allowing them to practice spelling and writing on the lines provided.

STEP 4
Comprehension and consolidation
15 mins

Book reading (5 mins)

- Reread Book 2: Tam has a Nap.
- Revisiting the book helps to reinforce familiarity with the text and supports phonetic recognition and comprehension.

Sequencing (5 mins)

- For this activity, the students will retell the story using in a small group.
- Divide students into pairs or small groups.
- Provide each group with a set of blank cards and pens.
- Ask each group to recall key events from the story or illustrate them on the cards.
- Once the cards are created, students will work together to arrange them in the correct sequence.
- Invite each group to retell the story using their arranged cards, encouraging them to use their own words to narrate the story.

Comprehension (5 mins)

- To check students' understanding of the story, conduct a group discussion.
- Ask the two comprehension questions at the back of the story ("Why doesn't Tam notice that the water is overflowing in the sink?" and "What is Tam dreaming about while she is napping?")
- Divide the class into small groups and ask each group to answer a question in turn.
- Encourage groups to explain their reasoning.
- Conclude with a brief discussion summarizing the key points of the story and reinforcing vocabulary.

Extension activities

- Ask students to complete the **Reading accuracy** activity (Activities, page 16). Students read the words in each box and circle the word that matches the picture.
- Ask students to complete the **Playing with sounds in real and nonsense CVC words** activity (page 20). Once a student has built a word, ask them to read it. Repeat the activity until the student has returned to the original word "mas."

STEP 5
Tracking progress

- Complete either the **4-in-a-row game** and **Stepping stones game** (Activities, pages 21–22).
- Depending on how the class performs with the games, optionally revisit some of the activities to reinforce any specific skill gaps.

4-in-a-row game

- This game is for two players: Play with two sets of colored counters. Players take turns to read a word or letter and put a counter on it.
- Encourage players to give the sound for the letter rather than the letter name
- The winner is the first to get four of their counters in a row in any direction.
- The winner places a counter on a pizza box.
- The game is played four times until all the pizza boxes are covered.

Stepping stones game

- This game is suitable for 1–4 players and requires counters and a die.
- Students place their counters at the start of the stepping stones path. They then take turns rolling the die. They move their counter according to the number rolled.
- Upon landing on a stepping stone, the student reads the word or letter sound on that stone aloud.
- If a student lands on a stone with a directional arrow, they follow the arrow forward or backward.
- The first student to reach the end of the stepping stones path wins.
- Provide positive feedback and encouragement throughout the game.
- For those needing more support, help them to blend the letter sound or word with assistance.

PARALLEL BOOKS

In addition to Book 2: Tam has a Nap, the following books also cover the focus sounds (/n/ /o/ /p/) and can be used for more practice of decoding, for book bags to take home.

Moon Dogs Set 1 Extras

Book 2a: The Tap

Book 2b: The Pot at the Top

Book 2c: Tim Is Not on Top

b, c, g, h

STEP 1
Preparation

20 mins

Reviewing sounds (3 mins)

- Using sound cards, review some of the previously learned sounds: /n/ /o/ /p/. For example, model blending "nap," reading it sound by sound and then the whole word. /n/ /a/ /p/ → "nap."

Learning goal (2 mins)

- Explain to the students that you will be teaching them to read and spell new words using the new sounds /b/ /c/ /g/ /h/ and the sounds they have previously learned.
- Introduce the book Moon Dogs Set 1 Book 3: Sim and the Bat.
- You will be completing some activities from Moon Dogs Set 1 Activities.

Preparation (15 mins)

- Model the new focus sounds: /b/ /c/ /g/ /h/

Word building and blending

- First demonstrate how to build a word. Use only three sound cards, e.g. for "bat."
- Draw three lines on the whiteboard, and tell the students that you are going to show them how to build the word "bat."
- As you say the word slowly, move your finger under the lines.
- Ask the students to listen to the first sound in the word "bat"—point to the first line. Emphasize the first sound as you say the whole word. The students respond—/b/.
- Then ask the students which letter spells the sound /b/. The students point to the letter (or you can tell them). Bring the letter down to the first line.
- Repeat with the second and last sounds in the word. Now ask the students to sound all three sounds and blend them into a word, moving your finger under the word: /b/ /a/ /t/ → "bat."

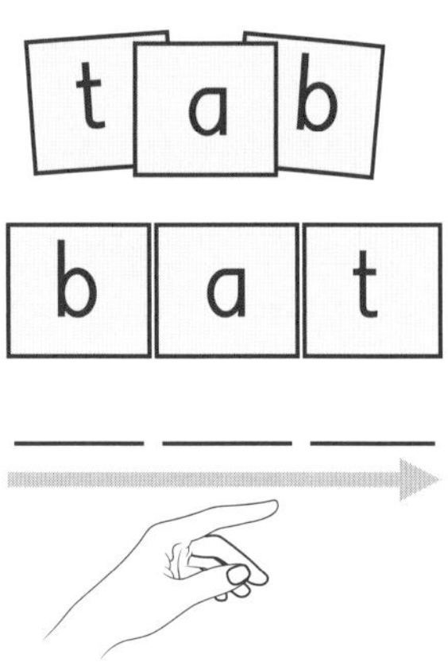

LESSON RESOURCES

Extension activities

1 Word reading

- Write the words you have created on the whiteboard. Then ask students to blend and read the words.
- Show how to say each sound individually and then blend them together to read the word. Model blending by using a swishing motion with your finger for blending.

2 Oral segmenting

- Say a word aloud (e.g. "hat") and ask students to a count the sounds in the word (3). Write the number of lines you need for all the sounds. Now ask students to listen to the sounds in the word and write a letter for every sound in the word as you spell the word.

3 Word chain

- Using sound cards or magnetic letters, demonstrate how to build the word "hit." Explain to the students that you will be making one change to the word. They must be "sound detectives" and notice if you have added a sound, taken away a sound, or swapped a sound.
- Say that you are going to change the word "hit" (moving your finger under the word) to "hat." Ask the students to listen carefully to where the change has occurred. Move your finger under the words as you say it slowly. Once the change has been identified, invite a student to swap the letter card or letter. Ask all the students to sound out the word and read the new word, e.g. /h/ /a/ /t/ → "hat."
- Introduce the new sounds gradually.
- Direct students through the following word-chain sequence: hit—hat—pat—tap—tip—hip—hit

4 Jumping Jack game

- Play the **Jumping Jack game** in Book 3: Sim and the Bat (page 7) to familiarize students with the vocabulary in the book.

STEP 2
Application for reading
25 mins

Before reading (3 mins)

- Revisit the vocabulary taught in Step 1 (e.g. "bat"). Clearly say the word: /b/ /a/ /t/.
- Explore different definitions of the word "bat."
- Ask questions such as "What is a bat?" and "What do you use a bat for?"
- Then write the word on the whiteboard and refer back to it throughout the week for reinforcement.

High-frequency words (2 mins)

- Pre-teach these high-frequency words: "has," "a," "is," and "cannot."
- Explain that these are high-frequency words that have tricky spellings the students will learn later. Read each high-frequency word aloud. Write the words on the board, showing the separate graphemes in each word

Application (10 mins)

- The chosen text for this reading activity is Book 3: Sim and the Bat. Briefly introduce the book to spark interest.
- Lead students through a directed reading of Book 3: Sim and the Bat. Encourage students to sound out each word carefully and then blend the sounds together to form the word.
- Provide support by modeling the blending.
- Encourage students to sound out each word and then blend to read.

Reading fluency (10 mins)

- Following the initial reading, revisit Book 3: Sim and the Bat with a focus on fluency.
- Reading the book again allows students to practice their newly acquired skills, this time with an emphasis on reading more smoothly and confidently.
- Create an interactive reading environment by inviting students to take turns reading aloud. Encourage them to point to each word as they read.
- As students read more fluently, support them to read with more expression and prosody, changing their pitch, pace, and emphasis according to the words and punctuation.

STEP 3
Application for spelling
20 mins

Segmenting and spelling (20 min)

- Invite students to complete the **Reading captions** activity (Activities, page 28). When reading high-frequency words, point to the grapheme the students do not yet know and sound it out for student, e.g. with the word "the," sound out /th/ and the schwa sound /uh/.
- Ask students to complete the following: **Writing captions** activity (Activities, page 29).
- Dictate the captions from the **Reading captions** activity in the previous page in the Activities book.
- Have students listen to the sounds in the words and say them aloud as they write them on the lines provided.
- This activity helps students connect spoken language with written text, enhancing their understanding of letter–sound correspondence.
- After students complete the activity, model the formation of each letter that was written during the activity on the whiteboard.
- Focus on the starting point, stroke direction, and completion of each letter to ensure proper handwriting techniques.
- Demonstrating proper letter formation is crucial for developing legible handwriting and building foundational writing skills.

Extension activities

- Ask students to complete the **Reading and spelling** activity (Activities, page 25).
- Fold the sheet along the dotted line. Instruct the student to read the words on the left side and check off the ones they read correctly. Then, turn the sheet over and dictate the words to the student. Ask them to spell the words by segmenting and sounding out each word as they write them on the lines. Finally, have the student open the sheet and check off the words they spelled correctly. This process reinforces phonetic skills and promotes self-assessment.
- For students who finish early or need additional practice spelling, provide extra activity sheets with different captions. Dictate these new captions to the students, allowing them to practice spelling and writing on the lines provided.

STEP 4
Comprehension and consolidation

15 mins

Book reading (5 mins)

- Reread Book 3: Sim and the Bat.
- Revisiting the book helps to reinforce familiarity with the text and supports phonetic recognition and comprehension.

Sequencing (5 mins)

- For this activity, the students will retell the story in a small group.
- Divide students into pairs or small groups.
- Provide each group with a set of blank cards and pens.
- Ask each group to recall key events from the story or illustrate them on the cards.
- Once the cards are created, students will work together to arrange them in the correct sequence.
- Invite each group to retell the story using their arranged cards, encouraging them to use their own words to narrate the story.

Comprehension (5 mins)

- To check students' understanding of the story, conduct a group discussion.
- Ask the two comprehension questions at the back of the story ("Why is Sim struggling to lift up the bat on page 3?" and "How do you think Sim is feeling on page 6?")
- Divide the class into small groups and ask each group to answer a question in turn.
- Encourage groups to explain their reasoning.
- Conclude with a brief discussion summarizing the key points of the story and reinforcing vocabulary.

Extension activities

- Ask students to complete the **Reading accuracy** activity (Activities, page 26). Students read the words in each box and circle the word that matches the picture.
- Ask students to complete the **Playing with sounds in real and nonsense CVC words** activity (page 30). Once a student has built a word, ask them to read it. Repeat the activity until the student has returned to the original word "pog."

STEP 5
Tracking progress

- Complete either the **4-in-a-row game** and **Stepping stones game** (Activities, pages 31–32).
- Depending on how the class performs with the games, optionally revisit some of the activities to reinforce any specific skill gaps.

4-in-a-row game

- This game is for two players: Play with two sets of colored counters. Players take turns to read a word or letter and put a counter on it.
- Encourage players to give the sound for the letter rather than the letter name.
- The winner is the first to get four of their counters in a row in any direction.
- The winner places a counter on a pizza box.
- The game is played four times until all the pizza boxes are covered.

Stepping stones game

- This game is suitable for 1–4 players and requires counters and a die.
- Students place their counters at the start of the stepping stones path. They then take turns rolling the die. They move their counter according to the number rolled.
- Upon landing on a stepping stone, the student reads the word or letter sound on that stone aloud.
- If a student lands on a stone with a directional arrow, they follow the arrow forward or backward.
- The first student to reach the end of the stepping stones path wins.
- Provide positive feedback and encouragement throughout the game.
- For those needing more support, help them to blend the letter sound or word with assistance.

PARALLEL BOOKS

In addition to Book 3: Sim and the Bat, the following books also cover the focus sounds (/b/ /c/ /g/ /h/) and can be used for more practice of decoding, for book bags to take home.

Moon Dogs Set 1 Extras

Book 3a: The Hat

Book 3b: Bob, the Cat

Book 3c: Sim and the Pan

d, e, f, v

STEP 1 Preparation

20 mins

Reviewing sounds (3 mins)

- Using sound cards, review some of the previously learned sounds: /b/ /c/ /g/ /h/. For example, model blending "bit," reading it sound by sound and then the whole word. /b/ /i/ /t/ → "bit."

Learning goal (2 mins)

- Explain to the students that you will be teaching them to read and spell new words using the new sounds /d/ /e/ /f/ /v/ and the sounds they have previously learned.
- Introduce the book Moon Dogs Set 1 Book 4: Ned, the Cat.
- You will be completing some activities from Moon Dogs Set 1 Activities.

Preparation (15 mins)

- Model the new focus sounds: /d/ /e/ /f/ /v/

Word building and blending

- First demonstrate how to build a word. Use only three sound cards, e.g. for "fed."
- Draw three lines on the whiteboard, and tell the students that you are going to show them how to build the word "fed."
- As you say the word slowly, move your finger under the lines.
- Ask the students to listen to the first sound in the word "fed"—point to the first line. Emphasize the first sound as you say the whole word. The students respond—/f/.
- Then ask the students which letter spells the sound /f/. The students point to the letter (or you can tell them). Bring the letter down to the first line.
- Repeat with the second and last sounds in the word. Now ask the students to sound all three sounds and blend them into a word, moving your finger under the word: /f/ /e/ /d/ → "fed."

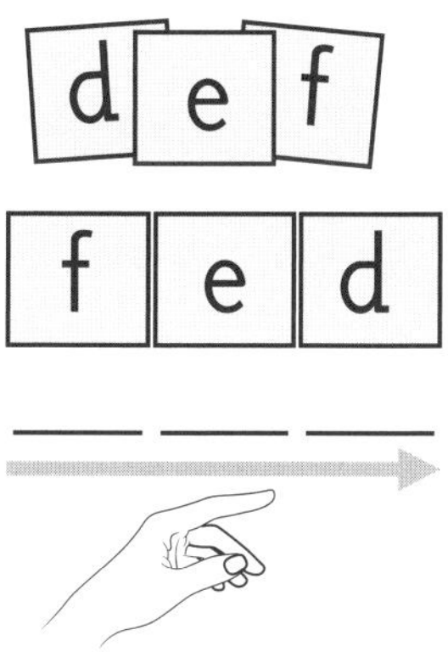

LESSON RESOURCES

Extension activities

1 Word reading

- Write the words you have created on the whiteboard. Then ask students to blend and read the words.
- Show how to say each sound individually and then blend them together to read the word. Model blending by pointing using a swishing motion with your finger.

2 Oral segmenting

- Say a word aloud (e.g. "den") and ask students to count the sounds in the word (3). Write the number of lines you need for all the sounds. Now ask students to listen to the sounds in the word and write a letter for every sound in the word as you spell the word.

3 Word chain

- Using sound cards or magnetic letters, demonstrate how to build the word "fed." Explain to the students that you will be making one change to the word. They must be "sound detectives" and notice if you have added a sound, taken away a sound, or swapped a sound.
- Say that you are going to change the word "fed" (moving your finger under the word) to "fad." Ask the students to listen carefully to where the change has occurred. Move your finger under the words as you say it slowly. Once the change has been identified, invite a student to swap the sound card or letter. Ask all the students to sound out the word and read the new word, e.g. /f/ /a/ /d/ → "fad."
- Introduce the new sounds gradually. This allows students to incorporate the letters and sounds they have learned so far.
- Direct students through the following word-chain sequence: ed—fad—bad—sad—sat—set—get—vet—bet—bed—fed

4 Reading game

- Play the **Jumping Jack** game in Book 4: Ned, the Cat (page 7).

STEP 2
Application for reading
25 mins

Before reading (3 mins)

- Revisit the vocabulary taught in Step 1 (e.g. "vet"). Clearly say the word: /v/ /e/ /t/.
- Provide a simple definition of the word "vet," such as, "A vet is a doctor who takes care of animals."
- Ask questions such as "What does a vet do?"
- Then write the word on the whiteboard and refer back to it throughout the week for reinforcement.

High-frequency words (2 mins)

- Pre-teach these high-frequency words: "has," "a," "off," "the," and "is."
- Explain that these are high-frequency words that have tricky spellings the students will learn later. Read each high-frequency word aloud. Write the words on the board, showing the separate graphemes in each word.

Application (10 mins)

- The chosen text for this reading activity is Book 4: Ned, the Cat. Briefly introduce the book to spark interest.
- Lead students through a directed reading of Book 4: Ned, the Cat. Encourage students to sound out each word carefully and then blend the sounds together to form the word.
- Provide support by modeling the blending.
- Encourage students to sound out each word and then blend to read.

Reading fluency (10 mins)

- Following the initial reading, revisit Book 4: Ned, the Cat with a focus on fluency.
- Reading the book again allows students to practice their newly acquired skills, this time with an emphasis on reading more smoothly and confidently.
- Create an interactive reading environment by inviting students to take turns reading aloud. Encourage them to point to each word as they read.
- As students read more fluently, support them to read with more expression and prosody, changing their pitch, pace, and emphasis according to the words and punctuation.

STEP 3
Application for spelling
20 mins

Segmenting and spelling (20 min)

- Invite students to complete the **Reading captions** activity (Activities, page 38). When reading high-frequency words, point to the grapheme the students do not yet know and sound it out for student, e.g. with the word "the," sound out /th/ and the schwa sound /uh/.
- Ask students to complete the following: **Writing captions** activity (Activities, page 39).
- Dictate the captions from the **Reading captions** activity in the previous page in the Activities book. Have students listen to the sounds in the words and say them aloud as they write them on the lines provided. This activity helps students connect spoken language with written text, enhancing their understanding of letter–sound correspondence.
- After students complete the activity, model the formation of each letter that was written during the activity on the whiteboard.
- Focus on the starting point, stroke direction, and completion of each letter to ensure proper handwriting techniques.
- Demonstrating proper letter formation is crucial for developing legible handwriting and building foundational writing skills.

Extension activities

- Ask students to complete the **Reading and spelling** activity (Activities, page 35).
- Fold the sheet along the dotted line. Instruct the student to read the words on the left side and check off the ones they read correctly.
- Then, turn the sheet over and dictate the words to the student. Ask them to spell the words by segmenting and sounding out each word as they write them on the lines.
- Finally, have the student open the sheet and check off the words they spelled correctly.
- This process reinforces phonetic skills and promotes self-assessment.
- For students who finish early or need additional practice spelling, provide extra activity sheets with different captions.
- Dictate these new captions to the students, allowing them to practice spelling and writing on the lines provided.

STEP 4
Comprehension and consolidation
15 mins

Book reading (5 mins)

- Reread Book 4: Ned, the Cat.
- Revisiting the book helps to reinforce familiarity with the text and supports phonetic recognition and comprehension.

Sequencing (5 mins)

- For this activity, the students will retell the story using in a small group.
- Divide students into pairs or small groups.
- Provide each group with a set of blank cards and pens.
- Ask each group to recall key events from the story or illustrate them on the cards.
- Once the cards are created, students will work together to arrange them in the correct sequence.
- Invite each group to retell the story using their arranged cards, encouraging them to use their own words to narrate the story.

Comprehension (5 mins)

- To check students' understanding of the story, conduct a group discussion.
- Ask the two comprehension questions at the back of the story ("Do you think Ned is good at following instructions?" and "Is Dan upset with Ned on page 6?")
- Divide the class into small groups and ask each group to answer a question in turn.
- Encourage groups to explain their reasoning.
- Conclude with a brief discussion summarizing the key points of the story and reinforcing vocabulary.

Extension activities

- Ask students to complete the **Reading accuracy** activity (Activities, page 36). Students read the words in each box and circle the word that matches the picture.
- Ask students to complete the **Playing with sounds in real and nonsense CVC words** activity (page 40). Once a student has built a word, ask them to read it. Repeat the activity until the student has returned to the original word "dep."

STEP 5
Tracking progress

- Complete either the **4-in-a-row game** and **Stepping stones game** (Activities, pages 41–42).
- Depending on how the class performs with the games, optionally revisit some of the activities to reinforce any specific skill gaps.

4-in-a-row game

- This game is for two players: Play with two sets of colored counters. Players take turns to read a word or letter and put a counter on it.
- Encourage players to give the sound for the letter rather than the letter name.
- The winner is the first to get four of their counters in a row in any direction.
- The winner places a counter on a pizza box.
- The game is played four times until all the pizza boxes are covered.

Stepping stones game

- This game is suitable for 1–4 players and requires counters and a die.
- Students place their counters at the start of the stepping stones path. They then take turns rolling the die. They move their counter according to the number rolled.
- Upon landing on a stepping stone, the student reads the word or letter sound on that stone aloud.
- If a student lands on a stone with a directional arrow, they follow the arrow forward or backward.
- The first student to reach the end of the stepping stones path wins.
- Provide positive feedback and encouragement throughout the game.
- For those needing more support, help them to blend the letter sound or word with assistance.

PARALLEL BOOKS

In addition to Book 4: Ned, the Cat, the following books also cover the focus sounds (/d/ /e/ /f/ /v/) and can be used for more practice of decoding, for book bags to take home.

Moon Dogs Set 1 Extras

Book 4a: The Van

Book 4b: Dan and the Cod

Book 4c: Dan Has a Pet

k, l, r, u

STEP 1
Preparation

20 mins

Reviewing sounds (3 mins)

- Using sound cards, review some of the previously learned sounds: /d/ /e/ /f/ /v/. For example, model blending "bed," reading it sound by sound and then the whole word. /b/ /e/ /d/ → "bed."

Learning goal (2 mins)

- Explain to the students that you will be teaching them to read and spell new words using the new sounds /k/ /l/ /r/ /u/ and the sounds they have previously learned.
- Introduce the book Moon Dogs Set 1 Book 5: Kip's Bad Leg.
- You will be completing some activities from Moon Dogs Set 1 Activities.

Preparation (15 mins)

- Model the new focus sounds: /k/ /l/ /r/ /u/

Word building and blending

- First demonstrate how to build a word. Use only three sound cards, e.g. for "rug."
- Draw three lines on the whiteboard, and tell the students that you are going to show them how to build the word "rug."
- As you say the word slowly, move your finger under the lines.
- Ask the students to listen to the first sound in the word "rug"—point to the first line. Emphasize the first sound as you say the whole word. The students respond—/r/.
- Then ask the students which letter spells the sound /r/. The students point to the letter (or you can tell them). Bring the letter down to the first line.
- Repeat with the second and last sounds in the word. Now ask the students to sound all three sounds and blend them into a word, moving your finger under the word: /r/ /u/ /g/ → "rug."

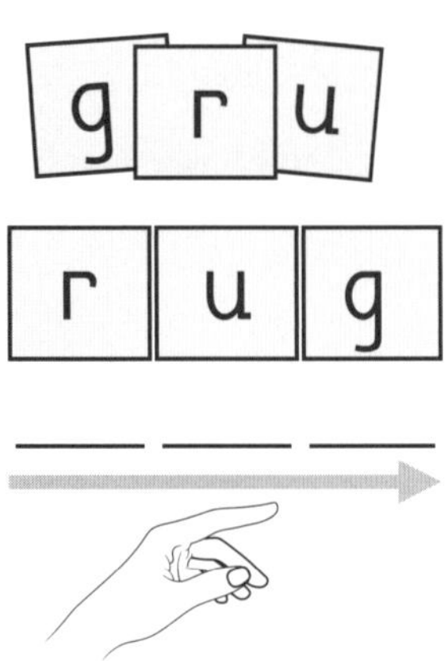

LESSON RESOURCES

Extension activities

1 Word reading

- Write the words you have created on the whiteboard. Then ask students to blend and read the words.
- Show how to say each sound individually and then blend them together to read the word. Model blending by using a swishing motion with your finger for blending.

2 Oral segmenting

- Say a word aloud (e.g. "leg") and ask students to a count the sounds in the word (3). Write the number of lines you need for all the sounds. Now ask students to listen to the sounds in the word and write a letter for every sound in the word as you spell the word.

3 Word chain

- Using sound cards or magnetic letters, demonstrate how to build the word "kin." Explain to the students that you will be making one change to the word. They must be "sound detectives" and notice if you have added a sound, taken away a sound, or swapped a sound.
- Say that you are going to change the word "kin" (moving your finger under the word) to "kid." Ask the students to listen carefully to where the change has occurred. Move your finger under the words as you say it slowly. Once the change has been identified, invite a student to swap the letter card or letter. Ask all the students to sound out the word and read the new word, e.g. /k/ /i/ /d/ → "kid."
- Introduce the new sounds gradually.
- Direct students through the following word-chain sequence: kin—kid—kip—sip—tip—tap—pat—pit—kit

4 Jumping Jack game

- Play the **Jumping Jack game** in Book 5: Kip's Bad Leg (page 7) to familiarize students with the vocabulary in the book.

STEP 2
Application for reading

25 mins

Before reading (3 mins)

- Revisit the vocabulary taught in Step 1 (e.g. "sun"). Clearly say the word: /s/ /u/ /n/
- Provide a simple definition of the word "sun," such as, "The sun is a star that gives us light and warmth."
- Ask questions such as "Why is the sun important?"
- Then write the word on the whiteboard and refer back to it throughout the week for reinforcement.

High-frequency words (2 mins)

- Pre-teach these high-frequency words: "is," "a," "his," "to," "the," "has," and "cannot."
- Explain that these are high-frequency words that have tricky spellings the students will learn later. Read each high-frequency word aloud. Write the words on the board, showing the separate graphemes in each word.

Application (10 mins)

- The chosen text for this reading activity is Book 5: Kip's Bad Leg. Briefly introduce the book to spark interest.
- Lead students through a directed reading of Book 5: Kip's Bad Leg. Encourage students to sound out each word carefully and then blend the sounds together to form the word.
- Provide support by modeling the blending.
- Encourage students to sound out each word and then blend to read.

Reading fluency (10 mins)

- Following the initial reading, revisit Book 5: Kip's Bad Leg with a focus on fluency.
- Reading the book again allows students to practice their newly acquired skills, this time with an emphasis on reading more smoothly and confidently.
- Create an interactive reading environment by inviting students to take turns reading aloud. Encourage them to point to each word as they read.
- As students read more fluently, support them to read with more expression and prosody, changing their pitch, pace, and emphasis according to the words and punctuation.

STEP 3
Application for spelling

20 mins

Segmenting and spelling (20 min)

- Invite students to complete the **Reading captions** activity (Activities, page 48). When reading high-frequency words, point to the grapheme the students do not yet know and sound it out for student, e.g. with the word "the," sound out /th/ and the schwa sound /uh/.
- Ask students to complete the following: **Writing captions** activity (Activities, page 49).
- Dictate the captions from the **Reading captions** activity in the previous page in the Activities book. Have students listen to the sounds in the words and say them aloud as they write them on the lines provided. This activity helps students connect spoken language with written text, enhancing their understanding of letter–sound correspondence.
- After students complete the activity, model the formation of each letter that was written during the activity on the whiteboard.
- Focus on the starting point, stroke direction, and completion of each letter to ensure proper handwriting techniques.
- Demonstrating proper letter formation is crucial for developing legible handwriting and building foundational writing skills.

Extension activities

- Ask students to complete the **Reading and spelling** activity (Activities, page 45).
- Fold the sheet along the dotted line. Instruct the student to read the words on the left side and check off the ones they read correctly.
- Then, turn the sheet over and dictate the words to the student. Ask them to spell the words by segmenting and sounding out each word as they write them on the lines.
- Finally, have the student open the sheet and check off the words they spelled correctly.
- This process reinforces phonetic skills and promotes self-assessment.
- For students who finish early or need additional practice spelling, provide extra activity sheets with different captions.
- Dictate these new captions to the students, allowing them to practice spelling and writing on the lines provided.

STEP 4
Comprehension and consolidation
15 mins

Book reading (5 mins)

- Reread Book 5: Kip's Bad Leg.
- Revisiting the book helps to reinforce familiarity with the text and supports phonetic recognition and comprehension.

Sequencing (5 mins)

- For this activity, the students will retell the story using in a small group.
- Divide students into pairs or small groups.
- Provide each group with a set of blank cards and pens.
- Ask each group to recall key events from the story or illustrate them on the cards.
- Once the cards are created, students will work together to arrange them in the correct sequence.
- Invite each group to retell the story using their arranged cards, encouraging them to use their own words to narrate the story.

Comprehension (5 mins)

- To check students' understanding of the story, conduct a group discussion.
- Ask the two comprehension questions at the back of the story ("What happens to Kip when he gets hit by the van?" and "Why is Kip sad on page 5?")
- Divide the class into small groups and ask each group to answer a question in turn.
- Encourage groups to explain their reasoning.
- Conclude with a brief discussion summarizing the key points of the story and reinforcing vocabulary.

Extension activities

- Ask students to complete the **Reading accuracy** activity (Activities, page 46). Students read the words in each box and circle the word that matches the picture.
- Ask students to complete the **Playing with sounds in real and nonsense CVC words** activity (page 50). Once a student has built a word, ask them to read it. Repeat the activity until the student has returned to the original word "lub."

STEP 5
Tracking progress

- Complete either the **4-in-a-row game** and **Stepping stones game** (Activities, pages 51–52).
- Depending on how the class performs with the games, optionally revisit some of the activities to reinforce any specific skill gaps.

4-in-a-row game

- This game is for two players: Play with two sets of colored counters. Players take turns to read a word or letter and put a counter on it.
- Encourage players to give the sound for the letter rather than the letter name.
- The winner is the first to get four of their counters in a row in any direction.
- The winner places a counter on a pizza box.
- The game is played four times until all the pizza boxes are covered.

Stepping stones game

- This game is suitable for 1–4 players and requires counters and a die.
- Students place their counters at the start of the stepping stones path. They then take turns rolling the die. They move their counter according to the number rolled.
- Upon landing on a stepping stone, the student reads the word or letter sound on that stone aloud.
- If a student lands on a stone with a directional arrow, they follow the arrow forward or backward.
- The first student to reach the end of the stepping stones path wins.
- Provide positive feedback and encouragement throughout the game.
- For those needing more support, help them to blend the letter sound or word with assistance.

PARALLEL BOOKS

In addition to Book 5: Kip's Bad Leg, the following books also cover the focus sounds (/k/ /l/ /r/ /u/) and can be used for more practice of decoding, for book bags to take home.

Moon Dogs Set 1 Extras

Book 5a: The Red Bag

Book 5b: The Log

Book 5c: The Rat

LESSON PLANS: Moon Dogs Set 1

j, w, z

STEP 1 Preparation

20 mins

Reviewing sounds (3 mins)

- Using sound cards, review some of the previously learned sounds: /k/ /l/ /r/ /u/. For example, model blending "kin," reading it sound by sound and then the whole word. /k/ /i/ /n/ → "kin."

Learning goal (2 mins)

- Explain to the students that you will be teaching them to read and spell new words using the new sounds /j/ /w/ /z/ and the sounds they have previously learned.
- Introduce the book Moon Dogs Set 1 Book 6: Jed's Bag.
- You will be completing some activities from Moon Dogs Set 1 Activities.

Preparation (15 mins)

- Model the new focus sounds: /j/ /w/ /z/

Word building and blending

- First demonstrate how to build a word. Use only three sound cards, e.g. for "wig."
- Draw three lines on the whiteboard, and tell the students that you are going to show them how to build the word "wig."
- As you say the word slowly, move your finger under the lines.
- Ask the students to listen to the first sound in the word "wig"—point to the first line. Emphasize the first sound as you say the whole word. The students respond—/w/.
- Then ask the students which letter spells the sound /w/. The students point to the letter (or you can tell them). Bring the letter down to the first line.
- Repeat with the second and last sounds in the word. Now ask the students to sound all three sounds and blend them into a word, moving your finger under the word: /w/ /i/ /g/ → "wig."

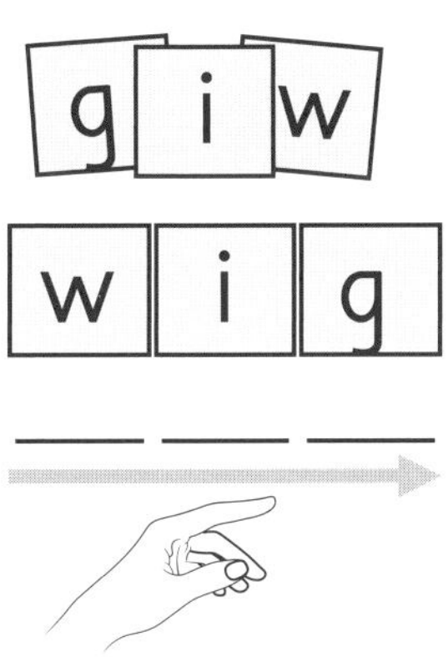

LESSON RESOURCES

Extension activities

1 Word reading

- Write the words you have created on the whiteboard. Then ask students to blend and read the words.
- Show how to say each sound individually and then blend them together to read the word. Model blending by pointing using a swishing motion with your finger.

2 Oral segmenting

- Say a word aloud (e.g. "jet") and ask students to count the sounds in the word (3). Write the number of lines you need for all the sounds. Now ask students to listen to the sounds in the word and write a letter for every sound in the word as you spell the word.

3 Word chain

- Using sound cards or magnetic letters, demonstrate how to build the word "zap." Explain to the students that you will be making one change to the word. They must be "sound detectives" and notice if you have added a sound, taken away a sound, or swapped a sound.
- Say that you are going to change the word "zap" (moving your finger under the word) to "zip." Ask the students to listen carefully to where the change has occurred. Move your finger under the words as you say it slowly. Once the change has been identified, invite a student to swap the sound card or letter. Ask all the students to sound out the word and read the new word, e.g. /z/ /i/ /p/ → "zip."
- Introduce the new sounds gradually. This allows students to incorporate the letters and sounds they have learned so far.
- Direct students through the following word-chain sequence: zap—zip—pip—pop—pep—pet—tap—zap

4 Reading game

- Play the **Jumping Jack** game in Book 6: Jed's Bag (page 7).

STEP 2
Application for reading
25 mins

Before reading (3 mins)

- Revisit the vocabulary taught in Step 1 (e.g. "jet"). Clearly say the word: /j/ /e/ /t/
- Provide a simple definition of the word "jet," such as, "A jet is an airplane."
- Ask questions such as "Can you name other types of transport?"
- Then write the word on the whiteboard and refer back to it throughout the week for reinforcement.

High-frequency words (2 mins)

- Pre-teach these high-frequency words: "has," "a," "the," "to," and "is."
- Explain that these are high-frequency words that have tricky spellings the students will learn later. Read each high-frequency word aloud. Write the words on the board, showing the separate graphemes in each word.

Application (10 mins)

- The chosen text for this reading activity is Book 6: Jed's Bag. Briefly introduce the book to spark interest.
- Lead students through a directed reading of Book 6: Jed's Bag. Encourage students to sound out each word carefully and then blend the sounds together to form the word.
- Provide support by modeling the blending.
- Encourage students to sound out each word and then blend to read.

Reading fluency (10 mins)

- Following the initial reading, revisit Book 6: Jed's Bag with a focus on fluency.
- Reading the book again allows students to practice their newly acquired skills, this time with an emphasis on reading more smoothly and confidently.
- Create an interactive reading environment by inviting students to take turns reading aloud. Encourage them to point to each word as they read.
- As students read more fluently, support them to read with more expression and prosody, changing their pitch, pace, and emphasis according to the words and punctuation.

STEP 3
Application for spelling
20 mins

Segmenting and spelling (20 min)

- Invite students to complete the **Reading captions** activity (Activities, page 58). When reading high-frequency words, point to the grapheme the students do not yet know and sound it out for student, e.g. with the word "the," sound out /th/ and the schwa sound /uh/.
- Ask students to complete the following: **Writing captions** activity (Activities, page 59).
- Dictate the captions from the **Reading captions** activity in the previous page in the Activities book. Have students listen to the sounds in the words and say them aloud as they write them on the lines provided. This activity helps students connect spoken language with written text, enhancing their understanding of letter–sound correspondence.
- After students complete the activity, model the formation of each letter that was written during the activity on the whiteboard.
- Focus on the starting point, stroke direction, and completion of each letter to ensure proper handwriting techniques.
- Demonstrating proper letter formation is crucial for developing legible handwriting and building foundational writing skills.

Extension activities

- Ask students to complete the **Reading and spelling** activity (Activities, page 55).
- Fold the sheet along the dotted line. Instruct the student to read the words on the left side and check off the ones they read correctly.
- Then, turn the sheet over and dictate the words to the student. Ask them to spell the words by segmenting and sounding out each word as they write them on the lines.
- Finally, have the student open the sheet and check off the words they spelled correctly.
- This process reinforces phonetic skills and promotes self-assessment.
- For students who finish early or need additional practice spelling, provide extra activity sheets with different captions.
- Dictate these new captions to the students, allowing them to practice spelling and writing on the lines provided.

STEP 4
Comprehension and consolidation
15 mins

Book reading (3 mins)

- Reread Book 6: Jed's Bag.
- Revisiting the book helps to reinforce familiarity with the text and supports phonetic recognition and comprehension.

Sequencing (5 mins)

- For this activity, the students will retell the story in a small group.
- Divide students into pairs or small groups.
- Provide each group with a set of blank cards and pens.
- Ask each group to recall key events from the story or illustrate them on the cards.
- Once the cards are created, students will work together to arrange them in the correct sequence.
- Invite each group to retell the story using their arranged cards, encouraging them to use their own words to narrate the story.

Comprehension (5 mins)

- To check students' understanding of the story, conduct a group discussion.
- Ask the two comprehension questions at the back of the story ("Why do Liz and Jed take their bags off?" and "How does Jed end up with the wrong bag?")
- Divide the class into small groups and ask each group to answer a question in turn.
- Encourage groups to explain their reasoning.
- Conclude with a brief discussion summarizing the key points of the story and reinforcing vocabulary.

Extension activities

- Ask students to complete the **Reading accuracy** activity (Activities, page 56). Students read the words in each box and circle the word that matches the picture.
- Ask students to complete the **Playing with sounds in real and nonsense CVC words** activity (page 60). Once a student has built a word, ask them to read it. Repeat the activity until the student has returned to the original word "jeb."

STEP 5
Tracking progress

- Complete either the **4-in-a-row game** and **Stepping stones game** (Activities, pages 61–62).
- Depending on how the class performs with the games, optionally revisit some of the activities to reinforce any specific skill gaps.

4-in-a-row game

- This game is for two players: Play with two sets of colored counters. Players take turns to read a word or letter and put a counter on it.
- Encourage players to give the sound for the letter rather than the letter name.
- The winner is the first to get four of their counters in a row in any direction.
- The winner places a counter on a pizza box.
- The game is played four times until all the pizza boxes are covered.

Stepping stones game

- This game is suitable for 1–4 players and requires counters and a die.
- Students place their counters at the start of the stepping stones path. They then take turns rolling the die. They move their counter according to the number rolled.
- Upon landing on a stepping stone, the student reads the word or letter sound on that stone aloud.
- If a student lands on a stone with a directional arrow, they follow the arrow forward or backward.
- The first student to reach the end of the stepping stones path wins.
- Provide positive feedback and encouragement throughout the game.
- For those needing more support, help them to blend the letter sound or word with assistance.

PARALLEL BOOKS

In addition to Book 6: Jed's Bag, the following books also cover the focus sounds (/j/ /w/ /z/) and can be used for more practice of decoding, for book bags to take home.

Moon Dogs Set 1 Extras

Book 6a: A Jog

Book 6b: Jam

Book 6c: A Pet for Jed

x, y, ff, ll, ss, zz

STEP 1
Preparation

20 mins

Reviewing sounds (3 mins)

- Using sound cards, review some of the previously learned sounds.

Learning goal (2 mins)

- Explain to the students that you will be teaching them to read and spell new words using the new sounds /x/ /y/ /ff/ /ll/ / ss/ /zz/ and the sounds they have previously learned.
- Introduce the book Moon Dogs Set 1 Book 7: The Big Hill.
- You will be completing some activities from Moon Dogs Set 1 Activities.

Preparation (15 mins)

- Model the new focus sounds.
- When introducing double consonants, show a card with the digraph (e.g. 'ff'). Explain that the two letters stand for one sound: this is an alternative way to spell the sound /f/.

Word building and blending

- First demonstrate how to build a word. Use only three sound cards, e.g. for "boss."
- Draw three lines on the whiteboard, and tell the students that you are going to show them how to build the word "boss."
- As you say the word slowly, move your finger under the lines.
- Ask the students to listen to the first sound in the word "boss"—point to the first line. Emphasize the first sound as you say the whole word. The students respond—/b/.
- Then ask the students which letter spells the sound /b/. The students point to the letter (or you can tell them). Bring the letter down to the first line.
- Repeat with the second and last sounds in the word. Now ask the students to sound all three sounds and blend them into a word, moving your finger under the word: /b/ /o/ /ss/ → "boss."

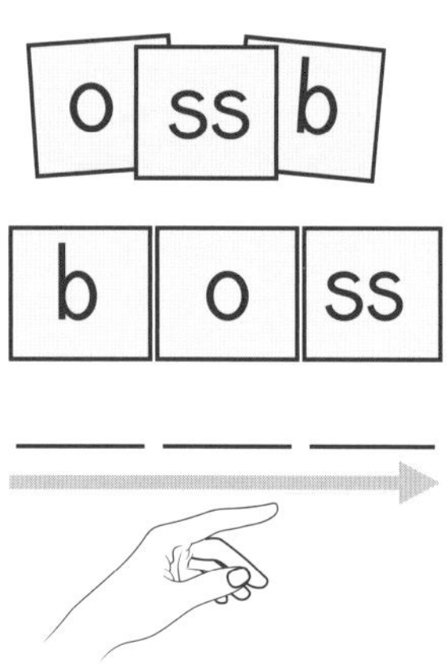

LESSON RESOURCES

Extension activities

1 Word reading

- Write the words you have created on the whiteboard. Then ask students to blend and read the words.
- Show how to say each sound individually and then blend them together to read the word. Model blending by using a swishing motion with your finger for blending.

2 Oral segmenting

- Say a word aloud (e.g. "fix") and ask students to a count the sounds in the word (3). Write the number of lines you need for all the sounds. Now ask students to listen to the sounds in the word and write a letter for every sound in the word as you spell the word.

3 Word chain

- Using sound cards or magnetic letters, demonstrate how to build the word "fox." Explain to the students that you will be making one change to the word. They must be "sound detectives" and notice if you have added a sound, taken away a sound, or swapped a sound.
- Say that you are going to change the word "fox" (moving your finger under the word) to "box." Ask the students to listen carefully to where the change has occurred. Move your finger under the words as you say it slowly. Once the change has been identified, invite a student to swap the letter card or letter. Ask all the students to sound out the word and read the new word, e.g. /b/ /o/ /x/ → "box."
- Introduce the new sounds gradually.
- Direct students through the following word-chain sequence: fox—box—boss—bess—bell—yell—tell—till—tiff—tizz

4 Jumping Jack game

- Play the **Jumping Jack game** in Book 7: The Big Hill (page 7) to familiarize students with the vocabulary in the book.

STEP 2
Application for reading
25 mins

Before reading (3 mins)

- Revisit the vocabulary taught in Step 1 (e.g. "fox"). Clearly say the word: /f/ /o/ /x/
- Provide a simple definition of the word "fox," such as, "A fox is an animal with a bushy tail."
- Ask questions such as "Where do foxes live?" and "What do foxes eat?"
- Then write the word on the whiteboard and refer back to it throughout the week for reinforcement.

High-frequency words (2 mins)

- Pre-teach these high-frequency words: "a," "is," "the," "has," "of," and "to."
- Explain that these are high-frequency words that have tricky spellings the students will learn later. Read each high-frequency word aloud. Write the words on the board, showing the separate graphemes in each word.

Application (10 mins)

- The chosen text for this reading activity is Book 7: The Big Hill. Briefly introduce the book to spark interest.
- Lead students through a directed reading of Book 7: The Big Hill. Encourage students to sound out each word carefully and then blend the sounds together to form the word.
- Provide support by modeling the blending.
- Encourage students to sound out each word and then blend to read.

Reading fluency (10 mins)

- Following the initial reading, revisit Book 7: The Big Hill with a focus on fluency.
- Reading the book again allows students to practice their newly acquired skills, this time with an emphasis on reading more smoothly and confidently.
- Create an interactive reading environment by inviting students to take turns reading aloud. Encourage them to point to each word as they read.
- As students read more fluently, support them to read with more expression and prosody, changing their pitch, pace, and emphasis according to the words and punctuation.

STEP 3
Application for spelling
20 mins

Segmenting and spelling (20 min)

- Invite students to complete the **Reading captions** activity (Activities, page 68). When reading high-frequency words, point to the grapheme the students do not yet know and sound it out for student, e.g. with the word "the," sound out /th/ and the schwa sound /uh/.
- Ask students to complete the following: **Writing captions** activity (Activities, page 69).
- Dictate the captions from the **Reading captions** activity in the previous page in the Activities book. Have students listen to the sounds in the words and say them aloud as they write them on the lines provided. This activity helps students connect spoken language with written text, enhancing their understanding of letter–sound correspondence.
- After students complete the activity, model the formation of each letter that was written during the activity on the whiteboard.
- Focus on the starting point, stroke direction, and completion of each letter to ensure proper handwriting techniques.
- Demonstrating proper letter formation is crucial for developing legible handwriting and building foundational writing skills.

Extension activities

- Ask students to complete the **Reading and spelling** activity (Activities, page 65).
- Fold the sheet along the dotted line. Instruct the student to read the words on the left side and check off the ones they read correctly.
- Then, turn the sheet over and dictate the words to the student. Ask them to spell the words by segmenting and sounding out each word as they write them on the lines.
- Finally, have the student open the sheet and check off the words they spelled correctly.
- This process reinforces phonetic skills and promotes self-assessment.
- For students who finish early or need additional practice spelling, provide extra activity sheets with different captions.
- Dictate these new captions to the students, allowing them to practice spelling and writing on the lines provided.

STEP 4
Comprehension and consolidation

15 mins

Book reading (5 mins)

- Reread Book 7: The Big Hill.
- Revisiting the book helps to reinforce familiarity with the text and supports phonetic recognition and comprehension.

Sequencing (5 mins)

- For this activity, the students will retell the story using in a small group.
- Divide students into pairs or small groups.
- Provide each group with a set of blank cards and pens.
- Ask each group to recall key events from the story or illustrate them on the cards.
- Once the cards are created, students will work together to arrange them in the correct sequence.
- Invite each group to retell the story using their arranged cards, encouraging them to use their own words to narrate the story.

Comprehension (5 mins)

- To check students' understanding of the story, conduct a group discussion.
- Ask the two comprehension questions at the back of the story ("Why are Sim and Liz tired on page 3?" and "How does Kip help Liz and Sim?")
- Divide the class into small groups and ask each group to answer a question in turn.
- Encourage groups to explain their reasoning.
- Conclude with a brief discussion summarizing the key points of the story and reinforcing vocabulary.

Extension activities

- Ask students to complete the **Reading accuracy** activity (Activities, page 66). Students read the words in each box and circle the word that matches the picture.
- Ask students to complete the **Playing with sounds in real and nonsense CVC words** activity (page 70). Once a student has built a word, ask them to read it. Repeat the activity until the student has returned to the original word "mell."

STEP 5
Tracking progress

- Complete either the **4-in-a-row game** and **Stepping stones game** (Activities, pages 71–72).
- Depending on how the class performs with the games, optionally revisit some of the activities to reinforce any specific skill gaps.

4-in-a-row game

- This game is for two players: Play with two sets of colored counters. Players take turns to read a word or letter and put a counter on it.
- Encourage players to give the sound for the letter rather than the letter name.
- The winner is the first to get four of their counters in a row in any direction.
- The winner places a counter on a pizza box.
- The game is played four times until all the pizza boxes are covered.

Stepping stones game

- This game is suitable for 1–4 players and requires counters and a die.
- Students place their counters at the start of the stepping stones path. They then take turns rolling the die. They move their counter according to the number rolled.
- Upon landing on a stepping stone, the student reads the word or letter sound on that stone aloud.
- If a student lands on a stone with a directional arrow, they follow the arrow forward or backward.
- The first student to reach the end of the stepping stones path wins.
- Provide positive feedback and encouragement throughout the game.
- For those needing more support, help them to blend the letter sound or word with assistance.

PARALLEL BOOKS

In addition to Book 7: The Big Hill, the following books also cover the focus sounds (/x/ /y/ /ff/ /ll/ /ss/ and /zz/) and can be used for more practice of decoding, for book bags to take home.

Moon Dogs Set 1 Extras

Book 7a: The Mess

Book 7b: Matt Can Fix It!

Book 7c: Six Buns

LESSON PLANS: Moon Dogs Set 1

All initial CVC sounds

STEP 1
Preparation

20 mins

LESSON RESOURCES

Learning goal (2 mins)

- Explain the lesson goal: reviewing all previously initial CVC sounds.
- Show the book Moon Dogs Set 1 Book 8: Ned is Bad.
- You will be completing some activities from Moon Dogs Set 1 Activities.

Word building activity (8 mins)

- Complete the **Word-building activity** on pages 74 of the Activities book.
- Distribute the activity on page 73 of the Activities book and cut into picture cards. You can also use sound cards from the previous chapters.
- Choose a word from one of the word lists on page 74.
- Demonstrate how to build a word. Use only three sound cards, e.g. for the word "mat."
- Draw three lines on the whiteboard, and tell the students that you are going to show them how to build the word "mat."
- As you say the word slowly, move your finger under the lines.
- Ask the students to listen to the first sound in the word "mat"—point to the first line. Emphasize the first sound as you say the whole word. The students respond—/m/.
- Then ask the students which letter spells the sound /m/. The students point to the letter (or you can tell them). Bring the letter down to the first line.
- Repeat with the second and last sounds in the word. Now ask the students to sound all three sounds and blend them into a word, moving your finger under the word: /m/ /a/ /t/ → "mat."
- The next time this is done, you can ask a student to participate and identify the sound and then letter and bring it down to the line.
- Note if the student is not forming the letters correctly and teach correct letter formation at another opportunity.

Extension activities

1 Word reading

- Write the words you have created on the whiteboard. Then ask students to blend and read the words.
- Show how to say each sound individually and then blend them together to read the word. Model blending by pointing using a swishing motion with your finger.

2 Oral segmenting

- Say a word aloud (e.g. "zap") and ask students to count the sounds in the word (3). Write the number of lines you need for all the sounds. Now ask students to listen to the sounds in the word and write a letter for every sound in the word as you spell the word.

3 Word chain

- Using sound cards or magnetic letters, demonstrate how to build the word "cod." Explain to the students that you will be making one change to the word. They must be "sound detectives" and notice if you have added a sound, taken away a sound, or swapped a sound.
- Say that you are going to change the word "cod" (moving your finger under the word) to "cot." Ask the students to listen carefully to where the change has occurred. Move your finger under the words as you say it slowly. Once the change has been identified, invite a student to swap the sound card or letter. Ask all the students to sound out the word and read the new word, e.g. /c/ /o/ /t/ → "cot."
- Introduce the new sounds gradually. This allows students to incorporate the letters and sounds they have learned so far.
- Direct students through the following word-chain sequence: cod—cot—pot—pit—pin—pan—pad—pod—tod—cod

4 Reading game

- Play the **Jumping Jack** game in Book 8: Ned is Bad (page 7).

STEP 2
Application for reading

25 mins

Before reading (3 mins)

- Revisit the vocabulary taught in Step 1 (e.g. "cot"). Clearly say the word: /c/ /o/ /t/
- Provide a simple definition of the word "cot," such as, "A cot is a small bed for a baby."
- Ask questions such as "Where might you find a cot?" and "When might someone use a cot?"
- Then write the word on the whiteboard and refer back to it throughout the week for reinforcement.

High-frequency words (2 mins)

- Pre-teach these high-frequency words: "a," "is," "the," "has," "of," and "to."
- Explain that these are high-frequency words that have tricky spellings the students will learn later. Read each high-frequency word aloud. Write the words on the board, showing the separate graphemes in each word.

Application (10 mins)

- The chosen text for this reading activity is Book 8: Ned is Bad. Briefly introduce the book to spark interest.
- Lead students through a guided reading of Book 8: Ned is Bad. Encourage students to sound out each word carefully and then blend the sounds together to form the word.
- Provide support by modeling the blending.
- Encourage students to sound out each word and then blend to read.

Reading fluency (10 mins)

- Following the initial reading, revisit Book 8: Ned is Bad with a focus on fluency.
- Reading the book again allows students to practice their newly acquired skills, this time with an emphasis on reading more smoothly and confidently.
- Create an interactive reading environment by inviting students to take turns reading aloud. Encourage them to point to each word as they read.
- As students read more fluently, support them to read with more expression and prosody, changing their pitch, pace, and emphasis according to the words and punctuation.

STEP 3
Application for spelling

20 mins

Segmenting and spelling (20 min)

- Invite students to complete the **Reading captions** activity (Activities, page 78). When reading high-frequency words, point to the grapheme the students do not yet know and sound it out for student, e.g. with the word "the," sound out /th/ and the schwa sound /uh/.
- Ask students to complete the following: **Writing captions** activity (Activities, page 79).
- Dictate the captions from the **Reading captions** activity in the previous page in the Activities book. Have students listen to the sounds in the words and say them aloud as they write them on the lines provided. This activity helps students connect spoken language with written text, enhancing their understanding of letter–sound correspondence.
- After students complete the activity, model the formation of each letter that was written during the activity on the whiteboard.
- Focus on the starting point, stroke direction, and completion of each letter to ensure proper handwriting techniques.
- Demonstrating proper letter formation is crucial for developing legible handwriting and building foundational writing skills.

Extension activities

- Ask students to complete the **Reading and spelling** activity (Activities, page 75).
- Fold the sheet along the dotted line. Instruct the student to read the words on the left side and check off the ones they read correctly.
- Then, turn the sheet over and dictate the words to the student. Ask them to spell the words by segmenting and sounding out each word as they write them on the lines.
- Finally, have the student open the sheet and check off the words they spelled correctly.
- This process reinforces phonetic skills and promotes self-assessment.
- For students who finish early or need additional practice spelling, provide extra activity sheets with different captions.
- Dictate these new captions to the students, allowing them to practice spelling and writing on the lines provided.

STEP 4
Comprehension and consolidation

15 mins

Book reading (5 mins)

- Reread Book 8: Ned is Bad.
- Revisiting the book helps to reinforce familiarity with the text and supports phonetic recognition and comprehension.

Sequencing (5 mins)

- For this activity, the students will retell the story in a small group.
- Divide students into pairs or small groups.
- Provide each group with a set of blank cards and pens.
- Ask each group to recall key events from the story or illustrate them on the cards.
- Once the cards are created, students will work together to arrange them in the correct sequence.
- Invite each group to retell the story using their arranged cards, encouraging them to use their own words to narrate the story.

Comprehension (5 mins)

- To check students' understanding of the story, conduct a group discussion.
- Ask the two comprehension questions at the back of the story ("Why does Ned climb up on the stool?" and "Why is Ned, the cat, sad on page 6?")
- Divide the class into small groups and ask each group to answer a question in turn.
- Encourage groups to explain their reasoning.
- Conclude with a brief discussion summarizing the key points of the story and reinforcing vocabulary.

Extension activities

- Ask students to complete the **Reading accuracy** activity (Activities, page 76). Students read the words in each box and circle the word that matches the picture.
- Ask students to complete the **Playing with sounds in real and nonsense CVC words** activity (page 80). Once a student has built a word, ask them to read it. Repeat the activity until the student has returned to the original word "mox."

STEP 5
Tracking progress

- Complete either the **4-in-a-row game** and **Stepping stones game** (Activities, pages 81–82).
- Depending on how the class performs with the games, optionally revisit some of the activities to reinforce any specific skill gaps.

4-in-a-row game

- This game is for two players: Play with two sets of colored counters. Players take turns to read a word or letter and put a counter on it.
- Encourage players to give the sound for the letter rather than the letter name
- The winner is the first to get four of their counters in a row in any direction.
- The winner places a counter on a pizza box.
- The game is played four times until all the pizza boxes are covered.

Stepping stones game

- This game is suitable for 1–4 players and requires counters and a die.
- Students place their counters at the start of the stepping stones path. They then take turns rolling the die. They move their counter according to the number rolled.
- Upon landing on a stepping stone, the student reads the word or letter sound on that stone aloud.
- If a student lands on a stone with a directional arrow, they follow the arrow forwards or backwards.
- The first student to reach the end of the stepping stones path wins.
- Provide positive feedback and encouragement throughout the game.
- For those needing more support, help them to blend the letter sound or word with assistance.

PARALLEL BOOKS

In addition to Book 8: Ned is Bad, the following books also provide revision of all initial CVC sounds and can be used for more practice of decoding, for book bags to take home.

Moon Dogs Set 1 Extras

Book 8a: The Gull

Book 8b: The Pit

Book 8c: The Den

VCC and CVCC

STEP 1
Preparation

20 mins

LESSON RESOURCES

Learning goal (2 mins)

- Explain the lesson goal: learning to read and spell VCC and CVCC words
- Show the book That Dog! Book 1: The Ramp.
- You will be completing some activities from That Dog! Activities.

Preparation (18 mins)

1 Word building

- First demonstrate how to build a word. Use only three sound cards, e.g. for the word "and."
- Draw three lines on the whiteboard, and tell the students that you are going to show them how to build the word "and."
- As you say the word slowly, move your finger under the lines.
- Ask the students to listen to the first sound in the word "and"—point to the first line. Emphasize the first sound as you say the whole word. The students respond—/a/.
- Then ask the students which letter spells the sound /a/. The students point to the letter (or you can tell them). Bring the letter down to the first line.
- Repeat with the second and last sounds in the word. Now ask the students to sound all three sounds and blend them into a word, moving your finger under the word: /a/ /n/ /d/ → "and."
- The next time this is done, you can ask a student to participate and identify the sound and then letter and bring it down to the line.

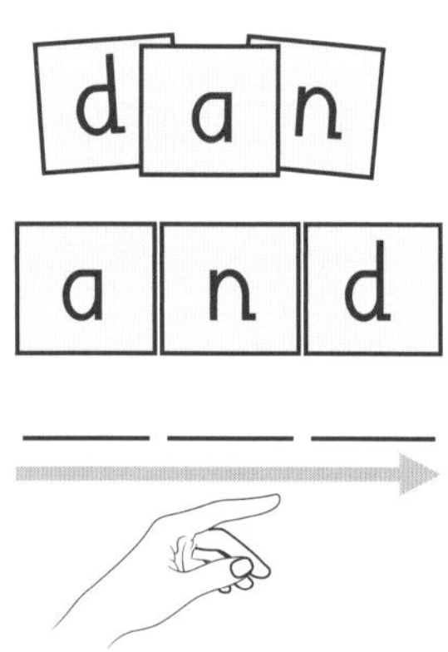

2 Word reading

- Write the words you have created on the whiteboard. Then ask students to blend and read the words.
- Show how to say each sound individually and then blend them together to read the word. Model blending by using a swishing motion with your finger.

3 Oral segmenting

- Say a word aloud (e.g. "sit") and ask students to a count the sounds in the word (3). Write the number of lines you need for all the sounds. Now ask students to listen to the sounds in the word and write a letter for every sound in the word as you spell the word.

4 Word chain

- Using sound cards or magnetic letters, demonstrate how to build the word "elk." Explain to the students that you will be making one change to the word. They must be "sound detectives" and notice if you have added a sound, taken away a sound, or swapped a sound.
- Say that you are going to change the word "elk" (moving your finger under the word) to "elf." Ask the students to listen carefully to where the change has occurred. Move your finger under the words as you say it slowly. Once the change has been identified, invite a student to swap the sound card or letter. Ask all the students to sound out the word and read the new word, e.g. /e/ /l/ /f/ → "elf."
- Introduce the new sounds gradually. This allows students to incorporate the letters and sounds they have learned so far.
- Guide students through the following word-chain sequence: elk—elf—self—sell—bell—well—elk

5 Reading practice cards

- Use the **Reading practice cards** (Activities, page 8) to provide students with additional practice of VCC words.
- Cut the words out and arrange them, so the student has them stacked in a pile (face down).
- Ask them to turn them over and read them one by one.
- The student can place the words they can read on the desk and the words they struggle with back at the bottom of the pile to try again.

STEP 2
Application for reading

25 mins

Before reading (3 mins)

- Revisit the vocabulary taught in Step 1 (e.g. "amp"). Clearly say the word: /a/ /m/ /p/.
- Then provide a simple definition, for example, "An amp is a device that increases electrical power."
- Ask questions such as "What does an amp do?" and "Who might use an amp?"
- Then write the word on the whiteboard and refer back to it throughout the week for reinforcement.

Vocabulary (6 mins)

- Pre-teach the words in the **Vocabulary** list in Book 1: The Ramp (page iv).
- Ensure students understand each word's pronunciation, meaning, and usage.

Application (8 mins)

- The chosen text for this reading activity is Book 1: The Ramp. Briefly introduce the book to spark interest.
- Lead students through a directed reading of Book 1: The Ramp. Encourage students to sound out each word carefully and then blend the sounds together to form the word.
- Provide support by modeling the blending. This hands-on practice is crucial for reinforcing phonetic skills and building fluency.
- Encourage students to sound out each word and then blend to read. This is crucial for reinforcing their learning and for building their confidence.

Reading fluency (8 mins)

- Following the initial reading, revisit Book 1: The Ramp with a focus on fluency.
- Reading the book again allows students to practice their newly acquired skills, this time with an emphasis on reading more smoothly and confidently.
- Create an interactive reading environment by inviting students to take turns reading aloud. Encourage them to point to each word as they read.
- As students read more fluently, support them to read with more expression and prosody, changing their pitch, pace, and emphasis according to the words and punctuation.

STEP 3
Application for spelling

20 mins

Reading and writing captions (20 min)

- Invite students to complete the **Reading captions** activity (Activities, page 9). Ask the student to read the captions and draw a line to the matching picture.
- Ask students to complete the following: **Writing captions** activity (Activities, page 10).
- Dictate the captions from the **Reading captions** activity in the previous page in the Activities book. Have students listen to the sounds in the words and say them aloud as they write them on the lines provided. This activity helps students connect spoken language with written text, enhancing their understanding of letter–sound correspondence.
- After students complete the activity, model the formation of each letter that was written during the activity on the whiteboard.
- Focus on the starting point, stroke direction, and completion of each letter to ensure proper handwriting techniques.
- Demonstrating proper letter formation is crucial for developing legible handwriting and building foundational writing skills.

Extension activities

- Ask students to complete the **Reading and spelling VCC words** activity (Activities, page 5).
- Fold the sheet along the dotted line. Instruct the student to read the words on the left side and check off the ones they read correctly.
- Then, turn the sheet over and dictate the words to the student. Ask them to spell the words by segmenting and sounding out each word as they write them on the lines.
- Finally, have the student open the sheet and check off the words they spelled correctly.
- This process reinforces phonetic skills and promotes self-assessment.
- For students who finish early or need additional practice spelling, provide extra activity sheets with different captions. Dictate these new captions to the students, allowing them to practice spelling and writing on the lines provided.
- For an introduction to spelling two-syllable words, ask students to complete the **Reading and spelling two-syllable words** activity (Activities, page 11).

STEP 4
Comprehension and consolidation
15 mins

Book reading (5 mins)

- Reread Book 1: The Ramp.
- Revisiting the book helps to reinforce familiarity with the text and supports phonetic recognition and comprehension.

Sequencing (5 mins)

- For this activity, the students are going to retell the story, using the pictures and words in the **Retell the story** activity (Activities, page 16).
- Divide students into small groups.
- Photocopy the activity page onto cardstock for each group.
- Decide whether to number the cards on the back to make sequencing easier for the students.
- Provide each group with a set of cards. Encourage collaboration as they work together to place the picture cards in the correct order of the story.
- Invite each group to retell the story using their arranged cards. Encourage them to use the word cards to narrate the story.
- Alternatively, after sequencing the story, the students can use the word cards to reinforce vocabulary. Ask students to match the word cards to the corresponding picture cards, promoting word recognition and comprehension.

Comprehension (5 mins)

- Check students have understood the story by completing the **Comprehension** activity (Activities, page 12).
- The aim of this activity is to test students' understanding of the story by answering the discussion questions.

Extension activities

- Ask students to complete the **Spot it!** activity (Activities, page 13). The students look at the picture and answer by circling the word "yes" or "no" for each question or statement.
- Invite students complete the **Sequence the story** activity (page 14). The students read the sentences carefully and sequence them in the order of the story in Book 1.
- They can also complete the **Fill in the missing words** activity (page 15). Encourage them to sound out the words as they write them on the lines.

STEP 5
Tracking progress

Stepping stone game

- Play the **Stepping stones game** (page 20).
- Provide positive feedback and encouragement throughout the game.
- For those needing more support, help them to blend the letter sound or word with assistance.
- Depending on how the class performs in the game, optionally revisit some of the activities to reinforce any specific skill gaps or assign one of the additional activities below.

Vocabulary activity

- Assign the **Vocabulary** activity (Activities, page 17). This covers the potentially challenging words that feature in Book 1: The Ramp.
- Cut the sentences into strips.
- Then ask the student to match the two parts of the sentence so that they make sense.
- This activity encourages students to think about the meaning of new words and to use them in the context of a complete sentence.

Punctuation activity

- Have students complete the **Punctuation** activity (Activities, page 19).
- Remind students that capital letters are used to begin sentences and periods come at the end of sentences.

PARALLEL BOOKS

In addition to Book 1: The Ramp, here are some books that also cover VCC or CVCC words and can be used for more practice of decoding, for book bags to take home.

Get Out of the Game
Book 1: Zap!

Magic Belt
Book 1: The Man in the Mist

Mel on Mars
Book 1: Dom Gets Lost

LESSON PLANS: That Dog!

CVCC

STEP 1
Preparation

25 mins

LESSON RESOURCES

Reviewing sounds (3 mins)

- Using sound cards, review some of the previously learned CVCC words: /r/ /a/ /m/ /p/. For example, model blending "ramp," reading it sound by sound and then the whole word.
  /r/ /a/ /m/ /p/ → "ramp."

Learning goal (2 mins)

- Explain the lesson goal: learning to read and spell CVCC words.
- Introduce the book That Dog! Book 2: The Lost Dog.
- You will be completing some activities from That Dog! Activities.

Preparation (20 mins)

1 Word building

- First demonstrate how to build a word. Use only four sound cards, e.g. for the word "sand."
- Draw four lines on the whiteboard, and tell the students that you are going to show them how to build the word "sand."
- As you say the word slowly, move your finger under the lines.
- Ask the students to listen to the first sound in the word "sand"—point to the first line. Emphasize the first sound as you say the whole word. The students respond—/s/.
- Then ask the students which letter spells the sound /s/. The students point to the letter (or you can tell them). Bring the letter down to the first line.
- Repeat with the remaining sounds in the word. Now ask the students to sound all four sounds and blend them into a word, moving your finger under the word:
  /s/ /a/ /n/ /d/ → "sand."
- The next time this is done, you can ask a student to participate and identify the sound and then letter and bring it down to the line.

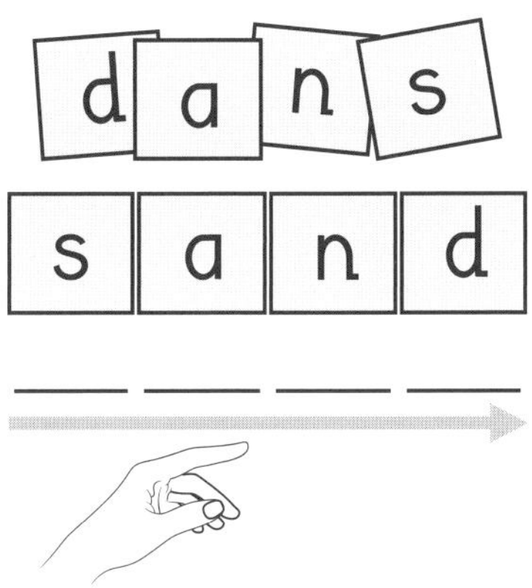

2 Word reading

- Write the words you have created on the whiteboard. Then ask students to blend and read the words.
- Show how to say each sound individually and then blend them together to read the word. Model blending by using a swishing motion with your finger.

3 Oral segmenting

- Say a word aloud (e.g. "nest") and ask students to a count the sounds in the word (4). Write the number of lines you need for all the sounds. Now ask students to listen to the sounds in the word and write a letter for every sound in the word as you spell the word.

4 Word chain

- Using sound cards or magnetic letters, demonstrate how to build the word "ramp." Explain to the students that you will be making one change to the word. They must be "sound detectives" and notice if you have added a sound, taken away a sound, or swapped a sound.
- Say that you are going to change the word "rant" (moving your finger under the word) to "ant." Ask the students to listen carefully to where the change has occurred. Move your finger under the words as you say it slowly. Once the change has been identified, invite a student to swap the sound card or letter. Ask all the students to sound out the word and read the new word, e.g. /a/ /n/ /t/ → "ant."
- Introduce the new sounds gradually. This allows students to incorporate the letters and sounds they have learned so far.
- Direct students through the following word-chain sequence: rant—ant—and—band—bank—sank—rank—rant

5 Reading practice cards

- Use the **Reading practice cards** (Activities, page 26) to provide students with additional practice of CVCC words.

STEP 2
Application for reading
25 mins

Before reading (3 mins)

- Revisit the vocabulary taught in Step 1 (e.g. "nest"). Clearly say the word: /n/ /e/ /s/ /t/.
- Then provide a simple definition, for example, "A nest is a made by birds to lay their eggs."
- Ask questions such as "Where might you find a nest?"
- Then write the word on the whiteboard and refer back to it throughout the week for reinforcement.

Vocabulary (6 mins)

- Pre-teach the words in the **Vocabulary** list in Book 2: The Lost Dog (page iv).
- Ensure students understand each word's pronunciation, meaning, and usage.

Application (8 mins)

- The chosen text for this reading activity is Book 2: The Lost Dog. Briefly introduce the book to spark interest.
- Lead students through a directed reading of Book 2: The Lost Dog. Encourage students to sound out each word carefully and then blend the sounds together to form the word.
- Provide support by modeling the blending. This hands-on practice is crucial for reinforcing phonetic skills and building fluency.
- Encourage students to sound out each word and then blend to read. This is crucial for reinforcing their learning and for building their confidence.

Reading fluency (8 mins)

- Following the initial reading, revisit Book 2: The Lost Dog with a focus on fluency.
- Reading the book again allows students to practice their newly acquired skills, this time with an emphasis on reading more smoothly and confidently.
- Create an interactive reading environment by inviting students to take turns reading aloud. Encourage them to point to each word as they read.
- As students read more fluently, support them to read with more expression and prosody, changing their pitch, pace, and emphasis according to the words and punctuation.

STEP 3
Application for spelling
20 mins

Segmenting and spelling (20 min)

- Invite students to complete the **Reading captions** activity (Activities, page 27). When reading high-frequency words, point to the grapheme the students do not yet know and sound it out for student, e.g. with the word "the," sound out /th/ and the schwa sound /uh/.
- Ask students to complete the following: **Writing captions** activity (Activities, page 28).
- Dictate the captions from the **Reading captions** activity in the previous page in the Activities book. Have students listen to the sounds in the words and say them aloud as they write them on the lines provided. This activity helps students connect spoken language with written text, enhancing their understanding of letter–sound correspondence.
- After students complete the activity, model the formation of each letter that was written during the activity on the whiteboard.
- Focus on the starting point, stroke direction, and completion of each letter to ensure proper handwriting techniques.
- Demonstrating proper letter formation is crucial for developing legible handwriting and building foundational writing skills.

Extension activities

- Ask students to complete the **Reading and spelling** activity (Activities, page 23).
- Fold the sheet along the dotted line. Instruct the student to read the words on the left side and check off the ones they read correctly.
- Then, turn the sheet over and dictate the words to the student. Ask them to spell the words by segmenting and sounding out each word as they write them on the lines.
- Finally, have the student open the sheet and check off the words they spelled correctly.
- This process reinforces phonetic skills and promotes self-assessment.
- For students who finish early or need additional practice spelling, provide extra activity sheets with different captions.
- Dictate these new captions to the students, allowing them to practice spelling and writing on the lines provided.

STEP 4
Comprehension and consolidation

15 mins

Book reading (5 mins)

- Reread Book 2: The Lost Dog.
- Revisiting the book helps to reinforce familiarity with the text and supports phonetic recognition and comprehension.

Sequencing (5 mins)

- For this activity, the students are going to retell the story, using the pictures and words in the **Sequence the story** activity (Activities, page 32).
- Cut out the sentences for each student or group.
- Ask the students to read the sentences carefully and sequence them in the order of the story in Book 2: The Lost Dog.
- The students then sticks them in the numbered boxes in the correct order.
- Some students may benefit from sequencing just two sentences at a time.

Comprehension (5 mins)

- Check students have understood the story by completing the **Comprehension** activity (Activities, page 30).
- The aim of this activity is to test students' understanding of the story by answering the discussion questions.

Extension activities

- Ask students to complete the **Spot it!** activity (Activities, page 31). The students look at the picture and answer by circling the word "yes" or "no" for each question or statement.
- They can also complete the **Fill in the missing words** activity (page 33). Encourage them to sound out the words as they write them on the lines.
- Invite students complete the **Retell the story** activity (page 34). The students read the sentences carefully and sequence them in the order of the story in Book 2.

STEP 5
Tracking progress

Stepping stone game

- Play the **Stepping stones game** (page 38).
- Provide positive feedback and encouragement throughout the game.
- For those needing more support, help them to blend the letter sound or word with assistance.
- Depending on how the class performs in the game, optionally revisit some of the activities to reinforce any specific skill gaps or assign an additional activity, such as the examples below.

Punctuation activity

- Have students complete the **Punctuation** activity (Activites, page 36)
- The student is given a passage of text that has its capital letters and periods removed.
- Ask the students to read the text and insert periods and capital letters where needed.
- Remind students that capital letters are used to begin sentences and periods come at the end of sentences.

Reading fluency activity

- Assign the **Reading fluency** activity (Activities, page 37).
- Fold the sheet on the dotted line.
- Ask the student to read the first passage. The first is for fluency.
- For the second reading, ask the student to read with expression.
- Put a check, sticker, or stamp in the boxes once this is done.
- The student can read the second passage on another day or both passages to develop reading stamina.

PARALLEL BOOKS

In addition to Book 2: The Lost Dog, here are some books that also cover VCC or CVCC words and can be used for more practice of decoding, for book bags to take home.

Get Out of the Game
Book 2: Bugs!

Magic Belt
Book 2: Ten Rocks

Mel on Mars
Book 2: Mel Lands on Mars

LESSON PLANS: That Dog!

CVCC

STEP 1
Preparation

25 mins

LESSON RESOURCES

Reviewing sounds (3 mins)

- Using sound cards, review some of the previously learned CVCC words: /s/ /a/ /n/ /d/. For example, model blending "ramp," reading it sound by sound and then the whole word.
  /s/ /a/ /n/ /d/ → "sand."

Learning goal (2 mins)

- Explain the lesson goal: learning to read and spell CVCC words.
- Introduce the book That Dog! Book 3: No Dogs!
- You will be completing some activities from That Dog! Activities.

Preparation (20 mins)

1 Word building

- First demonstrate how to build a word. Use only four sound cards, e.g. for the word "help."
- Draw four lines on the whiteboard, and tell the students that you are going to show them how to build the word "help."
- As you say the word slowly, move your finger under the lines.
- Ask the students to listen to the first sound in the word "help"—point to the first line. Emphasize the first sound as you say the whole word. The students respond—/h/.
- Then ask the students which letter spells the sound /h/. The students point to the letter (or you can tell them). Bring the letter down to the first line.
- Repeat with the remaining sounds in the word. Now ask the students to sound all four sounds and blend them into a word, moving your finger under the word: /h/ /e/ /l/ /p/ → "help."
- The next time this is done, you can ask a student to participate and identify the sound and then letter and bring it down to the line.

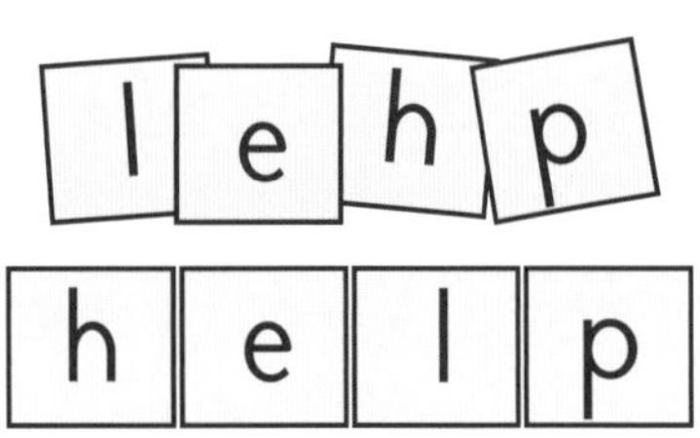

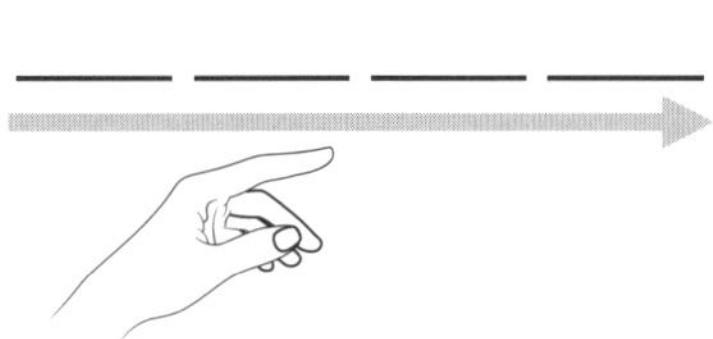

2 Word reading

- Write the words you have created on the whiteboard. Then ask students to blend and read the words.
- Show how to say each sound individually and then blend them together to read the word. Model blending by using a swishing motion with your finger.

3 Oral segmenting

- Say a word aloud (e.g. "silk") and ask students to a count the sounds in the word (4). Write the number of lines you need for all the sounds. Now ask students to listen to the sounds in the word and write a letter for every sound in the word as you spell the word.

4 Word chain

- Using sound cards or magnetic letters, demonstrate how to build the word "ramp." Explain to the students that you will be making one change to the word. They must be "sound detectives" and notice if you have added a sound, taken away a sound, or swapped a sound.
- Say that you are going to change the word "ramp" (moving your finger under the word) to "amp." Ask the students to listen carefully to where the change has occurred. Move your finger under the words as you say it slowly. Once the change has been identified, invite a student to swap the sound card or letter. Ask all the students to sound out the word and read the new word, e.g. /a/ /m/ /p/ → "amp."
- Introduce the new sounds gradually. This allows students to incorporate the letters and sounds they have learned so far.
- Direct students through the following word-chain sequence: ramp—amp—lamp—camp—damp—vamp—ramp.

5 Reading practice cards

- Use the **Reading practice cards** (Activities, page 44) to provide students with additional practice of CVCC words.

STEP 2
Application for reading

25 mins

Before reading (3 mins)

- Revisit the vocabulary taught in Step 1 (e.g. "wind"). Clearly say the word: /w/ /i/ /n/ /d/.
- Then provide a simple definition, for example, "Wind is the movement of air."
- Ask questions such as "What can you feel when there is wind?"
- Then write the word on the whiteboard and refer back to it throughout the week for reinforcement.

Vocabulary (6 mins)

- Pre-teach the words in the **Vocabulary** list in Book 3: No Dogs! (page iv).
- Ensure students understand each word's pronunciation, meaning, and usage.

Application (8 mins)

- The chosen text for this reading activity is Book 3: No Dogs! Briefly introduce the book to spark interest.
- Lead students through a directed reading of Book 3: No Dogs! Encourage students to sound out each word carefully and then blend the sounds together to form the word.
- Provide support by modeling the blending. This hands-on practice is crucial for reinforcing phonetic skills and building fluency.
- Encourage students to sound out each word and then blend to read. This is crucial for reinforcing their learning and for building their confidence.

Reading fluency (8 mins)

- Following the initial reading, revisit Book 3: No Dogs! with a focus on fluency.
- Reading the book again allows students to practice their newly acquired skills, this time with an emphasis on reading more smoothly and confidently.
- Create an interactive reading environment by inviting students to take turns reading aloud. Encourage them to point to each word as they read.
- As students read more fluently, support them to read with more expression and prosody, changing their pitch, pace, and emphasis according to the words and punctuation.

STEP 3
Application for spelling

20 mins

Reading and writing captions (20 min)

- Invite students to complete the **Reading captions** activity (Activities, page 45). Ask the student to read the captions and draw a line to the matching picture.
- Ask students to complete the following: **Writing captions** activity (Activities, page 46).
- Dictate the captions from the **Reading captions** activity in the previous page in the Activities book. Have students listen to the sounds in the words and say them aloud as they write them on the lines provided. This activity helps students connect spoken language with written text, enhancing their understanding of letter–sound correspondence.
- After students complete the activity, model the formation of each letter that was written during the activity on the whiteboard.
- Focus on the starting point, stroke direction, and completion of each letter to ensure proper handwriting techniques.
- Demonstrating proper letter formation is crucial for developing legible handwriting and building foundational writing skills.

Extension activities

- Ask students to complete the **Reading and spelling more CVCC words** activity (Activities, page 41).
- Fold the sheet along the dotted line. Instruct the student to read the words on the left side and check off the ones they read correctly.
- Then, turn the sheet over and dictate the words to the student. Ask them to spell the words by segmenting and sounding out each word as they write them on the lines.
- Finally, have the student open the sheet and check off the words they spelled correctly.
- This process reinforces phonetic skills and promotes self-assessment.
- For students who finish early or need additional practice spelling, provide extra activity sheets with different captions. Dictate these new captions to the students, allowing them to practice spelling and writing on the lines provided.
- For further practice of two-syllable words, ask students to complete the **Reading and spelling two-syllable words** activity (Activities, page 47).

STEP 4
Comprehension and consolidation

15 mins

Book reading (5 mins)

- Reread Book 3: No Dogs!
- Revisiting the book helps to reinforce familiarity with the text and supports phonetic recognition and comprehension.

Sequencing (5 mins)

- For this activity, the students are going to retell the story, using the pictures and words in the **Retell the story** activity (Activities, page 52).
- Divide students into small groups.
- Photocopy the activity page onto cardstock for each group.
- Decide whether to number the cards on the back to make sequencing easier for the students.
- Provide each group with a set of cards
- Encourage collaboration as they work together to place the picture cards in the correct order of the story.
- Invite each group to retell the story using their arranged cards. Encourage them to use the word cards to narrate the story.
- Alternatively, after sequencing the story, the students can use the word cards to reinforce vocabulary. Ask students to match the word cards to the corresponding picture cards, promoting word recognition and comprehension.

Comprehension (5 mins)

- Check students have understood the story by completing the **Comprehension** activity (Activities, page 48).
- The aim of this activity is to test students' understanding of the story by answering the discussion questions.

Extension activities

- Ask students to complete the **Spot it!** activity (Activities, page 49). The students look at the picture and answer by circling the word "yes" or "no" for each question or statement.
- Invite students complete the **Sequence the story** activity (page 50). The students read the sentences carefully and sequence them in the order of the story in Book 3.
- They can also complete the **Fill in the missing words** activity (page 51). Encourage them to sound out the words as they write them on the lines.

STEP 5
Tracking progress

Stepping stone game

- Play the **Stepping stones game** (page 56).
- Provide positive feedback and encouragement throughout the game.
- For those needing more support, help them to blend the letter sound or word with assistance.
- Depending on how the class performs in the game, optionally revisit some of the activities to reinforce any specific skill gaps or assign an additional activity, such as the examples below.

Vocabulary activity

- Assign the **Vocabulary** activity (Activities, page 53). This covers the potentially challenging words that feature in Book 3: No Dogs!
- Cut the sentences into strips.
- Then ask the student to match the two parts of the sentence so that they make sense.
- This activity encourages students to think about the meaning of new words and to use them in the context of a complete sentence.

Reading fluency activity

- Assign the **Reading fluency** activity (Activities, page 55).
- For the second reading, ask the student to read with expression.
- Put a check, sticker, or stamp in the boxes once this is done.
- The student can read the second passage on another day or both passages to develop reading stamina.

PARALLEL BOOKS

In addition to Book 3: No Dogs!, here are some books that also cover CVCC words and can be used for more practice of decoding, for book bags to take home.

Get Out of the Game
Book 3: Bats in the Mist

Magic Belt
Book 3: "Help Us!"

Mel on Mars
Book 3: Lost in the Dust

CCVC and -ed

STEP 1
Preparation

25 mins

LESSON RESOURCES

Reviewing sounds (3 mins)

- Using sound cards, review some of the previously learned CVCC words: /s/ /i/ /l/ /k/. For example, model blending "silk," reading it sound by sound and then the whole word.
  /s/ /i/ /l/ /k/ → "silk."

Learning goal (2 mins)

- Explain the lesson goal: learning to read and spell CCVC words and the suffix -ed.
- Introduce the book That Dog! Book 4: Drop It!
- You will be completing some activities from That Dog! Activities.

Preparation (20 mins)

1 Word building

- First demonstrate how to build a word. Use only four sound cards, e.g. for the word "drop."
- Draw four lines on the whiteboard, and tell the students that you are going to show them how to build the word "drop."
- As you say the word slowly, move your finger under the lines.
- Ask the students to listen to the first sound in the word "drop"—point to the first line. Emphasize the first sound as you say the whole word. The students respond—/d/.
- Then ask the students which letter spells the sound /d/. The students point to the letter (or you can tell them). Bring the letter down to the first line.
- Repeat with the remaining sounds in the word. Now ask the students to sound all four sounds and blend them into a word, moving your finger under the word:
  /d/ /r/ /o/ /p/ → "drop."
- The next time this is done, you can ask a student to participate and identify the sound and then letter and bring it down to the line.

2 Word reading

- Write the words you have created on the whiteboard. Then ask students to blend and read the words.
- Show how to say each sound individually and then blend them together to read the word. Model blending by using a swishing motion with your finger.

3 Oral segmenting

- Say a word aloud (e.g. "drum") and ask students to a count the sounds in the word (4). Write the number of lines you need for all the sounds. Now ask students to listen to the sounds in the word and write a letter for every sound in the word as you spell the word.

4 Introducing the three sounds of -ed

- Explain to students that the suffix -ed indicates that something has happened in the past. In the next activity, they are going to be "sound detectives" because -ed doesn't always sound the same.
- Introduce the three sounds: /t/, /d/, and /id/
- Explain that the sound of -ed depends on the last sound of the verb before the -ed is added. For example, for words ending in a voiced sound, the -ed sounds like /d/ (e.g. "hummed"); for words ending in a voiceless sound, the -ed sounds like /t/ ("kissed"); and for words ending in /t/ or /d/, the -ed is an extra syllable /id/ (e.g. "wanted").
- Next play the **Three sounds of -ed** game (Activities, page 66). In this activity, say the list of -ed words aloud and then the students sort them into the correct column depending on the sounds they make.

5 Reading practice cards

- Use the **Reading practice cards** (Activities, page 62) to provide students with additional practice of CCVC words.

STEP 2
Application for reading
25 mins

Before reading (3 mins)

- Revisit the vocabulary taught in Step 1 (e.g. "drum"). Clearly say the word: /d/ /r/ /u/ /m/.
- Then provide a simple definition, for example, "A drum is a musical instrument that you play by hitting it with sticks."
- Ask questions such as "What is a drum used for?" and "What sounds does a drum make?"
- Then write the word on the whiteboard and refer back to it throughout the week for reinforcement.

Vocabulary (6 mins)

- Pre-teach the words in the **Vocabulary** list in Book 4: Drop It! (page iv).
- Ensure students understand each word's pronunciation, meaning, and usage.

Application (8 mins)

- The chosen text for this reading activity is Book 4: Drop It!. Briefly introduce the book to spark interest.
- Lead students through a directed reading of Book 4: Drop It!. Encourage students to sound out each word carefully and then blend the sounds together to form the word.
- Provide support by modeling the blending. This hands-on practice is crucial for reinforcing phonetic skills and building fluency.
- Encourage students to sound out each word and then blend to read. This is crucial for reinforcing their learning and for building their confidence.

Reading fluency (8 mins)

- Following the initial reading, revisit Book 4: Drop It! with a focus on fluency.
- Reading the book again allows students to practice their newly acquired skills, this time with an emphasis on reading more smoothly and confidently.
- Create an interactive reading environment by inviting students to take turns reading aloud. Encourage them to point to each word as they read.
- As students read more fluently, support them to read with more expression and prosody, changing their pitch, pace, and emphasis according to the words and punctuation.

STEP 3
Application for spelling
20 mins

Reading and writing captions (20 min)

- Invite students to complete the **Reading captions** activity (Activities, page 63). Ask the student to read the captions and draw a line to the matching picture.
- Ask students to complete the following: **Writing captions** activity (Activities, page 64).
- Dictate the captions from the **Reading captions** activity in the previous page in the Activities book. Have students listen to the sounds in the words and say them aloud as they write them on the lines provided. This activity helps students connect spoken language with written text, enhancing their understanding of letter–sound correspondence.
- After students complete the activity, model the formation of each letter that was written during the activity on the whiteboard.
- Focus on the starting point, stroke direction, and completion of each letter to ensure proper handwriting techniques.
- Demonstrating proper letter formation is crucial for developing legible handwriting and building foundational writing skills.

Extension activities

- Ask students to complete the **Reading and spelling CCVC words** activity (Activities, page 59).
- Fold the sheet along the dotted line. Instruct the student to read the words on the left side and check off the ones they read correctly.
- Then, turn the sheet over and dictate the words to the student. Ask them to spell the words by segmenting and sounding out each word as they write them on the lines.
- Finally, have the student open the sheet and check off the words they spelled correctly.
- This process reinforces phonetic skills and promotes self-assessment.
- For students who finish early or need additional practice spelling, provide extra activity sheets with different captions. Dictate these new captions to the students, allowing them to practice spelling and writing on the lines provided.
- For further practice of two-syllable words, ask students to complete the **Reading and spelling two-syllable words** activity (Activities, page 65).

STEP 4
Comprehension and consolidation

15 mins

Book reading (5 mins)

- Reread Book 4: Drop It!
- Revisiting the book helps to reinforce familiarity with the text and supports phonetic recognition and comprehension.

Sequencing (5 mins)

- For this activity, the students are going to retell the story, using the pictures and words in the **Retell the story** activity (Activities, page 71).
- Divide students into small groups.
- Photocopy the activity page onto cardstock for each group.
- Decide whether to number the cards on the back to make sequencing easier for the students.
- Provide each group with a set of cards
- Encourage collaboration as they work together to place the picture cards in the correct order of the story.
- Invite each group to retell the story using their arranged cards. Encourage them to use the word cards to narrate the story.
- Alternatively, after sequencing the story, the students can use the word cards to reinforce vocabulary. Ask students to match the word cards to the corresponding picture cards, promoting word recognition and comprehension.

Comprehension (5 mins)

- Check students have understood the story by completing the **Comprehension** activity (Activities, page 67).
- The aim of this activity is to test students' understanding of the story by answering the discussion questions.

Extension activities

- Ask students to complete the **Spot it!** activity (Activities, page 68). The students look at the picture and answer by circling the word "yes" or "no" for each question or statement.
- Invite students complete the **Sequence the story** activity (page 69). The students read the sentences carefully and sequence them in the order of the story in Book 4.
- They can also complete the **Fill in the missing words** activity (page 70). Encourage them to sound out the words as they write them on the lines.

STEP 5
Tracking progress

Stepping stone game

- Play the **Stepping stones game** (page 75).
- Provide positive feedback and encouragement throughout the game.
- For those needing more support, help them to blend the letter sound or word with assistance.
- Depending on how the class performs in the game, optionally revisit some of the activities to reinforce any specific skill gaps or assign an additional activity, such as the examples below.

Vocabulary activity

- Assign the **Vocabulary** activity (Activities, page 72). This covers the potentially challenging words that feature in Book 4: Drop It!
- Cut the sentences into strips.
- Then ask the student to match the two parts of the sentence so that they make sense.
- This activity encourages students to think about the meaning of new words and to use them in the context of a complete sentence.

Reading fluency activity

- Assign the **Reading fluency** activity (Activities, page 74).
- Fold the sheet on the dotted line.
- Ask the student to read the first passage. The first is for fluency.
- For the second reading, ask the student to read with expression.
- Put a check, sticker, or stamp in the boxes once this is done.
- The student can read the second passage on another day or both passages to develop reading stamina.

PARALLEL BOOKS

In addition to Book 4: Drop It!, here are some books that also cover CCVC words and the suffix -ed and can be used for more practice of decoding, for book bags to take home.

Get Out of the Game
Book 4: Filled Up

Magic Belt
Book 4: The Clam

Mel on Mars
Book 4: Hunted at the Blob Dump

CCVCC

STEP 1
Preparation

25 mins

Reviewing sounds (3 mins)

- Using sound cards, review some of the previously learned CCVC words: /s/ /l/ /i/ /p/. For example, model blending “slip,” reading it sound by sound and then the whole word.
  /s/ /l/ /i/ /p/ → “slip.”

Learning goal (2 mins)

- Explain the lesson goal: learning to read and spell CCVCC words.
- Introduce the book That Dog! Book 5: Ben Gets Strict.
- You will be completing some activities from That Dog! Activities.

Preparation (20 mins)

1 Word building

- First demonstrate how to build a word. Use only five sound cards, e.g. for the word “drink.”
- Draw five lines on the whiteboard, and tell the students that you are going to show them how to build the word “drink.”
- As you say the word slowly, move your finger under the lines.
- Ask the students to listen to the first sound in the word “drink”—point to the first line. Emphasize the first sound as you say the whole word. The students respond—/d/.
- Then ask the students which letter spells the sound /d/. The students point to the letter (or you can tell them). Bring the letter down to the first line.
- Repeat with the remaining sounds in the word. Now ask the students to sound all four sounds and blend them into a word, moving your finger under the word: /d/ /r/ /i/ /n/ /k/ → “drink.”
- The next time this is done, you can ask a student to participate and identify the sound and then letter and bring it down to the line.

LESSON RESOURCES

2 Word reading

- Write the words you have created on the whiteboard. Then ask students to blend and read the words.
- Show how to say each sound individually and then blend them together to read the word. Model blending by using a swishing motion with your finger.

3 Oral segmenting

- Say a word aloud (e.g. “frost”) and ask students to a count the sounds in the word (5). Write the number of lines you need for all the sounds. Now ask students to listen to the sounds in the word and write a letter for every sound in the word as you spell the word.

4 Word chain

- Using sound cards or magnetic letters, demonstrate how to build the word “brand.” Explain to the students that you will be making one change to the word. They must be “sound detectives” and notice if you have added a sound, taken away a sound, or swapped a sound.
- Say that you are going to change the word “brand” (moving your finger under the word) to “bland.” Ask the students to listen carefully to where the change has occurred. Move your finger under the words as you say it slowly. Once the change has been identified, invite a student to swap the sound card or letter. Ask all the students to sound out the word and read the new word, e.g. /b/ /l/ /a/ /n/ /d/ → “bland.”
- Introduce the new sounds gradually. This allows students to incorporate the letters and sounds they have learned so far.
- Direct students through the following word-chain sequence: brand—bland—land—sand—stand—stan—clan—clam—clamp—cramp—cram—ram—ran—bran—brand

5 Reading practice cards

- Use the **Reading practice cards** (Activities, page 82) to provide students with additional practice of CCVCC words.

STEP 2
Application for reading

25 mins

Before reading (3 mins)

- Revisit the vocabulary taught in Step 1 (e.g. "frost"). Clearly say the word: /f/ /r/ /o/ /s/ /t/.
- Then provide a simple definition, for example, "Frost is a thin layer of ice that forms on surfaces."
- Ask questions such as "When does frost form?"
- Then write the word on the whiteboard and refer back to it throughout the week for reinforcement.

Vocabulary (6 mins)

- Pre-teach the words in the **Vocabulary** list in Book 5: Ben Gets Strict (page iv).
- Ensure students understand each word's pronunciation, meaning, and usage.

Application (8 mins)

- The chosen text for this reading activity is Book 5: Ben Gets Strict. Briefly introduce the book to spark interest.
- Lead students through a directed reading of Book 5: Ben Gets Strict. Encourage students to sound out each word carefully and then blend the sounds together to form the word.
- Provide support by modeling the blending. This hands-on practice is crucial for reinforcing phonetic skills and building fluency.
- Encourage students to sound out each word and then blend to read. This is crucial for reinforcing their learning and for building their confidence.

Reading fluency (8 mins)

- Following the initial reading, revisit Book 5: Ben Gets Strict with a focus on fluency.
- Reading the book again allows students to practice their newly acquired skills, this time with an emphasis on reading more smoothly and confidently.
- Create an interactive reading environment by inviting students to take turns reading aloud. Encourage them to point to each word as they read.
- As students read more fluently, support them to read with more expression and prosody, changing their pitch, pace, and emphasis according to the words and punctuation.

STEP 3
Application for spelling

20 mins

Reading and writing captions (20 min)

- Invite students to complete the **Reading captions** activity (Activities, page 83) Ask the student to read the captions and draw a line to the matching picture.
- Ask students to complete the following: **Writing captions** activity (Activities, page 84).
- Dictate the captions from the **Reading captions** activity in the previous page in the Activities book. Have students listen to the sounds in the words and say them aloud as they write them on the lines provided. This activity helps students connect spoken language with written text, enhancing their understanding of letter–sound correspondence.
- After students complete the activity, model the formation of each letter that was written during the activity on the whiteboard.
- Focus on the starting point, stroke direction, and completion of each letter to ensure proper handwriting techniques.
- Demonstrating proper letter formation is crucial for developing legible handwriting and building foundational writing skills.

Extension activities

- Ask students to complete the **Reading and spelling CCVCC words** activity (Activities, page 79).
- Fold the sheet along the dotted line. Instruct the student to read the words on the left side and check off the ones they read correctly.
- Then, turn the sheet over and dictate the words to the student. Ask them to spell the words by segmenting and sounding out each word as they write them on the lines.
- Finally, have the student open the sheet and check off the words they spelled correctly.
- This process reinforces phonetic skills and promotes self-assessment.
- For students who finish early or need additional practice spelling, provide extra activity sheets with different captions. Dictate these new captions to the students, allowing them to practice spelling and writing on the lines provided.
- For further practice of two-syllable words, ask students to complete the **Reading and spelling two-syllable words** activity (Activities, page 85).

STEP 4
Comprehension and consolidation

15 mins

Book reading (5 mins)

- Reread Book 5: Ben Gets Strict.
- Revisiting the book helps to reinforce familiarity with the text and supports phonetic recognition and comprehension.

Sequencing (5 mins)

- For this activity, the students are going to retell the story, using the pictures and words in the **Sequence the story** activity (Activities, page 88).
- Cut out the sentences for each student or group.
- Ask the students to read the sentences carefully and sequence them in the order of the story in Book 5: Ben Gets Strict.
- The students then sticks them in the numbered boxes in the correct order.
- Some students may benefit from sequencing just two sentences at a time.

Comprehension (5 mins)

- Check students have understood the story by completing the **Comprehension** activity (Activities, page 86).
- The aim of this activity is to test students' understanding of the story by answering the discussion questions.

Extension activities

- Ask students to complete the **Spot it!** activity (Activities, page 87). The students look at the picture and answer by circling the word "yes" or "no" for each question or statement.
- They can also complete the **Fill in the missing words** activity (page 89). Encourage them to sound out the words as they write them on the lines.
- Invite students complete the **Retell the story** activity (page 90). The students read the sentences carefully and sequence them in the order of the story in Book 5.

STEP 5
Tracking progress

Stepping stone game

- Play the **Stepping stones game** (page 94).
- Provide positive feedback and encouragement throughout the game.
- For those needing more support, help them to blend the letter sound or word with assistance.
- Depending on how the class performs in the game, optionally revisit some of the activities to reinforce any specific skill gaps or assign an additional activity, such as the examples below.

Punctuation activity

- Have the students complete the **Punctuation** activity (Activities, page 92).
- The student is given a passage of text that has its capital letters and periods removed.
- Ask the students to read the text and insert periods and capital letters where needed.
- Remind students that capital letters are used to begin sentences and periods come at the end of sentences.

Reading fluency activity

- Assign the **Reading fluency** activity (Activities, page 93).
- Fold the sheet on the dotted line.
- Ask the student to read the first passage. The first is for fluency.
- For the second reading, ask the student to read with expression.
- Put a check, sticker, or stamp in the boxes once this is done.
- The student can read the second passage on another day or both passages to develop reading stamina.

PARALLEL BOOKS

In addition to Book 5: The Lost Dog, here are some books that also cover CCVCC words and can be used for more practice of decoding, for book bags to take home.

Get Out of the Game
Book 5: Must Drink

Magic Belt
Book 5: Crabs!

Mel on Mars
Book 5: Trust Dr. Kim

LESSON PLANS: That Dog!

ch and tch

STEP 1
Preparation

25 mins

LESSON RESOURCES

Reviewing sounds (3 mins)

- Using sound cards, review some of the previously learned CCVCC words. For example, model blending "brink," reading it sound by sound and then the whole word. /b/ /r/ /i/ /n/ /k/ → "brink."

Learning goal (2 mins)

- Explain the lesson goal: learning the spellings 'ch' and 'tch' for the sound /ch/.
- Note that the sound /ch/ at the end of a word is usually spelled 'ch' when it comes after a consonant, e.g. "hunch," and 'tch' after a short vowel, e.g. "hutch". But there are exceptions e.g. "which," "rich," "much," and "such."
- Introduce the book That Dog! Book 6: Catch Me!
- You will be completing some activities from That Dog! Activities.

Preparation (20 mins)

1 Word building

- First demonstrate how to build a word. Use only three sound cards, e.g. for the word "chip."
- Draw three lines on the whiteboard, and tell the students that you are going to show them how to build the word "chip."
- As you say the word slowly, move your finger under the lines.
- Ask the students to listen to the first sound in the word "chip"—point to the first line. Emphasize the first sound as you say the whole word. The students respond—/ch/.
- Then ask the students which letters spell the sound /ch/. The students point to the letters (or you can tell them). Bring the letters down to the first line.
- Repeat with the second and last sounds in the word. Now ask the students to sound all three sounds and blend them into a word, moving your finger under the word: /ch/ /i/ /p/ → "chip."
- The next time this is done, you can ask a student to participate and identify the sound and then letter and bring it down to the line.

2 Word reading

- Write the words you have created on the whiteboard. Then ask students to blend and read the words.
- Show how to say each sound individually and then blend them together to read the word. Model blending by using a swishing motion with your finger.

3 Oral segmenting

- Say a word aloud (e.g. "munch") and ask students to a count the sounds in the word (4). Write the number of lines you need for all the sounds. Now ask students to listen to the sounds in the word and write a letter for every sound in the word as you spell the word.

4 Word chain

- Using sound cards or magnetic letters, demonstrate how to build the word "lunch." Explain to the students that you will be making one change to the word. They must be "sound detectives" and notice if you have added a sound, taken away a sound, or swapped a sound.
- Say that you are going to change the word "lunch" (moving your finger under the word) to "munch." Ask the students to listen carefully to where the change has occurred. Move your finger under the words as you say it slowly. Once the change has been identified, invite a student to swap the sound card or letter. Ask all the students to sound out the word and read the new word, e.g. /m/ /u/ /n/ /ch/ → "munch."
- Introduce the new sounds gradually. This allows students to incorporate the letters and sounds they have learned so far.
- Direct students through the following word-chain sequence: lunch—munch—punch—bunch—hunch—lunch

5 Reading practice cards

- Use the **Reading practice cards** (Activities, page 100) to provide students with additional practice of ch and tch words.

STEP 2
Application for reading
25 mins

Before reading (3 mins)

- Revisit the vocabulary taught in Step 1 (e.g. "match"). Clearly say the word: /m/ /a/ /ch/.
- Explore different definitions of word "match."
- Ask questions such as "What can you use a match for?" and "How do you strike a match?"
- Then write the word on the whiteboard and refer back to it throughout the week for reinforcement.

Vocabulary (6 mins)

- Pre-teach the words in the **Vocabulary** list in Book 6: Catch Me! (page iv).
- Ensure students understand each word's pronunciation, meaning, and usage.

Application (8 mins)

- The chosen text for this reading activity is Book 6: Catch Me!. Briefly introduce the book to spark interest.
- Lead students through a directed reading of Book 6: Catch Me!. Encourage students to sound out each word carefully and then blend the sounds together to form the word.
- Provide support by modeling the blending. This hands-on practice is crucial for reinforcing phonetic skills and building fluency.
- Encourage students to sound out each word and then blend to read. This is crucial for reinforcing their learning and for building their confidence.

Reading fluency (8 mins)

- Following the initial reading, revisit Book 6: Catch Me! with a focus on fluency.
- Reading the book again allows students to practice their newly acquired skills, this time with an emphasis on reading more smoothly and confidently.
- Create an interactive reading environment by inviting students to take turns reading aloud. Encourage them to point to each word as they read.
- As students read more fluently, support them to read with more expression and prosody, changing their pitch, pace, and emphasis according to the words and punctuation.

STEP 3
Application for spelling
20 mins

Reading and writing captions (20 min)

- Invite students to complete the **Reading captions** activity (Activities, page 101). Ask the student to read the captions and draw a line to the matching picture.
- Ask students to complete the following: **Writing captions** activity (Activities, page 102).
- Dictate the captions from the **Reading captions** activity in the previous page in the Activities book. Have students listen to the sounds in the words and say them aloud as they write them on the lines provided. This activity helps students connect spoken language with written text, enhancing their understanding of letter–sound correspondence.
- After students complete the activity, model the formation of each letter that was written during the activity on the whiteboard.
- Focus on the starting point, stroke direction, and completion of each letter to ensure proper handwriting techniques.
- Demonstrating proper letter formation is crucial for developing legible handwriting and building foundational writing skills.

Extension activities

- Ask students to complete the **Reading and spelling ch and tch** activity (Activities, page 97).
- Fold the sheet along the dotted line. Instruct the student to read the words on the left side and check off the ones they read correctly.
- Then, turn the sheet over and dictate the words to the student. Ask them to spell the words by segmenting and sounding out each word as they write them on the lines.
- Finally, have the student open the sheet and check off the words they spelled correctly.
- This process reinforces phonetic skills and promotes self-assessment.
- For students who finish early or need additional practice spelling, provide extra activity sheets with different captions. Dictate these new captions to the students, allowing them to practice spelling and writing on the lines provided.
- For further practice of two-syllable words, ask students to complete the **Reading and spelling two-syllable words** activity (Activities, page 103).

STEP 4
Comprehension and consolidation

15 mins

Book reading (5 mins)

- Reread Book 6: Catch Me!
- Revisiting the book helps to reinforce familiarity with the text and supports phonetic recognition and comprehension.

Sequencing (5 mins)

- For this activity, the students are going to retell the story, using the pictures and words in the **Sequence the story** activity (Activities, page 106).
- Cut out the sentences for each student or group.
- Ask the students to read the sentences carefully and sequence them in the order of the story in Book 6: Catch Me!.
- The students then sticks them in the numbered boxes in the correct order.
- Some students may benefit from sequencing just two sentences at a time.

Comprehension (5 mins)

- Check students have understood the story by completing the **Comprehension** activity (Activities, page 104).
- The aim of this activity is to test students' understanding of the story by answering the discussion questions.

Extension activities

- Ask students to complete the **Spot it!** activity (Activities, page 105). The students look at the picture and answer by circling the word "yes" or "no" for each question or statement.
- They can also complete the **Fill in the missing words** activity (page 107). Encourage them to sound out the words as they write them on the lines.
- Invite students complete the **Retell the story** activity (page 108). The students read the sentences carefully and sequence them in the order of the story in Book 6.

STEP 5
Tracking progress

Stepping stone game

- Play the **Stepping stones game** (page 112).
- Provide positive feedback and encouragement throughout the game.
- For those needing more support, help them to blend the letter sound or word with assistance.
- Depending on how the class performs in the game, optionally revisit some of the activities to reinforce any specific skill gaps or assign an additional activity, such as the examples below.

Punctuation activity

- Have the students complete the **Punctuation** activity (Activities, page 110).
- The student is given a passage of text that has its capital letters and periods removed.
- Ask the students to read the text and insert periods and capital letters where needed.
- Remind students that capital letters are used to begin sentences and periods come at the end of sentences.

Reading fluency activity

- Assign the **Reading fluency** activity (Activities, page 111).
- Fold the sheet on the dotted line.
- Ask the student to read the first passage. The first is for fluency.
- For the second reading, ask the student to read with expression.
- Put a check, sticker, or stamp in the boxes once this is done.
- The student can read the second passage on another day or both passages to develop reading stamina.

PARALLEL BOOKS

In addition to Book 6: Catch Me!, here are some books that also cover 'ch' and 'tch' words and can be used for more practice of decoding, for book bags to take home.

Get Out of the Game
Book 6: Glitch

Magic Belt
Book 6: Crunch!

Mel on Mars
Book 6: Catch the Torch!

sh

STEP 1
Preparation

25 mins

Reviewing sounds (3 mins)

- Using sound cards, review some of the previously learned ch and tch words. For example, model blending "itch," reading it sound by sound and then the whole word.
  /i/ /ch/ → "itch."

Learning goal (2 mins)

- Explain the lesson goal: learning to read and spell sh words.
- Introduce the book That Dog! Book 7: Fishing.
- You will be completing some activities from That Dog! Activities.

Preparation (20 mins)

1 Word building

- First demonstrate how to build a word. Use only three sound cards, e.g. for the word "ship."
- Draw three lines on the whiteboard, and tell the students that you are going to show them how to build the word "ship."
- As you say the word slowly, move your finger under the lines.
- Ask the students to listen to the first sound in the word "ship"—point to the first line. Emphasize the first sound as you say the whole word. The students respond—/sh/.
- Then ask the students which letters spell the sound /sh/. The students point to the letters (or you can tell them). Bring the letters down to the first line.
- Repeat with the remaining sounds in the word. Now ask the students to sound all three sounds and blend them into a word, moving your finger under the word: /sh/ /i/ /p/ → "ship."
- The next time this is done, you can ask a student to participate and identify the sound and then letter and bring it down to the line.

LESSON RESOURCES

2 Word reading

- Write the words you have created on the whiteboard. Then ask students to blend and read the words.
- Show how to say each sound individually and then blend them together to read the word. Model blending by using a swishing motion with your finger.

3 Oral segmenting

- Say a word aloud (e.g. "shell") and ask students to a count the sounds in the word (3). Write the number of lines you need for all the sounds. Now ask students to listen to the sounds in the word and write a letter for every sound in the word as you spell the word.

4 Word chain

- Using sound cards or magnetic letters, demonstrate how to build the word "wish." Explain to the students that you will be making one change to the word. They must be "sound detectives" and notice if you have added a sound, taken away a sound, or swapped a sound.
- Say that you are going to change the word "wish" (moving your finger under the word) to "dish." Ask the students to listen carefully to where the change has occurred. Move your finger under the words as you say it slowly. Once the change has been identified, invite a student to swap the sound card or letter. Ask all the students to sound out the word and read the new word, e.g. /d/ /i/ /sh/ → "dish."
- Introduce the new sounds gradually. This allows students to incorporate the letters and sounds they have learned so far.
- Direct students through the following word-chain sequence: wish—dish—dash—ash—cash—clash—flash—lash—lush—blush—brush—rush—mush—mash—dash—dish—wish

5 Reading practice cards

- Use the **Reading practice cards** (Activities, page 118) for additional practice.

STEP 2 Application for reading

25 mins

Before reading (3 mins)

- Revisit the vocabulary taught in Step 1 (e.g. "shell"). Clearly say the word: /sh/ /e/ /ll/.
- Provide a simple definition of the word "shell," such as "A shell is the hard outer covering of some animals."
- Ask questions such as "What animals have shells?"
- Then write the word on the whiteboard and refer back to it throughout the week for reinforcement.

Vocabulary (5 mins)

- Pre-teach the words in the **Vocabulary** list in Book 7: Fishing (page iv).
- Ensure students understand each word's pronunciation, meaning, and usage.

Application (8 mins)

- The chosen text for this reading activity is Book 7: Fishing. Briefly introduce the book to spark interest.
- Lead students through a guided reading of Book 7: Fishing. Encourage students to sound out each word carefully and then blend the sounds together to form the word.
- Provide support by modeling the blending. This hands-on practice is crucial for reinforcing phonetic skills and building fluency.
- Encourage students to sound out each word and then blend to read. This is crucial for reinforcing their learning and for building their confidence.

Reading fluency (8 mins)

- Following the initial reading, revisit Book 7: Fishing with a focus on fluency.
- Reading the book again allows students to practice their newly acquired skills, this time with an emphasis on reading more smoothly and confidently.
- Create an interactive reading environment by inviting students to take turns reading aloud. Encourage them to point to each word as they read.
- As students read more fluently, support them to read with more expression and prosody, changing their pitch, pace, and emphasis according to the words and punctuation.

STEP 3 Application for spelling

20 mins

Reading and writing captions (20 min)

- Invite students to complete the **Reading captions** activity (Activities, page 119). Ask the student to read the captions and draw a line to the matching picture.
- Ask students to complete the following: **Writing captions** activity (Activities, page 120).
- Dictate the captions from the **Reading captions** activity in the previous page in the Activities book. Have students listen to the sounds in the words and say them aloud as they write them on the lines provided. This activity helps students connect spoken language with written text, enhancing their understanding of letter–sound correspondence.
- After students complete the activity, model the formation of each letter that was written during the activity on the whiteboard.
- Focus on the starting point, stroke direction, and completion of each letter to ensure proper handwriting techniques.
- Demonstrating proper letter formation is crucial for developing legible handwriting and building foundational writing skills.

Extension activities

- Ask students to complete the **Reading and spelling /sh/** activity (Activities, page 115).
- Fold the sheet along the dotted line. Instruct the student to read the words on the left side and check off the ones they read correctly.
- Then, turn the sheet over and dictate the words to the student. Ask them to spell the words by segmenting and sounding out each word as they write them on the lines.
- Finally, have the student open the sheet and check off the words they spelled correctly.
- This process reinforces phonetic skills and promotes self-assessment.
- For students who finish early or need additional practice spelling, provide extra activity sheets with different captions. Dictate these new captions to the students, allowing them to practice spelling and writing on the lines provided.
- For further practice of two-syllable words, ask students to complete the **Reading and spelling two-syllable words** activity (Activities, page 121).

STEP 4
Comprehension and consolidation

15 mins

Book reading (5 mins)

- Reread Book 7: Fishing.
- Revisiting the book helps to reinforce familiarity with the text and supports phonetic recognition and comprehension.

Sequencing (5 mins)

- For this activity, the students are going to retell the story, using the pictures and words in the **Retell the story** activity (Activities, page 126).
- Divide students into small groups.
- Photocopy the activity page onto cardstock for each group.
- Decide whether to number the cards on the back to make sequencing easier for the students.
- Provide each group with a set of cards.
- Encourage collaboration as they work together to place the picture cards in the correct order of the story.
- Invite each group to retell the story using their arranged cards. Encourage them to use the word cards to narrate the story.
- Alternatively, after sequencing the story, the students can use the word cards to reinforce vocabulary. Ask students to match the word cards to the corresponding picture cards, promoting word recognition and comprehension.

Comprehension (5 mins)

- Check students have understood the story by completing the **Comprehension** activity (Activities, page 122).
- The aim of this activity is to test students' understanding of the story by answering the discussion questions.

Extension activities

- Ask students to complete the **Spot it!** activity (Activities, page 123). The students look at the picture and answer by circling the word "yes" or "no" for each question or statement.
- Invite students complete the **Sequence the story** activity (page 124). The students read the sentences carefully and sequence them in the order of the story in Book 7.
- They can also complete the **Fill in the missing words** activity (page 125). Encourage them to sound out the words as they write them on the lines.

STEP 5
Tracking progress

Stepping stone game

- Play the **Stepping stones game** (page 130).
- Provide positive feedback and encouragement throughout the game.
- For those needing more support, help them to blend the letter sound or word with assistance.
- Depending on how the class performs in the game, optionally revisit some of the activities to reinforce any specific skill gaps or assign an additional activity, such as the examples below.

Punctuation activity

- Have the students complete the **Punctuation** activity (Activities, page 128).
- The student is given a passage of text that has its capital letters and periods removed.
- Ask the students to read the text and insert periods and capital letters where needed.
- Remind students that capital letters are used to begin sentences and periods come at the end of sentences.

Reading fluency activity

- Assign the **Reading fluency** activity (Activities, page 129).
- Fold the sheet on the dotted line.
- Ask the student to read the first passage. The first is for fluency.
- For the second reading, ask the student to read with expression.
- Put a check, sticker, or stamp in the boxes once this is done.
- The student can read the second passage on another day or both passages to develop reading stamina.

PARALLEL BOOKS

In addition to Book 7: Fishing, here are some books that also cover /sh/ words and can be used for more practice of decoding, for book bags to take home.

Get Out of the Game
Book 7: Crash and Bash

Magic Belt
Book 7: Hush!

Mel on Mars
Book 7: Will the Ship Crash?

LESSON PLANS: That Dog!

th

STEP 1
Preparation

25 mins

Reviewing sounds (3 mins)

- Using sound cards, review some of the previously learned sh words. For example, model blending "dish," reading it sound by sound and then the whole word. /d/ /i/ /sh/ → "dish."

Learning goal (2 mins)

- Introduce and model the new focus sound: /th/.
- 'th' can spell two different sounds: /th/ as in "that" which is voiced, and /th/ as in "thin" which is non-voiced. Ask students to listen to you say the word "that" and hear the voiced sound /th/ at the beginning of the word. Then ask them to listen to the word "thin" and hear just the air flowing at the beginning of the word.
- Introduce the book That Dog! Book 8: Cherished Things.
- You will be completing some activities from That Dog! Activities.

Preparation (20 mins)

1 Word building

- First demonstrate how to build a word. Use only three sound cards, e.g. for the word "thin."
- Draw three lines on the whiteboard, and tell the students that you are going to show them how to build the word "thin."
- As you say the word slowly, move your finger under the lines.
- Ask the students to listen to the first sound in the word "thin"—point to the first line. Emphasize the first sound as you say the whole word. The students respond—/th/.
- Then ask the students which letter spells the sound /th/. The students point to the letter (or you can tell them). Bring the letter down to the first line.
- Repeat with the second and last sounds in the word.
- Now ask the students to sound all three sounds and blend them into a word, moving your finger under the word: /th/ /i/ /n/ → "thin."
- The next time this is done, you can ask a student to participate and identify the sound and then letter and bring it down to the line.

2 Word reading

- Write the words you have created on the whiteboard. Then ask students to blend and read the words.
- Show how to say each sound individually and then blend them together to read the word. Model blending by using a swishing motion with your finger.

3 Oral segmenting

- Say a word aloud (e.g. "thud") and ask students to a count the sounds in the word (3). Write the number of lines you need for all the sounds. Now ask students to listen to the sounds in the word and write a letter for every sound in the word as you spell the word.

4 Word chain

- Using sound cards or magnetic letters, demonstrate how to build the word "that." Explain to the students that you will be making one change to the word. They must be "sound detectives" and notice if you have added a sound, taken away a sound, or swapped a sound.
- Say that you are going to change the word "that" (moving your finger under the word) to "at." Ask the students to listen carefully to where the change has occurred. Move your finger under the word as you say it slowly. Once the change has been identified, invite a student to swap the sound card or letter. Ask all the students to sound out the word and read the new word. e.g. /a/ /t/ → "at."
- Direct students through the following word-chain sequence: that—at—bat—bit—bin—thin—think—thank—bank—ban—than—that

5 Reading practice cards

- Use the **Reading practice cards** (Activities, page 136) to provide students with additional practice of /th/ words.

LESSON RESOURCES

STEP 2
Application for reading

25 mins

Before reading (3 mins)

- Revisit the vocabulary taught in Step 1 (e.g. "thud"). Clearly say the word: /th/ /u/ /d/.
- Provide a simple definition of the word "thud," such as "A thud is a dull sound made when something heavy falls or hits something."
- Ask questions such as "What objects might make a thudding noise when they fall?"
- Then write the word on the whiteboard and refer back to it throughout the week for reinforcement.

Vocabulary (5 mins)

- Pre-teach the words in the **Vocabulary** list in Book 8: Cherished Things (page iv).
- Ensure students understand each word's pronunciation, meaning, and usage.

Application (8 mins)

- The chosen text for this reading activity is Book 8: Cherished Things. Briefly introduce the book to spark interest.
- Lead students through a directed reading of Book 8: Cherished Things. Encourage students to sound out each word carefully and then blend the sounds together to form the word.
- Provide support by modeling the blending. This hands-on practice is crucial for reinforcing phonetic skills and building fluency.
- Encourage students to sound out each word and then blend to read. This is crucial for reinforcing their learning and for building their confidence.

Reading fluency (8 mins)

- Following the initial reading, revisit Book 8: Cherished Things with a focus on fluency.
- Reading the book again allows students to practice their newly acquired skills, this time with an emphasis on reading more smoothly and confidently.
- Create an interactive reading environment by inviting students to take turns reading aloud. Encourage them to point to each word as they read.
- As students read more fluently, support them to read with more expression and prosody, changing their pitch, pace, and emphasis according to the words and punctuation.

STEP 3
Application for spelling

20 mins

Reading and writing captions (20 min)

- Invite students to complete the **Reading captions** activity (Activities, page 137). Ask the student to read the captions and draw a line to the matching picture.
- Ask students to complete the following: **Writing captions** activity (Activities, page 138).
- Dictate the captions from the **Reading captions** activity in the previous page in the Activities book. Have students listen to the sounds in the words and say them aloud as they write them on the lines provided. This activity helps students connect spoken language with written text, enhancing their understanding of letter–sound correspondence.
- After students complete the activity, model the formation of each letter that was written during the activity on the whiteboard.
- Focus on the starting point, stroke direction, and completion of each letter to ensure proper handwriting techniques.
- Demonstrating proper letter formation is crucial for developing legible handwriting and building foundational writing skills.

Extension activities

- Ask students to complete the **Reading and spelling th** activity (Activities, page 133).
- Fold the sheet along the dotted line. Instruct the student to read the words on the left side and check off the ones they read correctly.
- Then, turn the sheet over and dictate the words to the student. Ask them to spell the words by segmenting and sounding out each word as they write them on the lines.
- Finally, have the student open the sheet and check off the words they spelled correctly.
- This process reinforces phonetic skills and promotes self-assessment.
- For students who finish early or need additional practice spelling, provide extra activity sheets with different captions. Dictate these new captions to the students, allowing them to practice spelling and writing on the lines provided.
- Ask students to complete the **Reading accuracy** activity (Activities, page 134).

STEP 4
Comprehension and consolidation
15 mins

Book reading (5 mins)

- Reread Book 8: Cherished Things.
- Revisiting the book helps to reinforce familiarity with the text and supports phonetic recognition and comprehension.

Sequencing (5 mins)

- For this activity, the students are going to retell the story, using the pictures and words in the **Retell the story** activity (Activities, page 143).
- Divide students into small groups.
- Photocopy the activity page onto cardstock for each group.
- Decide whether to number the cards on the back to make sequencing easier for the students.
- Provide each group with a set of cards. Encourage collaboration as they work together to place the picture cards in the correct order of the story.
- Invite each group to retell the story using their arranged cards. Encourage them to use the word cards to narrate the story.
- Alternatively, after sequencing the story, the students can use the word cards to reinforce vocabulary. Ask students to match the word cards to the corresponding picture cards, promoting word recognition and comprehension.

Comprehension (5 mins)

- Check students have understood the story by completing the **Comprehension** activity (Activities, page 139).
- The aim of this activity is to test students' understanding of the story by answering the discussion questions.

Extension activities

- Ask students to complete the **Spot it!** activity (Activities, page 140). The students look at the picture and answer by circling the word "yes" or "no" for each question or statement.
- Invite students complete the **Sequence the story** activity (page 141). The students read the sentences carefully and sequence them in the order of the story in Book 8.
- They can also complete the **Fill in the missing words** activity (page 142). Encourage them to sound out the words as they write them on the lines.

STEP 5
Tracking progress

Stepping stone game

- Play the **Stepping stones game** (page 147).
- Provide positive feedback and encouragement throughout the game.
- For those needing more support, help them to blend the letter sound or word with assistance.
- Depending on how the class performs in the game, optionally revisit some of the activities to reinforce any specific skill gaps or assign an additional activity, such as the examples below.

Punctuation activity

- Have students complete the **Punctuation** activity (Activities, page 145)
- The student is given a passage of text that has its capital letters and periods removed.
- Ask the students to read the text and insert periods and capital letters where needed.
- Remind students that capital letters are used to begin sentences and periods come at the end of sentences.

Reading fluency activity

- Assign the **Reading fluency** activity (Activities, page 146).
- Fold the sheet on the dotted line.
- Ask the student to read the first passage. The first is for fluency.
- For the second reading, ask the student to read with expression.
- Put a check, sticker, or stamp in the boxes once this is done.
- The student can read the second passage on another day or both passages to develop reading stamina.

PARALLEL BOOKS

In addition to Book 8: Cherished Things, here are some books that also cover /th/ words and can be used for more practice of decoding, for book bags to take home.

Get Out of the Game
Book 8: Find the Path

Magic Belt
Book 8: The Sixth Rock

Mel on Mars
Book 8: Thox

LESSON PLANS: That Dog!

ck and qu

STEP 1
Preparation

25 mins

Reviewing sounds (3 mins)

- Using sound cards, review some of the previously learned th words. For example, model blending "thin," reading it sound by sound and then the whole word. /th/ /i/ /n/ → "thin."

Learning goal (2 mins)

- Explain the lesson goal: learning to read and spell ck and qu words.
- Explain that we have already learned two other ways to spell the sound /k/ (e.g. "cat" and "king").
- Explain that 'ck' is an alternative spelling for the sound /k/. The visual representation should make clear that the /k/ sound, while represented by two letters ('c' and 'k'), functions as a single sound.
- Note: the letters 'qu' spell two sounds (/k/ and /w/), but we teach them together because they usually appear together in words.
- Introduce the book That Dog! Book 9: Good and Bad Luck.
- You will be completing some activities from That Dog! Activities.

Preparation (20 mins)

1 Word building

- First demonstrate how to build a word. Use only three sound cards, e.g. for the word "quip."
- Draw three lines on the whiteboard, and tell the students that you are going to show them how to build the word "quip."
- As you say the word slowly, move your finger under the lines.
- Ask the students to listen to the first two sounds in the word "quip"—point to the first line. Emphasize the first two sounds as you say the whole word. The students respond—/k/ /w/.
- Then ask the students which letters spell the sounds /k/ and /w/ together. The students point to the letters (or you can tell them). Bring the letters down to the first line.
- Repeat with the remaining sounds in the word. Now ask the students to sound all four sounds and blend them into a word, moving your finger under the word: /k/ /w/ /i/ /p/ → "quip."

LESSON RESOURCES

2 Word reading

- Write the words you have created on the whiteboard. Then ask students to blend and read the words.
- Show how to say each sound individually and then blend them together to read the word. Model blending by using a swishing motion with your finger.

3 Oral segmenting

- Say a word aloud (e.g. "quill") and ask students to a count the sounds in the word (4). Write the number of lines you need for all the sounds. Now ask students to listen to the sounds in the word and write a letter for every sound in the word as you spell the word.

4 Word chain

- Using sound cards or magnetic letters, demonstrate how to build the word "lick." Explain to the students that you will be making one change to the word. They must be "sound detectives" and notice if you have added a sound, taken away a sound, or swapped a sound.
- Say that you are going to change the word "lick" (moving your finger under the word) to "click." Ask the students to listen carefully to where the change has occurred. Move your finger under the words as you say it slowly. Once the change has been identified, invite a student to swap the sound card or letter. Ask all the students to sound out the word and read the new word, e.g. /c/ /l/ /i/ /k/ → "click."
- Introduce the new sounds gradually. This allows students to incorporate the letters and sounds they have learned so far.
- Direct students through the following word-chain sequence: lick—click—slick—slack—lack—lock—clock—clack—black—back—rack—track—trick—tick—lick

5 Reading practice cards

- Use the **Reading practice cards** (Activities, page 154) for additional practice.

STEP 2
Application for reading

25 mins

Before reading (3 mins)

- Revisit the vocabulary taught in Step 1 (e.g. "quill"). Clearly say the word: /k/ /w/ /i/ /ll/.
- Provide a simple definition of "quill," such as "A quill is a feather from a bird, traditionally used as a writing tool."
- Ask questions such as "What animals have quills?"
- Then write the word on the whiteboard and refer back to it throughout the week for reinforcement.

Vocabulary (5 mins)

- Pre-teach the words in the **Vocabulary** list in Book 9: Good and Bad Luck (page iv).
- Ensure students understand each word's pronunciation, meaning, and usage.

Application (8 mins)

- The chosen text for this reading activity is Book 9: Good and Bad Luck. Briefly introduce the book to spark interest.
- Lead students through a guided reading of Book 9: Good and Bad Luck. Encourage students to sound out each word carefully and then blend the sounds together to form the word.
- Provide support by modeling the blending. This hands-on practice is crucial for reinforcing phonetic skills and building fluency.
- Encourage students to sound out each word and then blend to read. This is crucial for reinforcing their learning and for building their confidence.

Reading fluency (8 mins)

- Following the initial reading, revisit Book 9: Good and Bad Luck with a focus on fluency.
- Reading the book again allows students to practice their newly acquired skills, this time with an emphasis on reading more smoothly and confidently.
- Create an interactive reading environment by inviting students to take turns reading aloud. Encourage them to point to each word as they read.
- As students read more fluently, support them to read with more expression and prosody, changing their pitch, pace, and emphasis according to the words and punctuation.

STEP 3
Application for spelling

20 mins

Reading and writing captions (20 min)

- Invite students to complete the **Reading captions** activity (Activities, page 155). Ask the student to read the captions and draw a line to the matching picture.
- Ask students to complete the following: **Writing captions** activity (Activities, page 156).
- Dictate the captions from the **Reading captions** activity in the previous page in the Activities book. Have students listen to the sounds in the words and say them aloud as they write them on the lines provided. This activity helps students connect spoken language with written text, enhancing their understanding of letter–sound correspondence.
- After students complete the activity, model the formation of each letter that was written during the activity on the whiteboard.
- Focus on the starting point, stroke direction, and completion of each letter to ensure proper handwriting techniques.
- Demonstrating proper letter formation is crucial for developing legible handwriting and building foundational writing skills.

Extension activities

- Ask students to complete the **Reading and spelling qu** activity (Activities, page 158).
- Fold the sheet along the dotted line. Instruct the student to read the words on the left side and check off the ones they read correctly.
- Then, turn the sheet over and dictate the words to the student. Ask them to spell the words by segmenting and sounding out each word as they write them on the lines.
- Finally, have the student open the sheet and check off the words they spelled correctly.
- This process reinforces phonetic skills and promotes self-assessment.
- For students who finish early or need additional practice spelling, provide extra activity sheets with different captions. Dictate these new captions to the students, allowing them to practice spelling and writing on the lines provided.
- Ask students to complete the **Reading and spelling ck** activity (Activities, page 151).

STEP 4
Comprehension and consolidation

15 mins

Book reading (5 mins)

- Reread Book 9: Good and Bad Luck.
- Revisiting the book helps to reinforce familiarity with the text and supports phonetic recognition and comprehension.

Sequencing (5 mins)

- For this activity, the students are going to retell the story, using the pictures and words in the **Sequence the story** activity (Activities, page 162).
- Cut out the sentences for each student or group.
- Ask the students to read the sentences carefully and sequence them in the order of the story in Book 9: Good and Bad Luck.
- The students then sticks them in the numbered boxes in the correct order.
- Some students may benefit from sequencing just two sentences at a time.

Comprehension (5 mins)

- Check students have understood the story by completing the **Comprehension** activity (Activities, page 160).
- The aim of this activity is to test students' understanding of the story by answering the discussion questions.

Extension activities

- Ask students to complete the **Spot it!** activity (Activities, page 161). The students look at the picture and answer by circling the word "yes" or "no" for each question or statement.
- They can also complete the **Fill in the missing words** activity (page 163). Encourage them to sound out the words as they write them on the lines.
- Invite students complete the **Retell the story** activity (page 164). The students read the sentences carefully and sequence them in the order of the story in Book 9.

STEP 5
Tracking progress

Stepping stone game

- Play the **Stepping stones game** (page 168).
- Provide positive feedback and encouragement throughout the game.
- For those needing more support, help them to blend the letter sound or word with assistance.
- Depending on how the class performs in the game, optionally revisit some of the activities to reinforce any specific skill gaps or assign an additional activity, such as the examples below.

Punctuation activity

- Have students complete the Punctuation activity (Activities, page 166).
- The student is given a passage of text that has its capital letters and periods removed.
- Ask the students to read the text and insert periods and capital letters where needed.
- Remind students that capital letters are used to begin sentences and periods come at the end of sentences.

Reading fluency activity

- Assign the **Reading fluency** activity (Activities, page 167).
- Fold the sheet on the dotted line.
- Ask the student to read the first passage. The first is for fluency.
- For the second reading, ask the student to read with expression.
- Put a check, sticker, or stamp in the boxes once this is done.
- The student can read the second passage on another day or both passages to develop reading stamina.

PARALLEL BOOKS

In addition to Book 9: Good and Bad Luck, here are some books that also cover 'ck' and 'qu' words and can be used for more practice of decoding, for book bags to take home.

Get out of the Game
Book 9: Run, Quick! Rats!

Magic Belt
Book 9: Golem of the Rocks

Mel on Mars
Book 9: The Quest for Quock Rocks

ng

STEP 1
Preparation

25 mins

LESSON RESOURCES

Reviewing sounds (3 mins)

- Using sound cards, review some of the previously learned ck and qu words. For example, model blending "duck," reading it sound by sound and then the whole word. /d/ /u/ /k/ → "duck."

Learning goal (2 mins)

- Explain the lesson goal: learning to read and spell ng words.
- Note that the /ng/ sound, while represented by two letters ('n' and 'g') functions as a single sound.
- Introduce the book That Dog! Book 10: The Long, Thin Boat.
- You will be completing some activities from That Dog! Activities.

Preparation (20 mins)

1 Word building

- First demonstrate how to build a word. Use only four sound cards, e.g. for the word "sting."
- Draw four lines on the whiteboard, and tell the students that you are going to show them how to build the word "sting."
- As you say the word slowly, move your finger under the lines.
- Ask the students to listen to the first sound in the word "sting"—point to the first line. Emphasize the first sound as you say the whole word. The students respond—/s/.
- Then ask the students which letter spells the sound /s/. The students point to the letter (or you can tell them). Bring the letter down to the first line.
- Repeat with the remaining sounds in the word. Now ask the students to sound all four sounds and blend them into a word, moving your finger under the word:
  /s/ /t/ /i/ /ng/ → "sting."

2 Word reading

- Write the words you have created on the whiteboard. Then ask students to blend and read the words.
- Show how to say each sound individually and then blend them together to read the word. Model blending by using a swishing motion with your finger.

3 Oral segmenting

- Say a word aloud (e.g. "song") and ask students to a count the sounds in the word (3). Write the number of lines you need for all the sounds. Now ask students to listen to the sounds in the word and write a letter for every sound in the word as you spell the word.

4 Word chain

- Using sound cards or magnetic letters, demonstrate how to build the word "sing." Explain to the students that you will be making one change to the word. They must be "sound detectives" and notice if you have added a sound, taken away a sound, or swapped a sound.
- Say that you are going to change the word "sing" (moving your finger under the word) to "sling." Ask the students to listen carefully to where the change has occurred. Move your finger under the words as you say it slowly. Once the change has been identified, invite a student to swap the sound card or letter. Ask all the students to sound out the word and read the new word, e.g.
  /s/ /l/ /i/ /ng/ → "sling."
- Introduce the new sounds gradually. This allows students to incorporate the letters and sounds they have learned so far.
- Direct students through the following word-chain sequence: sing—sling—slang—sang—song—pong—ping—wing—swing—sing

5 Reading practice cards

- Use the **Reading practice cards** (Activities, page 174) to provide students with additional practice of /ng/ words.

STEP 2
Application for reading
25 mins

Before reading (3 mins)

- Provide a simple definition of the word "sting," such as "A sting is a sharp feeling of pain."
- Ask questions such as "What insects or animals can sting?"
- Then write the word on the whiteboard and refer back to it throughout the week for reinforcement.

Vocabulary (5 mins)

- Pre-teach the words in the **Vocabulary** list in Book 10: The Long, Thin Boat (page iv).
- Ensure students understand each word's pronunciation, meaning, and usage.

Application (8 mins)

- The chosen text for this reading activity is Book 10: The Long, thin Boat. Briefly introduce the book to spark interest.
- Lead students through a directed reading of Book 10: The Long, thin Boat. Encourage students to sound out each word carefully and then blend the sounds together to form the word.
- Provide support by modeling the blending. This hands-on practice is crucial for reinforcing phonetic skills and building fluency.
- Encourage students to sound out each word and then blend to read. This is crucial for reinforcing their learning and for building their confidence.

Reading fluency (8 mins)

- Following the initial reading, revisit Book 10: The Long, thin Boat with a focus on fluency.
- Reading the book again allows students to practice their newly acquired skills, this time with an emphasis on reading more smoothly and confidently.
- Create an interactive reading environment by inviting students to take turns reading aloud. Encourage them to point to each word as they read.
- As students read more fluently, support them to read with more expression and prosody, changing their pitch, pace, and emphasis according to the words and punctuation.

STEP 3
Application for spelling
20 mins

Reading and writing captions (20 min)

- Invite students to complete the **Reading captions** activity (Activities, page 175). Ask the student to read the captions and draw a line to the matching picture.
- Ask students to complete the following: **Writing captions** activity (Activities, page 176).
- Dictate the captions from the **Reading captions** activity in the previous page in the Activities book. Have students listen to the sounds in the words and say them aloud as they write them on the lines provided. This activity helps students connect spoken language with written text, enhancing their understanding of letter–sound correspondence.
- After students complete the activity, model the formation of each letter that was written during the activity on the whiteboard.
- Focus on the starting point, stroke direction, and completion of each letter to ensure proper handwriting techniques.
- Demonstrating proper letter formation is crucial for developing legible handwriting and building foundational writing skills.

Extension activities

- Ask students to complete the **Reading and spelling /ng/** activity (Activities, page 171).
- Fold the sheet along the dotted line. Instruct the student to read the words on the left side and check off the ones they read correctly.
- Then, turn the sheet over and dictate the words to the student. Ask them to spell the words by segmenting and sounding out each word as they write them on the lines.
- Finally, have the student open the sheet and check off the words they spelled correctly.
- This process reinforces phonetic skills and promotes self-assessment.
- For students who finish early or need additional practice spelling, provide extra activity sheets with different captions. Dictate these new captions to the students, allowing them to practice spelling and writing on the lines provided.
- For further spelling practice, assign the **Reading and spelling two-syllable words** activity (Activities, page 177).

STEP 4
Comprehension and consolidation

15 mins

Book reading (5 mins)

- Reread Book 10: The Long, thin Boat.
- Revisiting the book helps to reinforce familiarity with the text and supports phonetic recognition and comprehension.

Sequencing (5 mins)

- For this activity, the students are going to retell the story, using the pictures and words in the **Retell the story** activity (Activities, page 182).
- Divide students into small groups.
- Photocopy the activity page onto cardstock for each group.
- Decide whether to number the cards on the back to make sequencing easier for the students.
- Provide each group with a set of cards.
- Encourage collaboration as they work together to place the picture cards in the correct order of the story.
- Invite each group to retell the story using their arranged cards. Encourage them to use the word cards to narrate the story.
- Alternatively, after sequencing the story, the students can use the word cards to reinforce vocabulary. Ask students to match the word cards to the corresponding picture cards, promoting word recognition and comprehension.

Comprehension (5 mins)

- Check students have understood the story by completing the **Comprehension** activity (Activities, page 178).
- The aim of this activity is to test students' understanding of the story by answering the discussion questions.

Extension activities

- Ask students to complete the **Spot it!** activity (Activities, page 179). The students look at the picture and answer by circling the word "yes" or "no" for each question or statement.
- Invite students to complete the **Sequence the story** activity (page 180). The students read the sentences carefully and sequence them in the order of the story in Book 10.
- They can also complete the **Fill in the missing words** activity (page 181). Encourage them to sound out the words as they write them on the lines.

STEP 5
Tracking progress

Stepping stone game

- Play the **Stepping stones game** (page 186).
- Provide positive feedback and encouragement throughout the game.
- For those needing more support, help them to blend the letter sound or word with assistance.
- Depending on how the class performs in the game, optionally revisit some of the activities to reinforce any specific skill gaps or assign an additional activity, such as the examples below.

Punctuation activity

- Have students complete the **Punctuation** activity (Activities, page 184).
- The student is given a passage of text that has its capital letters and periods removed.
- Ask the students to read the text and insert periods and capital letters where needed.
- Remind students that capital letters are used to begin sentences and periods come at the end of sentences.

Reading fluency activity

- Assign the **Reading fluency** activity (Activities, page 185).
- Fold the sheet on the dotted line.
- Ask the student to read the first passage. The first is for fluency.
- For the second reading, ask the student to read with expression.
- Put a check, sticker, or stamp in the boxes once this is done.
- The student can read the second passage on another day or both passages to develop reading stamina.

PARALLEL BOOKS

In addition to Book 10: The Long, thin Boat, here are some books that also cover /ng/ words and can be used for more practice of decoding, for book bags to take home.

Get Out of the Game
Book 10: Wings, Kings, and Fangs

Magic Belt
Book 10: Dung!

Mel on Mars
Book 10: The Winged Thing with Fangs

LESSON PLANS: That Dog!

wh and -ing

STEP 1
Preparation

25 mins

LESSON RESOURCES

Reviewing sounds (3 mins)

- Using sound cards, review some of the previously learned /ng/ words. For example, model blending "sing," reading it sound by sound and then the whole word. /s/ /i/ /ng/ → "sing."

Learning goal (2 mins)

- Explain the lesson goal: learning to read and spell words with wh and the suffix -ing.
- Explain that 'wh' is an alternative spelling for the sound /w/. The visual representation should make clear that the /w/ sound, while represented by two letters ('w' and 'h'), functions as a single sound.
- Introduce the book That Dog! Book 11: Shopping for Props.
- You will be completing some activities from That Dog! Activities.

Preparation (20 mins)

1 Word building

- First demonstrate how to build a word. Use only three sound cards, e.g. for the word "whip."
- Draw three lines on the whiteboard, and tell the students that you are going to show them how to build the word "whip."
- As you say the word slowly, move your finger under the lines.
- Ask the students to listen to the first sound in the word "whip"—point to the first line. Emphasize the first sound as you say the whole word. The students respond—/w/.
- Then ask the students which letters spell the sound /w/. The students point to the letters (or you can tell them). Bring the letters down to the first line.
- Repeat with the remaining sounds in the word. Now ask the students to sound all three sounds and blend them into a word, moving your finger under the word: /w/ /i/ /p/ → "whip."

2 Word reading

- Write the words you have created on the whiteboard. Then ask students to blend and read the words.
- Show how to say each sound individually and then blend them together to read the word. Model blending by using a swishing motion with your finger.

3 Oral segmenting

- Say a word aloud (e.g. "whiz") and ask students to a count the sounds in the word (3). Write the number of lines you need for all the sounds. Now ask students to listen to the sounds in the word and write a letter for every sound in the word as you spell the word.

4 Introducing the suffix -ing

- Explain that we add -ing to the end of verbs to talk about different things.
- The -ing suffix can be used to tell us about something we do, for example, "Dancing makes me happy." (Here, "dancing" acts as a noun.)
- The -ing suffix can also tell us about what someone is doing now. For example: "He is drinking." (The sentence is in the present continuous tense and -ing is the present participle of the verb.)
- The -ing suffix can also be used to describe things or how they make us feel. For example: "This movie is exciting." (Here, "exciting" is an adjective that describes the movie.)
- Explain that -ing is made up of two sounds /i/ and /ng/.
- Model how to say the sounds correctly and "purely" and ask students to copy.
- Have students watch you as they pronounce /i/ /ng/.
- Read this list of words: "blending," "asking," and "running."

Reading practice cards

- For extension, assign the **Word-building with the suffix -ing** (Activities, page 190).

STEP 2 Application for reading

25 mins

Before reading (3 mins)

- Revisit the vocabulary taught in Step 1 (e.g. "whiz"). Clearly say the word: /wh/ /i/ /z/.
- Provide a simple definition of "whiz," such as "To whiz means to move quickly through the air with a humming or buzzing sound."
- Ask questions such as "What objects might whiz through the air?"
- Then write the word on the whiteboard and refer back to it throughout the week for reinforcement.

Vocabulary (5 mins)

- Pre-teach the words in the **Vocabulary** list in Book 11: Shopping for Props (page iv).
- Ensure students understand each word's pronunciation, meaning, and usage.

Application (8 mins)

- The chosen text for this reading activity is Book 11: Shopping for Props. Briefly introduce the book to spark interest.
- Lead students through a guided reading of Book 11: Shopping for Props. Encourage students to sound out each word carefully and then blend the sounds together to form the word.
- Provide support by modeling the blending. This hands-on practice is crucial for reinforcing phonetic skills and building fluency.
- Encourage students to sound out each word and then blend to read. This is crucial for reinforcing their learning and for building their confidence.

Reading fluency (8 mins)

- Following the initial reading, revisit Book 11: Shopping for Props with a focus on fluency.
- Reading the book again allows students to practice their newly acquired skills, this time with an emphasis on reading more smoothly and confidently.
- Create an interactive reading environment by inviting students to take turns reading aloud. Encourage them to point to each word as they read.
- As students read more fluently, support them to read with more expression and prosody, changing their pitch, pace, and emphasis according to the words and punctuation.

STEP 3 Application for spelling

20 mins

Reading and writing captions (20 min)

- Invite students to complete the **Reading captions** activity (Activities, page 194) Ask the student to read the captions and draw a line to the matching picture.
- Ask students to complete the following: **Writing captions** activity (Activities, page 195).
- Dictate the captions from the **Reading captions** activity in the previous page in the Activities book. Have students listen to the sounds in the words and say them aloud as they write them on the lines provided. This activity helps students connect spoken language with written text, enhancing their understanding of letter–sound correspondence.
- After students complete the activity, model the formation of each letter that was written during the activity on the whiteboard.
- Focus on the starting point, stroke direction, and completion of each letter to ensure proper handwriting techniques.
- Demonstrating proper letter formation is crucial for developing legible handwriting and building foundational writing skills.

Extension activities

- Ask students to complete the **Reading and spelling wh** activity (Activities, page 158).
- Fold the sheet along the dotted line. Instruct the student to read the words on the left side and check off the ones they read correctly.
- Then, turn the sheet over and dictate the words to the student. Ask them to spell the words by segmenting and sounding out each word as they write them on the lines.
- Finally, have the student open the sheet and check off the words they spelled correctly.
- This process reinforces phonetic skills and promotes self-assessment.
- For students who finish early or need additional practice spelling, provide extra activity sheets with different captions. Dictate these new captions to the students, allowing them to practice spelling and writing on the lines provided.
- Ask students to complete the **Reading and spelling with the suffix -ing** activity (Activities, page 191).

STEP 4
Comprehension and consolidation

15 mins

Book reading (5 mins)

- Reread Book 11: Shopping for Props.
- Revisiting the book helps to reinforce familiarity with the text and supports phonetic recognition and comprehension.

Sequencing (5 mins)

- For this activity, the students are going to retell the story, using the pictures and words in the **Sequence the story** activity (Activities, page 199).
- Cut out the sentences for each student or group.
- Ask the students to read the sentences carefully and sequence them in the order of the story in Book 11: Shopping for Props.
- The students then sticks them in the numbered boxes in the correct order.
- Some students may benefit from sequencing just two sentences at a time.

Comprehension (5 mins)

- Check students have understood the story by completing the **Comprehension** activity (Activities, page 197).
- The aim of this activity is to test students' understanding of the story by answering the discussion questions.

Extension activities

- Ask students to complete the **Spot it!** activity (Activities, page 198). The students look at the picture and answer by circling the word "yes" or "no" for each question or statement.
- They can also complete the **Fill in the missing words** activity (page 200). Encourage them to sound out the words as they write them on the lines.
- Invite students to complete the **Retell the story** activity (page 201). The students read the sentences carefully and sequence them in the order of the story in Book 11.

STEP 5
Tracking progress

Stepping stone game

- Play the **Stepping stones game** (page 205).
- Provide positive feedback and encouragement throughout the game.
- For those needing more support, help them to blend the letter sound or word with assistance.
- Depending on how the class performs in the game, optionally revisit some of the activities to reinforce any specific skill gaps or assign an additional activity, such as the examples below.

Punctuation activity

- Assign the **Punctuation** activity (page 203).
- The student is given a passage of text that has its capital letters and periods removed.
- Ask the students to read the text and insert periods and capital letters where needed.
- Remind students that capital letters are used to begin sentences and periods come at the end of sentences.

Reading fluency activity

- Assign the **Reading fluency** activity (Activities, page 204).
- Fold the sheet on the dotted line.
- Ask the student to read the first passage. The first is for fluency.
- For the second reading, ask the student to read with expression.
- Put a check, sticker, or stamp in the boxes once this is done.
- The student can read the second passage on another day or both passages to develop reading stamina.

PARALLEL BOOKS

In addition to Book 11: Shopping for Props, here are some books that also cover 'wh' and the suffix -ing and can be used for more practice of decoding, for book bags to take home.

Get Out of the Game
Book 11: What's Going On?

Magic Belt
Book 11: The Spitting Pot

Mel on Mars
Book 11: The Singing Wind

le

STEP 1
Preparation

25 mins

Reviewing sounds (3 mins)

- Using sound cards, review some of the previously learned wh and -ing words. For example, model blending "when," reading it sound by sound and then the whole word.
  /w/ /e/ /n/ → "when."

Learning goal (2 mins)

- Explain the lesson goal: learning to read and spell two-syllable words with the spelling 'le' and sounds they have previously learned.
- Introduce the book That Dog! Book 12: Dog in Trouble.
- You will be completing some activities from That Dog! Activities.

Preparation (20 mins)

- Introduce the spelling 'le.'
- Read this list of words: "apple," "cuddle," and "ankle."

1 Word building

- Place sound cards or magnetic letters needed to spell a 'le' word on the board (for example, "apple.")
- Draw two lines on the board—one for each syllable. Ask the students to listen to the word. You say "apple." Move your finger under the two lines as you say the word. Point to the first line—what is the first syllable in the word "apple"?
- Students say "app." Ask a student to build the syllable "app" with the letters on the board.
- Now listen to the second syllable.
- You say "apple." Move your finger under the word. Students say "le."
- Ask a student to build the syllable "le" with the letters on the board. Now ask the students to read the syllables together ("app" "le") and say the word quickly "apple."

pp | a | le

______ ______

LESSON RESOURCES

- Now ask the students to spell the word "apple" by drawing two lines on the board, writing each syllable they hear and then writing the whole word underneath without a gap.

2 Word reading

- Write the words you have created on the whiteboard. Then ask students to blend and read the words.
- Show how to say each syllable individually and then blend them together to read the word. Model blending by using a swishing motion with your finger.
- Encourage students to follow your example with these words: "cuddle," "candle," and "dimple."

3 Oral segmenting

- Say a word aloud (e.g. "single") and ask students to count the syllables in the word (2). Write two lines—one for each syllable. Now ask students to listen to the syllables in the word and write the letters for each syllable on the lines as you spell the word.

4 Reading accuracy

- Ask students to complete the **Reading accuracy** activity (Activities, page 210).
- Ask the students to read the words in each box and circle the word that matches the picture.

5 Reading practice cards

- Use the **Reading practice cards** (Activities, page 211) to provide students with additional practice of 'le' words.

STEP 2
Application for reading
25 mins

Before reading (3 mins)

- Revisit the vocabulary taught in Step 1 (e.g. "candle").
- Provide a simple definition of "candle," such as "A candle is a stick of wax with a wick that burns to give light."
- Ask questions such as "When might you use a candle?"
- Then write the word on the whiteboard and refer back to it throughout the week for reinforcement.

Vocabulary (5 mins)

- Pre-teach the words in the **Vocabulary** list in Book 12: Dog in Trouble (page iv).
- Ensure students understand each word's pronunciation, meaning, and usage.

Application (8 mins)

- The chosen text for this reading activity is Book 12: Dog in Trouble. Briefly introduce the book to spark interest.
- Lead students through a directed reading of Book 12: Dog in Trouble. Encourage students to sound out each word carefully and then blend the sounds together to form the word.
- Provide support by modeling the blending. This hands-on practice is crucial for reinforcing phonetic skills and building fluency.
- Encourage students to sound out each word and then blend to read. This is crucial for reinforcing their learning and for building their confidence.

Reading fluency (8 mins)

- Following the initial reading, revisit Book 12: Dog in Trouble with a focus on fluency.
- Reading the book again allows students to practice their newly acquired skills, this time with an emphasis on reading more smoothly and confidently.
- Create an interactive reading environment by inviting students to take turns reading aloud. Encourage them to point to each word as they read.
- As students read more fluently, support them to read with more expression and prosody, changing their pitch, pace, and emphasis according to the words and punctuation.

STEP 3
Application for spelling
20 mins

Reading and writing captions (20 min)

- Invite students to complete the **Reading captions** activity (Activities, page 212) Ask the student to read the captions and draw a line to the matching picture.
- Ask students to complete the following: **Writing captions** activity (Activities, page 213).
- Dictate the captions from the **Reading captions** activity in the previous page in the Activities book. Have students listen to the sounds in the words and say them aloud as they write them on the lines provided. This activity helps students connect spoken language with written text, enhancing their understanding of letter–sound correspondence.
- After students complete the activity, model the formation of each letter that was written during the activity on the whiteboard.
- Focus on the starting point, stroke direction, and completion of each letter to ensure proper handwriting techniques.
- Demonstrating proper letter formation is crucial for developing legible handwriting and building foundational writing skills.

Extension activities

- Ask students to complete the **Reading and spelling le** activity (Activities, page 209).
- Fold the sheet along the dotted line. Instruct the student to read the words on the left side and check off the ones they read correctly.
- Then, turn the sheet over and dictate the words to the student. Ask them to spell the words by segmenting and sounding out each word as they write them on the lines.
- Finally, have the student open the sheet and check off the words they spelled correctly.
- This process reinforces phonetic skills and promotes self-assessment.
- For students who finish early or need additional practice spelling, provide extra activity sheets with different captions. Dictate these new captions to the students, allowing them to practice spelling and writing on the lines provided.

STEP 4
Comprehension and consolidation

15 mins

Book reading (5 mins)

- Reread Book 12: Dog in Trouble.
- Revisiting the book helps to reinforce familiarity with the text and supports phonetic recognition and comprehension.

Sequencing (5 mins)

- For this activity, the students are going to retell the story, using the pictures and words in the **Sequence the story** activity (Activities, page 216).
- Cut out the sentences for each student or group.
- Ask the students to read the sentences carefully and sequence them in the order of the story in Book 12: Dog in Trouble.
- The students then sticks them in the numbered boxes in the correct order.
- Some students may benefit from sequencing just two sentences at a time.

Comprehension (5 mins)

- Check students have understood the story by completing the **Comprehension** activity (Activities, page 214).
- The aim of this activity is to test students' understanding of the story by answering the discussion questions.

Extension activities

- Ask students to complete the **Spot it!** activity (Activities, page 215). The students look at the picture and answer by circling the word "yes" or "no" for each question or statement.
- They can also complete the **Fill in the missing words** activity (page 217). Encourage them to sound out the words as they write them on the lines.
- Invite students to complete the **Retell the story** activity (page 218). The students read the sentences carefully and sequence them in the order of the story in Book 12.

STEP 5
Tracking progress

Stepping stone game

- Play the **Stepping stones game** (page 222).
- Provide positive feedback and encouragement throughout the game.
- For those needing more support, help them to blend the letter sound or word with assistance.
- Depending on how the class performs in the game, optionally revisit some of the activities to reinforce any specific skill gaps or assign an additional activity, such as the examples below.

Punctuation activity

- Assign the **Punctuation** activity (page 220).
- The student is given a passage of text that has its capital letters and periods removed.
- Ask the students to read the text and insert periods and capital letters where needed.
- Remind students that capital letters are used to begin sentences and periods come at the end of sentences.

Reading fluency activity

- Assign the **Reading fluency** activity (Activities, page 221).
- Fold the sheet on the dotted line.
- Ask the student to read the first passage. The first is for fluency.
- For the second reading, ask the student to read with expression.
- Put a check, sticker, or stamp in the boxes once this is done.
- The student can read the second passage on another day or both passages to develop reading stamina.

PARALLEL BOOKS

In addition to Book 12: Dog in Trouble, here are some books that also cover the ending 'le' and can be used for more practice of decoding, for book bags to take home.

Get Out of the Game
Book 12: The Last Puzzle

Magic Belt
Book 12: The Simple Plot

Mel on Mars
Book 12: Up from the Rubble

a–e

STEP 1
Preparation

20 mins

LESSON RESOURCES

Learning goal (2 mins)

- Explain the lesson goal: learning the a–e spelling for the sound /ae/.
- Introduce the book Moon Dogs VCe Spellings Book 1: The Shape Game.
- Inform students they will also be completing some activities from Moon Dogs VCe Spellings Activities.

Preparation (18 mins)

- Introduce the new focus spelling 'a–e' for the sound /ae/.
- Have students watch you as they pronounce /ae/.
- Read this list of words: "cake," "make," and "fate."
- For each, point to the letters as you slowly pronounce them, demonstrating how the 'a' and 'e' work together to form the /ae/ sound.
- Use your thumb and third finger to visually link these letters.

1 Word building and blending

- Begin by demonstrating how to build the word "gate."
- Draw four lines on the whiteboard.
- Explain to the students that you will show them how to build the word "gate."
- As you say the word slowly, move your finger under the lines.
- Ask the students to listen to the first sound in the word "gate." Point to the first line and emphasize the first sound as you say the whole word. The students respond with /g/.
- Then ask the students which letter spells the sound /g/. The students point to the letter (or you can tell them). Bring the letter down to the first line.
- Repeat the process with the second sound /ae/ and the last sound /t/.
- Now ask the students to sound out all three sounds and blend them into a word while you move your finger under the word: /g/ /ae/ /t/ → "gate."

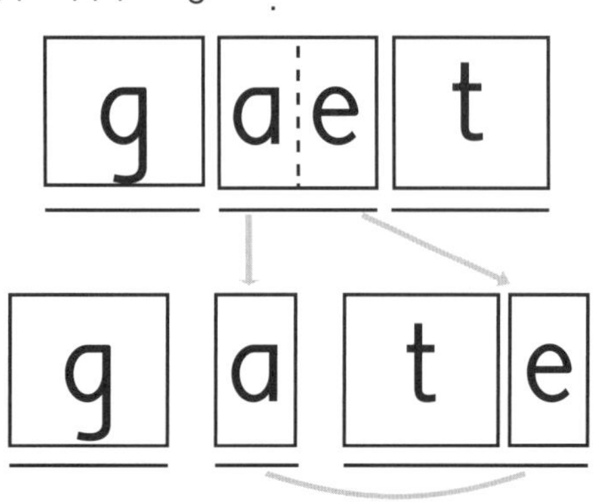

- Explain the spelling rule: In words like "gate," even though a consonant ('t') separates the vowels, the 'a' and 'e' still work together to form the /ae/ sound, which occurs right before the consonant.
- The next time this is done, you can ask a student to participate. Have them identify the sound, then the letter, and bring it down to the line.

2 Word reading

- Write the words you have created on the whiteboard. Then ask students to blend and read the words.
- Show how to say each sound individually and then blend them together to read the word. Model blending by pointing using a swishing motion with your finger.

3 Oral segmenting

- Say a word aloud (e.g. "cake") and count the sounds in the word (3). Write the number of lines you need for all the sounds. Now ask students to listen to the sounds in the word and write a letter for every sound in the word as you spell the word.

Extension activities

1 Reading practice cards

- Assign the **Reading practice** cards activity (Activities, pages 8–9).
- Distribute the acitivity by cutting the reading cards for eaach student or small group.
- On page 8, the 'a–e' spelling is highlighted for initial introduction. On page 9, the 'a–e' spelling is not highlighted.

2 Reading and sorting words

- Assign the **Reading and sorting: words with a and a–e** activity (Activities, page 10).
- This activity involves students distinguishing between words with the 'a' spelling (as in "hat") and words with the 'a–e' spelling (as in "hate").

STEP 2
Application for reading
25 mins

Before reading (3 mins)

- Revisit the vocabulary taught in Step 1 (e.g. "gate"). Clearly say the word: /g/ /ae/ /t/.
- Then provide a simple definition, for example, "A gate is a barrier used to close an opening in a fence or wall."
- Ask questions such as "What is a gate?" and "Where can we find gates?"
- Then write the word on the whiteboard and refer back to it throughout the week for reinforcement.

Vocabulary (2 mins)

- Pre-teach the words in the **Vocabulary** list in Book 1: The Shape Game (page iv).
- Ensure students understand each word's pronunciation, meaning, and usage.

Application (10 mins)

- The chosen text for this reading activity is Book 1: The Shape Game. Briefly introduce the book to spark interest.
- Lead students through a directed reading of Book 1: The Shape Game. Encourage students to sound out each word carefully and then blend the sounds together to form the word.
- Provide support by modeling the blending.
- Encourage students to sound out each word and then blend to read.

Reading fluency (10 mins)

- Following the initial reading, revisit Book 1: The Shape Game with a focus on fluency.
- Reading the book again allows students to practice their newly acquired skills, this time with an emphasis on reading more smoothly and confidently.
- Create an interactive reading environment by inviting students to take turns reading aloud. Encourage them to point to each word as they read.
- As students read more fluently, support them to read with more expression and prosody, changing their pitch, pace, and emphasis according to the words and punctuation.

STEP 3
Application for spelling
20 mins

Segmenting and spelling (10 mins)

- Invite students to complete the **Segmenting and spelling** activity (Activities, page 7).
- In this activity, the student writes the missing word for each picture by putting one spelling in each square.
- Cut or fold the sheet along the dotted line before giving to the student.
- After students complete the activity, model the formation of each letter that was written during the activity on the whiteboard.
- Focus on the starting point, stroke direction, and completion of each letter to ensure proper handwriting techniques.
- Demonstrating proper letter formation is crucial for developing legible handwriting and building foundational writing skills.

Sentence dictation (10 mins)

- Ask students to complete the **Dictation** activity (Activities, page 19).
- Use the text at the bottom of the activity for dictation.
- Cut and fold along the dotted line before giving it to the students.
- Ask students to write the spelling of each sound on the provided write-on lines.
- Remind the students that some sounds can be spelled by more than one letter.
- A longer line indicates the spelling has more than one letter.
- The curved lines running underneath the write-on lines indicate a VCe spelling.
- For students who finish early or need additional practice, create additional activity sheets with your own passages of text and dictate these new passages to them.

Extension

- Ask students to complete the **Splitting two-syllable words with a–e** activity for additional spelling practice (Activities, page 14).

STEP 4
Comprehension and consolidation

15 mins

Book reading (5 mins)

- Reread Book 1: The Shape Game.
- Revisiting the book helps to reinforce familiarity with the text and supports phonetic recognition and comprehension.

Comprehension (5 mins)

- To check students' understanding of the story, conduct a group discussion.
- Ask the three comprehension questions at the back of the story ("What does Sim make in the sand?", "What does Tam make in the sand?", and "Why doesn't Tam see the wave?")
- Divide the class into small groups and ask each group to answer a question in turn.
- Encourage groups to explain their reasoning.
- Conclude with a brief discussion summarizing the key points of the story and reinforcing vocabulary.

Sequencing (5 mins)

- For this activity, the students will retell the story using in a small group.
- Divide students into pairs or small groups.
- Provide each group with a set of blank cards and pens.
- Ask each group to recall key events from the story or illustrate them on the cards.
- Once the cards are created, students will work together to arrange them in the correct sequence.
- Invite each group to retell the story using their arranged cards, encouraging them to use their own words to narrate the story.

Extension activities

There are a range of comprehension activities in the Activities book that can be used for extended learning:

- **Is it true?** (Activities, page 11) Students check the sentences for accuracy.
- **Make a page for a comic** (page 15) Students draw a picture to match the text in each box.
- **What happens next?** (page 16) Students underline their favorite part in the passage, then draw an illustration in the box.
- **Find the untruths** (page 17) Students underline the four untruths that have been planted in the passage.
- **Write the story in your own words** (page 21) Students retell the story orally before writing it.

STEP 5
Tracking progress

- Assign the **Spelling assessment and bookmarks** (Activities, page 24) to quickly evaluate each student's progress.
- Ask students to complete the **Timed word reading** (Activities, page 12) to assess their reading speed.
- Have students complete the **Reading fluency** activity (Activities, page 18)
- Depending on the class's performance, revisit specific activities to address skill gaps or encourage students to play one of the games below.

Extension activities

1 Stepping stones game (Activities, page 22)

- This game is suitable for 1–4 players and requires counters and a die.
- Students place their counters at the start of the stepping stones path. They then take turns rolling the die. They move their counter according to the number rolled.
- Upon landing on a stepping stone, the student reads the word or letter sound on that stone aloud.
- If a student lands on a stone with a directional arrow, they follow the arrow forward or backward.
- The first student to reach the end of the stepping stones path wins.
- Provide positive feedback and encouragement throughout the game.
- For those needing more support, help them to blend the letter sound or word with assistance.

2 4-in-a-row game (Activities, page 23)

- This game is for two players: Play with two sets of colored counters. Players take turns to read a word or letter and put a counter on it.
- Encourage players to give the sound for the letter rather than the letter name
- The winner is the first to get four of their counters in a row in any direction.
- The winner places a counter on a pizza box.
- The game is played four times until all the pizza boxes are covered.

e–e

STEP 1
Preparation 20 mins

LESSON RESOURCES

Learning goal (2 mins)

- Explain the lesson goal: learning the e–e spelling for the sound /ee/.
- Introduce the book Moon Dogs VCe Spellings Book 2: These Things.
- Inform students they will also be completing some activities from Moon Dogs VCe Spellings Activities.

Preparation (18 mins)

- Introduce the new focus spelling 'e–e' for the sound /ee/.
- Have students watch you as they pronounce /ee/.
- Read this list of names: "Pete," "Eve," and "Steve."
- For each, point to the letters as you slowly pronounce them, demonstrating how the 'e' and 'e' work together to form the /ee/ sound.
- Use your thumb and third finger to visually link these letters.

1 Word building and blending

- Begin by demonstrating how to build the word "Pete."
- Draw four lines on the whiteboard.
- Explain to the students that you will show them how to build the word "Pete."
- As you say the word slowly, move your finger under the lines.
- Ask the students to listen to the first sound in the word "Pete." Point to the first line and emphasize the first sound as you say the whole word. The students respond with /p/.
- Then ask the students which letter spells the sound /p/. The students point to the letter (or you can tell them). Bring the letter down to the first line.
- Repeat the process with the second sound /ee/ and the last sound /t/.
- Now ask the students to sound out all three sounds and blend them into a word while you move your finger under the word: /p/ /ee/ /t/ → "Pete."

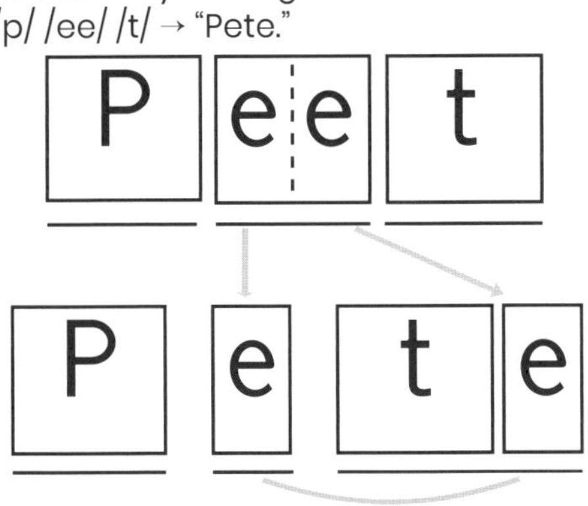

- Explain the spelling rule: even though the letter 't' separates the vowels, the 'e' and 'e' still work together to form the /ee/ sound.
- The next time this is done, you can ask a student to participate. Have them identify the sound, then the letter, and bring it down to the line.

2 Word reading

- Write the words you have created on the whiteboard. Then ask students to blend and read the words.
- Show how to say each sound individually and then blend them together to read the word. Model blending by pointing using a swishing motion with your finger.

3 Oral segmenting

- Say a word aloud (e.g. "these") and count the sounds in the word (3). Write the number of lines you need for all the sounds. Now ask students to listen to the sounds in the word and write a letter for every sound in the word as you spell the word.

Extension activities

1 Reading practice cards

- Assign the **Reading practice** cards activity (Activities, pages 28–29).
- Distribute the acitivity by cutting the reading cards for each student or small group.
- On page 28, the 'e–e' spelling is highlighted for initial introduction. On page 29, the e–e spelling is not highlighted.

2 Reading and sorting words

- Assign the **Reading and sorting: words with e and e–e** activity (Activities, page 30).
- This activity involves students distinguishing between words with the 'e' spelling (as in "pet") and words with the 'e–e' spelling (as in "Pete").

STEP 2
Application for reading

25 mins

Before reading (3 mins)

- Revisit the vocabulary taught in Step 1 (e.g. "eve"). Clearly say the word: /ee/ /v/.
- Then provide a simple definition, for example, "Eve means the day or evening before an event."
- Ask questions such as "Can you remember the eve before a special event?" and "How did you feel?"
- Then write the word on the whiteboard and refer back to it throughout the week for reinforcement.

Vocabulary (2 mins)

- Pre-teach the words in the **Vocabulary** list in Book 2: These Things (page iv).
- Ensure students understand each word's pronunciation, meaning, and usage.

Application (10 mins)

- The chosen text for this reading activity is Book 2: These Things. Briefly introduce the book to spark interest.
- Lead students through a directed reading of Book 2: These Things. Encourage students to sound out each word carefully and then blend the sounds together to form the word.
- Provide support by modeling the blending.
- Encourage students to sound out each word and then blend to read.

Reading fluency (10 mins)

- Following the initial reading, revisit Book 2: These Things with a focus on fluency.
- Reading the book again allows students to practice their newly acquired skills, this time with an emphasis on reading more smoothly and confidently.
- Create an interactive reading environment by inviting students to take turns reading aloud. Encourage them to point to each word as they read.
- As students read more fluently, support them to read with more expression and prosody, changing their pitch, pace, and emphasis according to the words and punctuation.

STEP 3
Application for spelling

20 mins

Segmenting and spelling (10 mins)

- Invite students to complete the **Splitting two-syllable words with ‹e–e›** activity (Activities, page 34).
- In this activity, the student splits each word into two syllables by writing each syllable in the box.
- Encourage students to write the whole word while saying the syllables.
- After students complete the activity, model the formation of each letter that was written during the activity on the whiteboard.
- Focus on the starting point, stroke direction, and completion of each letter to ensure proper handwriting techniques.
- Demonstrating proper letter formation is crucial for developing legible handwriting and building foundational writing skills.

Sentence dictation (10 mins)

- Ask students to complete the **Dictation** activity (Activities, page 39).
- Use the text at the bottom of the activity for dictation.
- Cut and fold along the dotted line before giving it to the students.
- Ask students to write the spelling of each sound on the provided write-on lines.
- Remind the students that some sounds can be spelled by more than one letter.
- A longer line indicates the spelling has more than one letter.
- The curved lines running underneath the write-on lines indicate a VCe spelling.
- For students who finish early or need additional practice, create additional activity sheets with your own passages of text and dictate these new passages to them.

STEP 4
Comprehension and consolidation
15 mins

Book reading (5 mins)
- Reread Book 2: These Things.
- Revisiting the book helps to reinforce familiarity with the text and supports phonetic recognition and comprehension.

Comprehension (5 mins)
- To check students' understanding of the story, conduct a group discussion.
- Ask the three comprehension questions at the back of the story ("What did Dan use his computer for?", "How did Pete deliver Dan's box of purchases?", and "Why would the vet like all of Dan's gifts?")
- Divide the class into small groups and ask each group to answer a question in turn.
- Encourage groups to explain their reasoning.
- Conclude with a brief discussion summarizing the key points of the story and reinforcing vocabulary.

Sequencing (5 mins)
- For this activity, the students will retell the story in a small group.
- Divide students into pairs or small groups.
- Provide each group with a set of blank cards and pens.
- Ask each group to recall key events from the story or illustrate them on the cards.
- Once the cards are created, students will work together to arrange them in the correct sequence.
- Invite each group to retell the story using their arranged cards, encouraging them to use their own words to narrate the story.

Extension activities

There are a range of comprehension activities in the Activities book that can be used for extended learning:
- **Is it true?** (Activities, page 31) Students check the sentences for accuracy.
- **Make a page for a comic** (page 35) Students draw a picture to match the text in each box.
- **What happens next?** (page 36) Students underline their favorite part in the passage, then draw an illustration in the match.
- **Find the untruths** (page 37) Students underline the four untruths that have been planted in the passage.
- **Write the story in your own words** (page 41) Students retell the story orally before writing it.

STEP 5
Tracking progress

- Assign the **Spelling assessment and bookmarks** (Activities, page 44) to quickly evaluate each student's progress.
- Ask students to complete the **Timed word reading** (Activities, page 32) to assess their reading speed.
- Have students complete the **Reading fluency** activity (Activities, page 38)
- Depending on the class's performance, revisit specific activities to address skill gaps or encourage students to play one of the games below.

Extension activities

1 Stepping stones game (Activities, page 42)
- This game is suitable for 1–4 players and requires counters and a die.
- Students place their counters at the start of the stepping stones path. They then take turns rolling the die. They move their counter according to the number rolled.
- Upon landing on a stepping stone, the student reads the word or letter sound on that stone aloud.
- If a student lands on a stone with a directional arrow, they follow the arrow forward or backward.
- The first student to reach the end of the stepping stones path wins.
- Provide positive feedback and encouragement throughout the game.
- For those needing more support, help them to blend the letter sound or word with assistance.

2 4-in-a-row-game (Activities, page 43)
- This game is for two players: Play with two sets of colored counters. Players take turns to read a word or letter and put a counter on it.
- Encourage players to give the sound for the letter rather than the letter name
- The winner is the first to get four of their counters in a row in any direction.
- The winner places a counter on a pizza box.
- The game is played four times until all the pizza boxes are covered.

i–e

STEP 1
Preparation

20 mins

LESSON RESOURCES

Learning goal (2 mins)

- Explain the lesson goal: learning the i–e spelling for the sound /ie/.
- Introduce the book Moon Dogs VCe Spellings Book 3: Bike Ride.
- Inform students they will also be completing some activities from Moon Dogs VCe Spellings Activities.

Preparation (18 mins)

- Introduce the new focus spelling 'i–e' for the sound /ie/.
- Have students watch you as they pronounce /ie/.
- Read this list of words: "bike," "ride," and "side."
- For each, point to the letters as you slowly pronounce them, demonstrating how the 'i' and 'e' work together to form the /ie/ sound.
- Use your thumb and third finger to visually link these letters.

1 Word building and blending

- Begin by demonstrating how to build the word "ride."
- Draw four lines on the whiteboard.
- Explain to the students that you will show them how to build the word "ride."
- As you say the word slowly, move your finger under the lines.
- Ask the students to listen to the first sound in the word "ride." Point to the first line and emphasize the first sound as you say the whole word. The students respond with /r/.
- Then ask the students which letter spells the sound /r/. The students point to the letter (or you can tell them). Bring the letter down to the first line.
- Repeat the process with the second sound /ie/ and the last sound /d/.
- Now ask the students to sound out all three sounds and blend them into a word while you move your finger under the word: /r/ /ie/ /d/ → "ride."

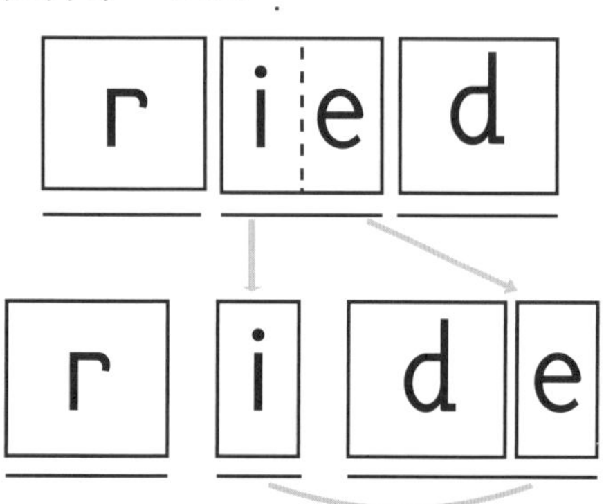

- Explain the spelling rule: In words like "ride," even though a consonant ('d') separates the vowels, the 'i' and 'e' still work together to form the /ie/ sound, which occurs right before the consonant.
- The next time this is done, you can ask a student to participate. Have them identify the sound, then the letter, and bring it down to the line.

2 Word reading

- Write the words you have created on the whiteboard. Then ask students to blend and read the words.
- Show how to say each sound individually and then blend them together to read the word. Model blending by pointing using a swishing motion with your finger.

3 Oral segmenting

- Say a word aloud (e.g. "time") and count the sounds in the word (3). Write the number of lines you need for all the sounds. Now ask students to listen to the sounds in the word and write a letter for every sound in the word as you spell the word.

Extension activities

1 Reading practice cards

- Assign the **Reading practice** cards activity (Activities, pages 48–49).
- Distribute the acitivity by cutting the reading cards for each student or small group.
- On page 48, the 'i–e' spelling is highlighted for initial introduction. On page 49, the 'i–e' spelling is not highlighted.

2 Reading and sorting words

- Assign the **Reading and sorting: words with i and i–e** activity (Activities, page 50).
- This activity involves students distinguishing between words with the 'i' spelling (as in "pin") and words with the 'i–e' spelling (as in "pine").

STEP 2
Application for reading
25 mins

Before reading (3 mins)

- Revisit the vocabulary taught in Step 1 (e.g. "pine"). Clearly say the word: /p/ /ie/ /n/.
- Explore different definitions of the word "pine."
- Ask questions such as "What does it mean to pine for something?"
- Then write the word on the whiteboard and refer back to it throughout the week for reinforcement.

Vocabulary (2 mins)

- Pre-teach the words in the **Vocabulary** list in Book 3: Bike Ride (page iv).
- Ensure students understand each word's pronunciation, meaning, and usage.

Application (10 mins)

- The chosen text for this reading activity is Book 3: Bike Ride. Briefly introduce the book to spark interest.
- Lead students through a directed reading of Book 3: Bike Ride. Encourage students to sound out each word carefully and then blend the sounds together to form the word.
- Provide support by modeling the blending.
- Encourage students to sound out each word and then blend to read.

Reading fluency (10 mins)

- Following the initial reading, revisit Book 3: Bike Ride with a focus on fluency.
- Reading the book again allows students to practice their newly acquired skills, this time with an emphasis on reading more smoothly and confidently.
- Create an interactive reading environment by inviting students to take turns reading aloud. Encourage them to point to each word as they read.
- As students read more fluently, support them to read with more expression and prosody, changing their pitch, pace, and emphasis according to the words and punctuation.

STEP 3
Application for spelling
20 mins

Segmenting and spelling (10 mins)

- Invite students to complete the **Segmenting and spelling** activity (Activities, page 47).
- In this activity, the student writes the missing word for each picture by putting one spelling in each square.
- Cut or fold the sheet along the dotted line before giving to the student.
- After students complete the activity, model the formation of each letter that was written during the activity on the whiteboard.
- Focus on the starting point, stroke direction, and completion of each letter to ensure proper handwriting techniques.
- Demonstrating proper letter formation is crucial for developing legible handwriting and building foundational writing skills.

Sentence dictation (10 mins)

- Ask students to complete the **Dictation** activity (Activities, page 59).
- Use the text at the bottom of the activity for dictation.
- Cut and fold along the dotted line before giving it to the students.
- Ask students to write the spelling of each sound on the provided write-on lines.
- Remind the students that some sounds can be spelled by more than one letter.
- A longer line indicates the spelling has more than one letter.
- The curved lines running underneath the write-on lines indicate a VCe spelling.
- For students who finish early or need additional practice, create additional activity sheets with your own passages of text and dictate these new passages to them.

Extension

- Ask students to complete the **Splitting two-syllable words with i–e** activity for additional spelling practice (Activities, page 54).

STEP 4
Comprehension and consolidation
15 mins

Book reading (5 mins)
- Reread Book 3: Bike Ride.
- Revisiting the book helps to reinforce familiarity with the text and supports phonetic recognition and comprehension.

Comprehension (5 mins)
- To check students' understanding of the story, conduct a group discussion.
- Ask the three comprehension questions at the back of the story ("Why can't Matt and Win ride in the rain?", "What did they find in the woods to keep them dry?", and "What did Matt and Win do while they waited for the rain to stop?")
- Divide the class into small groups and ask each group to answer a question in turn.
- Encourage groups to explain their reasoning.
- Conclude with a brief discussion summarizing the key points of the story and reinforcing vocabulary.

Sequencing (5 mins)
- For this activity, the students will retell the story in a small group.
- Divide students into pairs or small groups.
- Provide each group with a set of blank cards and pens.
- Ask each group to recall key events from the story or illustrate them on the cards.
- Once the cards are created, students will work together to arrange them in the correct sequence.
- Invite each group to retell the story using their arranged cards, encouraging them to use their own words to narrate the story.

Extension activities

There are a range of comprehension activities in the Activities book that can be used for extended learning:
- **Is it true?** (page 51) Students check the sentences for accuracy.
- **Make a page for a comic** (page 55) Students draw a picture to match the text in each box.
- **What happens next?** (page 56) Students underline their favorite part in the passage, then draw an illustration in the box.
- **Find the untruths** (page 57) Students underline the four untruths that have been planted in the passage.
- **Write the story in your own words** (page 61) Students retell the story orally before writing it.

STEP 5
Tracking progress

- Assign the **Spelling assessment and bookmarks** (Activities, page 64) to quickly evaluate each student's progress.
- Ask students to complete the **Timed word reading** (Activities, page 52) to assess their reading speed.
- Have students complete the **Reading fluency** activity (Activities, page 58).
- Depending on the class's performance, revisit specific activities to address skill gaps or encourage students to play one of the games below.

Extension activities

1 Stepping stones game (Activities, page 62)
- This game is suitable for 1–4 players and requires counters and a die.
- Students place their counters at the start of the stepping stones path. They then take turns rolling the die. They move their counter according to the number rolled.
- Upon landing on a stepping stone, the student reads the word or letter sound on that stone aloud.
- If a student lands on a stone with a directional arrow, they follow the arrow forward or backward.
- The first student to reach the end of the stepping stones path wins.
- Provide positive feedback and encouragement throughout the game.
- For those needing more support, help them to blend the letter sound or word with assistance.

2 4-in-a-row game (Activities, page 63)
- This game is for two players: Play with two sets of colored counters. Players take turns to read a word or letter and put a counter on it.
- Encourage players to give the sound for the letter rather than the letter name
- The winner is the first to get four of their counters in a row in any direction.
- The winner places a counter on a pizza box.
- The game is played four times until all the pizza boxes are covered.

o–e

LESSON RESOURCES

STEP 1
Preparation

20 mins

Learning goal (2 mins)

- Explain the lesson goal: learning the o–e spelling for the sound /oe/.
- Introduce the book Moon Dogs VCe Spellings Book 4: A Good Nose.
- Inform students they will also be completing some activities from Moon Dogs VCe Spellings Activities.

Preparation (18 mins)

- Introduce the new focus spelling 'o–e' for the sound /oe/.
- Have students watch you as they pronounce /oe/.
- Read this list of names: "nose," "hole," and "rope."
- For each, point to the letters as you slowly pronounce them, demonstrating how the 'o' and 'e' work together to form the /oe/ sound.
- Use your thumb and third finger to visually link these letters.

1 Word building and blending

- Begin by demonstrating how to build the word "rope."
- Draw four lines on the whiteboard.
- Explain to the students that you will show them how to build the word "rope."
- As you say the word slowly, move your finger under the lines.
- Ask the students to listen to the first sound in the word "rope." Point to the first line and emphasize the first sound as you say the whole word. The students respond with /r/.
- Then ask the students which letter spells the sound /r/. The students point to the letter (or you can tell them). Bring the letter down to the first line.
- Repeat the process with the second sound /oe/ and the last sound /p/.
- Now ask the students to sound out all three sounds and blend them into a word while you move your finger under the word: /r/ /oe/ /p/ → "rope."

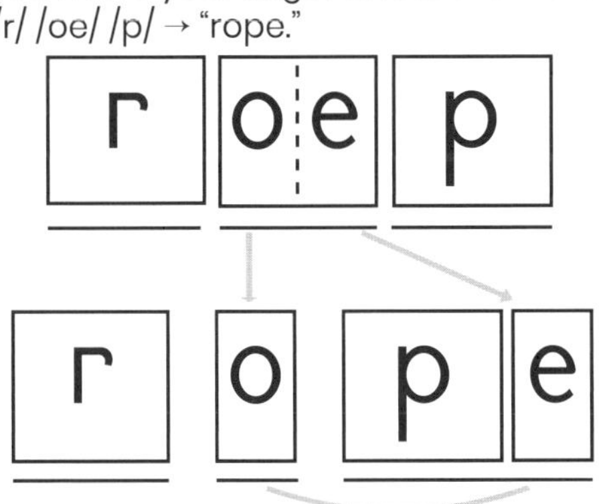

- Explain the spelling rule: even though the letter 'p' separates the vowels, the 'o' and 'e' still work together to form the /oe/ sound.
- The next time this is done, you can ask a student to participate. Have them identify the sound, then the letter, and bring it down to the line.

2 Word reading

- Write the words you have created on the whiteboard. Then ask students to blend and read the words.
- Show how to say each sound individually and then blend them together to read the word. Model blending by pointing using a swishing motion with your finger.

3 Oral segmenting

- Say a word aloud (e.g. "hole") and count the sounds in the word (3). Write the number of lines you need for all the sounds. Now ask students to listen to the sounds in the word and write a letter for every sound in the word as you spell the word.

Extension activities

1 Reading practice cards

- Assign the **Reading practice** cards activity (Activities, pages 68–69).
- Distribute the acitivity by cutting the reading cards for each student or small group.
- On page 68, the 'o–e' spelling is highlighted for initial introduction. On page 69, the 'o–e' spelling is not highlighted.

2 Reading and sorting words

- Assign the **Reading and sorting: words with o and o–e** activity (Activities, page 70).
- This activity involves students distinguishing between words with the 'o' spelling (as in "hop") and words with the 'o–e' spelling (as in "hope").

STEP 2
Application for reading
25 mins

Before reading (3 mins)

- Revisit the vocabulary taught in Step 1 (e.g. "rope"). Clearly say the word: /r/ /oe/ /p/.
- Then provide a simple definition, for example, "rope is a strong, thick string made of long twisted threads."
- Ask questions such as "Where might we use ropes?"
- Then write the word on the whiteboard and refer back to it throughout the week for reinforcement.

Vocabulary (2 mins)

- Pre-teach the words in the **Vocabulary** list in Book 4: A Good Nose (page iv).
- Ensure students understand each word's pronunciation, meaning, and usage.

Application (10 mins)

- The chosen text for this reading activity is Book 4: A Good Nose. Briefly introduce the book to spark interest.
- Lead students through a directed reading of Book 4: A Good Nose. Encourage students to sound out each word carefully and then blend the sounds together to form the word.
- Provide support by modeling the blending.
- Encourage students to sound out each word and then blend to read.

Reading fluency (10 mins)

- Following the initial reading, revisit Book 4: A Good Nose with a focus on fluency.
- Reading the book again allows students to practice their newly acquired skills, this time with an emphasis on reading more smoothly and confidently.
- Create an interactive reading environment by inviting students to take turns reading aloud. Encourage them to point to each word as they read.
- As students read more fluently, support them to read with more expression and prosody, changing their pitch, pace, and emphasis according to the words and punctuation.

STEP 3
Application for spelling
20 mins

Segmenting and spelling (10 mins)

- Invite students to complete the **Segmenting and spelling** activity (Activities, page 67).
- In this activity, the student writes the missing word for each picture by putting one spelling in each square.
- Cut or fold the sheet along the dotted line before giving to the student.
- After students complete the activity, model the formation of each letter that was written during the activity on the whiteboard.
- Focus on the starting point, stroke direction, and completion of each letter to ensure proper handwriting techniques.
- Demonstrating proper letter formation is crucial for developing legible handwriting and building foundational writing skills.

Sentence dictation (10 mins)

- Ask students to complete the **Dictation** activity (Activities, page 79).
- Use the text at the bottom of the activity for dictation.
- Cut and fold along the dotted line before giving it to the students.
- Ask students to write the spelling of each sound on the provided write-on lines.
- Remind the students that some sounds can be spelled by more than one letter.
- A longer line indicates the spelling has more than one letter.
- The curved lines running underneath the write-on lines indicate a VCe spelling.
- For students who finish early or need additional practice, create additional activity sheets with your own passages of text and dictate these new passages to them.

Extension

- Ask students to complete the **Splitting two-syllable words with o–e** activity for additional spelling practice (Activities, page 74).

STEP 4
Comprehension and consolidation
15 mins

Book reading (5 mins)

- Reread Book 4: A Good Nose.
- Revisiting the book helps to reinforce familiarity with the text and supports phonetic recognition and comprehension.

Comprehension (5 mins)

- To check students' understanding of the story, conduct a group discussion.
- Ask the three comprehension questions at the back of the story ("Why did Rose stop?", "How did the fire start?", and "What was Frank doing when the fire started?")
- Divide the class into small groups and ask each group to answer a question in turn.
- Encourage groups to explain their reasoning.
- Conclude with a brief discussion summarizing the key points of the story and reinforcing vocabulary.

Sequencing (5 mins)

- For this activity, the students will retell the story in a small group.
- Divide students into pairs or small groups.
- Provide each group with a set of blank cards and pens.
- Ask each group to recall key events from the story or illustrate them on the cards.
- Once the cards are created, students will work together to arrange them in the correct sequence.
- Invite each group to retell the story using their arranged cards, encouraging them to use their own words to narrate the story.

Extension activities

There are a range of comprehension activities in the Activities book that can be used for extended learning:

- **Is it true?** (page 71) Students check the sentences for accuracy.
- **Make a page for a comi**c (page 75) Students draw a picture to match the text in each box.
- **What happens next?** (page 76) Students underline their favorite part in the passage, then draw an illustration in the box.
- **Find the untruths** (page 77) Students underline the four untruths that have been planted in the passage.
- **Write the story in your own words** (page 81) Students retell the story orally before writing it.

STEP 5
Tracking progress

- Assign the **Spelling assessment and bookmarks** (Activities, page 84) to quickly evaluate each student's progress.
- Ask students to complete the **Timed word reading** (Activities, page 72) to assess their reading speed.
- Have students complete the **Reading fluency** activity (Activities, page 78).
- Depending on the class's performance, revisit specific activities to address skill gaps or encourage students to play one of the games below.

Extension activities

1 Stepping stones game (Activities, page 82)

- This game is suitable for 1–4 players and requires counters and a die.
- Students place their counters at the start of the stepping stones path. They then take turns rolling the die. They move their counter according to the number rolled.
- Upon landing on a stepping stone, the student reads the word or letter sound on that stone aloud.
- If a student lands on a stone with a directional arrow, they follow the arrow forward or backward.
- The first student to reach the end of the stepping stones path wins.
- Provide positive feedback and encouragement throughout the game.
- For those needing more support, help them to blend the letter sound or word with assistance.

2 4-in-a-row-game (Activities, page 83)

- This game is for two players: Play with two sets of colored counters. Players take turns to read a word or letter and put a counter on it.
- Encourage players to give the sound for the letter rather than the letter name
- The winner is the first to get four of their counters in a row in any direction.
- The winner places a counter on a pizza box.
- The game is played four times until all the pizza boxes are covered.

u–e

STEP 1
Preparation

20 mins

LESSON RESOURCES

Learning goal (2 mins)

- Explain the lesson goal: learning the u–e spelling for the sounds /oo/ and /ue/.
- Introduce the book Moon Dogs VCe Spellings Book 5: A Useful Bag.
- Inform students they will also be completing some activities from Moon Dogs VCe Spellings Activities.

Preparation (18 mins)

- Introduce the new focus spelling 'u–e' for the sounds /oo/ (e.g. "rule) and /ue/ (e.g. "cute").
- Have students watch you as they pronounce each sound.
- Read this list of words: "flute" and "cube."
- For each, point to the letters as you slowly pronounce them, demonstrating how the 'u' and 'e' work together to form both sounds.
- Use your thumb and third finger to visually link these letters.

1 Word building and blending

- Begin by demonstrating how to build the word "mute."
- Draw four lines on the whiteboard.
- Explain to the students that you will show them how to build the word "mute."
- As you say the word slowly, move your finger under the lines.
- Ask the students to listen to the first sound in the word "mute." Point to the first line and emphasize the first sound as you say the whole word. The students respond with /m/.
- Then ask the students which letter spells the sound /m/. The students point to the letter (or you can tell them). Bring the letter down to the first line.
- Repeat the process with the second sound /ue/ and the last sound /t/.
- Now ask the students to sound out all three sounds and blend them into a word while you move your finger under the word: /m/ /ue/ /t/ → "mute."

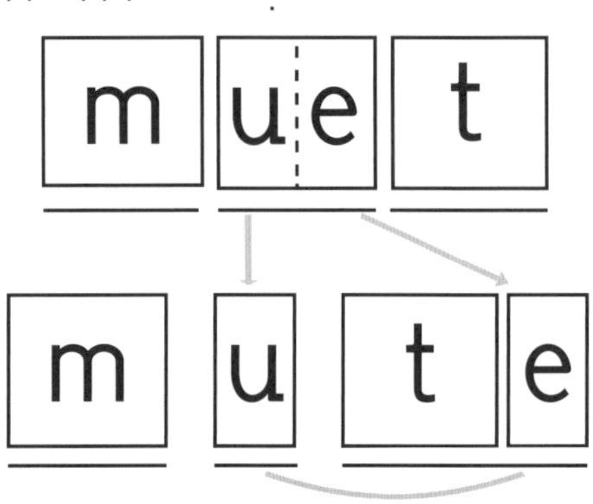

- Explain the spelling rule: In words like "mute," even though a consonant ('t') separates the vowels, the 'u' and 'e' still work together to form the /ue/ sound, which occurs right before the consonant.
- The next time this is done, you can ask a student to participate. Have them identify the sound, then the letter, and bring it down to the line.

2 Word reading

- Write the words you have created on the whiteboard. Then ask students to blend and read the words.
- Show how to say each sound individually and then blend them together to read the word. Model blending by pointing using a swishing motion with your finger.

3 Oral segmenting

- Say a word aloud (e.g. "flute") and count the sounds in the word (4). Write the number of lines you need for all the sounds. Now ask students to listen to the sounds in the word and write a letter for every sound in the word as you spell the word.

Extension activities

1 Reading practice cards

- Assign the **Reading practice** cards activity (Activities, pages 88–89).
- Distribute the acitivity by cutting the reading cards for each student or small group.
- On page 88, the 'u–e' spelling is highlighted for initial introduction. On page 89, the 'u–e' spelling is not highlighted.

2 Reading and sorting words

- Assign the **Reading and sorting: words with the two sounds for the spelling u and u–e** activity (Activities, page 90).
- This activity involves students distinguishing between words spelled 'u–e' with the sound /oo/ (e.g. "flute") and with the sound /u–e/ (as in "cube").

STEP 2
Application for reading
25 mins

Before reading (3 mins)

- Revisit the vocabulary taught in Step 1 (e.g. "flute"). Clearly say the word: /f/ /l /oo/ /t/.
- Then provide a simple definition, for example, "A flute is a musical instrument that you play by blowing across a hole at one end while pressing keys to change the notes."
- Ask questions such as "Can you think of any other wind instruments?"
- Then write the word on the whiteboard and refer back to it throughout the week for reinforcement.

Vocabulary (2 mins)

- Pre-teach the words in the **Vocabulary** list in Book 5: A Useful Bag (page iv).
- Ensure students understand each word's pronunciation, meaning, and usage.

Application (10 mins)

- The chosen text for this reading activity is Book 5: A Useful Bag. Briefly introduce the book to spark interest.
- Lead students through a directed reading of Book 5: A Useful Bag. Encourage students to sound out each word carefully and then blend the sounds together to form the word.
- Provide support by modeling the blending.
- Encourage students to sound out each word and then blend to read.

Reading fluency (10 mins)

- Following the initial reading, revisit Book 5: A Useful Bag with a focus on fluency.
- Reading the book again allows students to practice their newly acquired skills, this time with an emphasis on reading more smoothly and confidently.
- Create an interactive reading environment by inviting students to take turns reading aloud. Encourage them to point to each word as they read.
- As students read more fluently, support them to read with more expression and prosody, changing their pitch, pace, and emphasis according to the words and punctuation.

STEP 3
Application for spelling
20 mins

Segmenting and spelling (10 mins)

- Invite students to complete the **Segmenting and spelling** activity (Activities, page 87).
- In this activity, the student writes the missing word for each picture by putting one spelling in each square.
- Cut or fold the sheet along the dotted line before giving to the student.
- After students complete the activity, model the formation of each letter that was written during the activity on the whiteboard.
- Focus on the starting point, stroke direction, and completion of each letter to ensure proper handwriting techniques.
- Demonstrating proper letter formation is crucial for developing legible handwriting and building foundational writing skills.

Sentence dictation (10 mins)

- Ask students to complete the **Dictation** activity (Activities, page 99).
- Use the text at the bottom of the activity for dictation.
- Cut and fold along the dotted line before giving it to the students.
- Ask students to write the spelling of each sound on the provided write-on lines.
- Remind the students that some sounds can be spelled by more than one letter.
- A longer line indicates the spelling has more than one letter.
- The curved lines running underneath the write-on lines indicate a VCe spelling.
- For students who finish early or need additional practice, create additional activity sheets with your own passages of text and dictate these new passages to them.

Extension

- Ask students to complete the **Splitting two-syllable words with u–e** activity for additional spelling practice (Activities, page 94).

STEP 4
Comprehension and consolidation

15 mins

Book reading (5 mins)

- Reread Book 5: A Useful Bag.
- Revisiting the book helps to reinforce familiarity with the text and supports phonetic recognition and comprehension.

Comprehension (5 mins)

- To check students' understanding of the story, conduct a group discussion.
- Ask the three comprehension questions at the back of the story ("What do you think Jed thought was in Tam's big bag?", "How does fog make hill walking difficult?", and "What instrument would you bring to help in the fog?")
- Divide the class into small groups and ask each group to answer a question in turn.
- Encourage groups to explain their reasoning.
- Conclude with a brief discussion summarizing the key points of the story and reinforcing vocabulary.

Sequencing (5 mins)

- For this activity, the students will retell the story in a small group.
- Divide students into pairs or small groups.
- Provide each group with a set of blank cards and pens.
- Ask each group to recall key events from the story or illustrate them on the cards.
- Once the cards are created, students will work together to arrange them in the correct sequence.
- Invite each group to retell the story using their arranged cards, encouraging them to use their own words to narrate the story.

Extension activities

There are a range of comprehension activities in the Activities book that can be used for extended learning:

- **Is it true?** (page 91) Students check the sentences for accuracy.
- **Make a page for a comic** (page 95) Students draw a picture to match the text in each box.
- **What happens next?** (page 96) Students underline their favorite part in the passage, then draw an illustration in the box.
- **Find the untruths** (page 97) Students underline the four untruths that have been planted in the passage.
- **Write the story in your own words** (page 101) Students retell the story orally before writing it.

STEP 5
Tracking progress

- Assign the **Spelling assessment and bookmarks** (Activities, page 104) to quickly evaluate each student's progress.
- Ask students to complete the **Timed word reading** (Activities, page 92) to assess their reading speed.
- Have students complete the **Reading fluency** activity (Activities, page 98).
- Depending on the class's performance, revisit specific activities to address skill gaps or encourage students to play one of the games below.

Extension activities

1 Stepping stones game (Activities, page 102).

- This game is suitable for 1–4 players and requires counters and a die.
- Students place their counters at the start of the stepping stones path. They then take turns rolling the die. They move their counter according to the number rolled.
- Upon landing on a stepping stone, the student reads the word or letter sound on that stone aloud.
- If a student lands on a stone with a directional arrow, they follow the arrow forward or backward.
- The first student to reach the end of the stepping stones path wins.
- Provide positive feedback and encouragement throughout the game.
- For those needing more support, help them to blend the letter sound or word with assistance.

2 4-in-a-row game (Activities, page 103).

- This game is for two players: Play with two sets of colored counters. Players take turns to read a word or letter and put a counter on it.
- Encourage players to give the sound for the letter rather than the letter name
- The winner is the first to get four of their counters in a row in any direction.
- The winner places a counter on a pizza box.
- The game is played four times until all the pizza boxes are covered.

LESSON PLANS: Moon Dogs VCe Spellings

a–e, e–e, i–e, o–e, u–e

STEP 1
Preparation

20 mins

LESSON RESOURCES

Learning goal (2 mins)

- Explain the lesson goal: revising all the VCe spellings previously learned.
- Introduce the book Moon Dogs VCe Spellings Book 6: A Place to Hide.
- Inform students they will also be completing some activities from Moon Dogs VCe Spellings Activities.

Preparation (18 mins)

- Explain that this lesson is revising all VCe spellings and that they're starting with a–e.
- Have students watch you as they say /ae/.
- Read this list of words: "bake" and "name."
- For each, point to the letters as you slowly pronounce them, demonstrating how the 'a' and 'e' work together to form the /ae/ sound.
- Use your thumb and third finger to visually link these letters.
- Repeat this process with e–e, i–e, o–e, and u–e.

1 Word building and blending

- Begin by demonstrating how to build the word "wipe."
- Draw four lines on the whiteboard.
- Explain to the students that you will show them how to build the word "wipe."
- As you say the word slowly, move your finger under the lines.
- Ask the students to listen to the first sound in the word "wipe." Point to the first line and emphasize the first sound as you say the whole word. The students respond with /w/.
- Then ask the students which letter spells the sound /w/. The students point to the letter (or you can tell them). Bring the letter down to the first line.
- Repeat the process with the second sound /ie/ and the last sound /p/.
- Now ask the students to sound out all three sounds and blend them into a word while you move your finger under the word: /w/ /ie/ /p/ → "wipe."

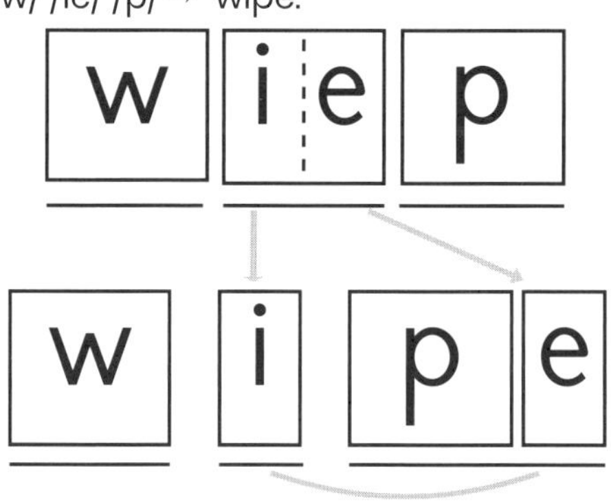

- Explain the spelling rule: In words like "wipe," even though a consonant ('p') separates the vowels, the 'i' and 'e' still work together to form the /ie/ sound, which occurs right before the consonant.
- The next time this is done, you can ask a student to participate. Have them identify the sound, then the letter, and bring it down to the line.

2 Word reading

- Write the words you have created on the whiteboard. Then ask students to blend and read the words.
- Show how to say each sound individually and then blend them together to read the word. Model blending by pointing using a swishing motion with your finger.

3 Oral segmenting

- Say a word aloud (e.g. "mole") and count the sounds in the word (3). Write the number of lines you need for all the sounds. Now ask students to listen to the sounds in the word and write a letter for every sound in the word as you spell the word.

Extension activities

1 Reading practice cards

- Assign the **Reading practice** cards activity (Activities, pages 108–109).
- Distribute the acitivity by cutting the reading cards for each student or small group.
- On page 108, the VCe spelling is highlighted for initial introduction. On page 109, the VCe spelling is not highlighted.

2 Reading and sorting words

- Assign the **Reading and sorting: VCe spellings** activity (Activities, page 110).
- This activity involves students distinguishing between words with different VCe spellings

STEP 2
Application for reading
25 mins

Before reading (3 mins)

- Revisit the vocabulary taught in Step 1 (e.g. "bake"). Clearly say the word: /b/ /ae/ /k/.
- Then provide a simple definition, for example, "Bake means to cook food in the oven."
- Ask questions such as "What kinds of food can we bake?"
- Then write the word on the whiteboard and refer back to it throughout the week for reinforcement.

Vocabulary (2 mins)

- Pre-teach the words in the **Vocabulary** list in Book 6: A Place to Hide (page iv).
- Ensure students understand each word's pronunciation, meaning, and usage.

Application (10 mins)

- The chosen text for this reading activity is Book 6: A Place to Hide. Briefly introduce the book to spark interest.
- Lead students through a directed reading of Book 6: A Place to Hide. Encourage students to sound out each word carefully and then blend the sounds together to form the word.
- Provide support by modeling the blending.
- Encourage students to sound out each word and then blend to read.

Reading fluency (10 mins)

- Following the initial reading, revisit Book 6: A Place to Hide with a focus on fluency.
- Reading the book again allows students to practice their newly acquired skills, this time with an emphasis on reading more smoothly and confidently.
- Create an interactive reading environment by inviting students to take turns reading aloud. Encourage them to point to each word as they read.
- As students read more fluently, support them to read with more expression and prosody, changing their pitch, pace, and emphasis according to the words and punctuation.

STEP 3
Application for spelling
20 mins

Segmenting and spelling (10 mins)

- Invite students to complete the **Segmenting and spelling** activity (Activities, page 107).
- In this activity, the student writes the missing word for each picture by putting one spelling in each square.
- Cut or fold the sheet along the dotted line before giving to the student.
- After students complete the activity, model the formation of each letter that was written during the activity on the whiteboard.
- Focus on the starting point, stroke direction, and completion of each letter to ensure proper handwriting techniques.
- Demonstrating proper letter formation is crucial for developing legible handwriting and building foundational writing skills.

Sentence dictation (10 mins)

- Ask students to complete the **Dictation** activity (Activities, page 119).
- Use the text at the bottom of the activity for dictation.
- Cut and fold along the dotted line before giving it to the students.
- Ask students to write the spelling of each sound on the provided write-on lines.
- Remind the students that some sounds can be spelled by more than one letter.
- A longer line indicates the spelling has more than one letter.
- The curved lines running underneath the write-on lines indicate a VCe spelling.
- For students who finish early or need additional practice, create additional activity sheets with your own passages of text and dictate these new passages to them.

Extension

- Ask students to complete the **Splitting two-syllable words with all VCe spellings** activity for additional spelling practice (Activities, page 114).

STEP 4
Comprehension and consolidation
15 mins

Book reading (5 mins)

- Reread Book 6: A Place to Hide.
- Revisiting the book helps to reinforce familiarity with the text and supports phonetic recognition and comprehension.

Comprehension (5 mins)

- To check students' understanding of the story, conduct a group discussion.
- Ask the three comprehension questions at the back of the story ("What is the name of the game the kids play?", "What encourages Moon to find the other kids?", and "Who has the best hiding place?")
- Divide the class into small groups and ask each group to answer a question in turn.
- Encourage groups to explain their reasoning.
- Conclude with a brief discussion summarizing the key points of the story and reinforcing vocabulary.

Sequencing (5 mins)

- For this activity, the students will retell the story in a small group.
- Divide students into pairs or small groups.
- Provide each group with a set of blank cards and pens.
- Ask each group to recall key events from the story or illustrate them on the cards.
- Once the cards are created, students will work together to arrange them in the correct sequence.
- Invite each group to retell the story using their arranged cards, encouraging them to use their own words to narrate the story.

Extension activities

There are a range of comprehension activities in the Activities book that can be used for extended learning:

- **Is it true?** (page 111) Students check the sentences for accuracy.
- **Make a page for a comic** (page 115) Students draw a picture to match the text in each box.
- **What happens next?** (page 116) Students underline their favorite part in the passage, then draw an illustration in the match.
- **Find the untruths** (page 117) Students underline the four untruths that have been planted in the passage.
- **Write the story in your own words** (page 121) Students retell the story orally before writing it.

STEP 5
Tracking progress

- Assign the **Spelling assessment and bookmarks** (Activities, page 124) to quickly evaluate each student's progress.
- Ask students to complete the **Timed word reading** (Activities, page 112) to assess their reading speed.
- Have students complete the **Reading fluency** activity (Activities, page 118)
- Depending on the class's performance, revisit specific activities to address skill gaps or encourage students to play one of the games below.

Extension activities

1 Stepping stones game (Activities, page 122)

- This game is suitable for 1–4 players and requires counters and a die.
- Students place their counters at the start of the stepping stones path. They then take turns rolling the die. They move their counter according to the number rolled.
- Upon landing on a stepping stone, the student reads the word or letter sound on that stone aloud.
- If a student lands on a stone with a directional arrow, they follow the arrow forward or backward.
- The first student to reach the end of the stepping stones path wins.
- Provide positive feedback and encouragement throughout the game.
- For those needing more support, help them to blend the letter sound or word with assistance.

2 4-in-a-row-game (Activities, page 123)

- This game is for two players: Play with two sets of colored counters. Players take turns to read a word or letter and put a counter on it.
- Encourage players to give the sound for the letter rather than the letter name
- The winner is the first to get four of their counters in a row in any direction.
- The winner places a counter on a pizza box.
- The game is played four times until all the pizza boxes are covered.

ai, ay

STEP 1
Preparation

20 mins

Learning goal (2 mins)

- Explain that in English there is more than one way to spell a sound. In this lesson we will learn two ways to spell the sound /ae/: 'ai' and 'ay.'
- Introduce the book Moon Dogs Vowel Spellings Book 1: Wet Day in Spain.
- Inform students they will also be completing some activities from Moon Dogs Vowel Spellings Activities.

Preparation (18 mins)

- Introduce the new focus spellings 'ai' and 'ay' for the sound /ae/.
- Model the sound correctly and ask pupils to copy.
- Have students watch you as they pronounce /ae/.
- Read these lists of words: "rain," "play," "spray," and "plain."

1 Word building and blending

- Use the same word building procedure as in previous chapters.
- For example, first build words with the grapheme 'ai.' If the student can learn another spelling alternative, introduce 'ay' and build word with this grapheme.
- Place the words in two columns and ask the student to read the words in one column and then the next.
- For word-building instructions see page 9 of the Activities book.

LESSON RESOURCES

2 Word reading

- Write the words you have created on the whiteboard. Then ask students to blend and read the words.
- Show how to say each sound individually and then blend them together to read the word. Model blending by pointing using a swishing motion with your finger.

3 Oral segmenting

- Say a word aloud (e.g. "spray") and count the sounds in the word (4). Write the number of lines you need for all the sounds. Now ask students to listen to the sounds in the word and write a letter for every sound in the word as you spell the word.

Extension activities

- If the student is learning one spelling at a time, use decodable passages in the Activities book on pages 11 (**Story with 'ai' words**) and 13 (**Story with 'ay' words**).

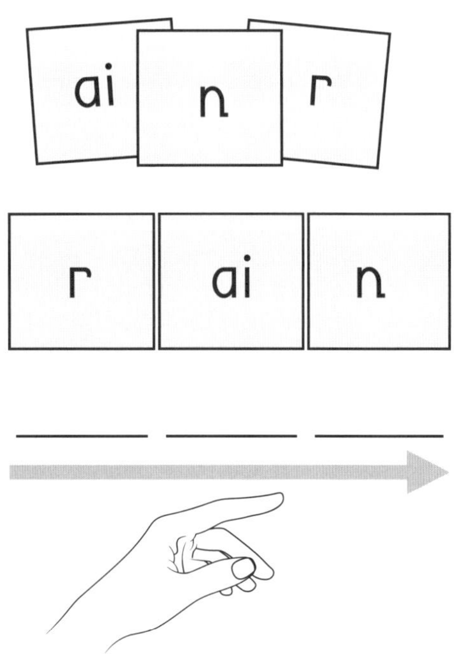

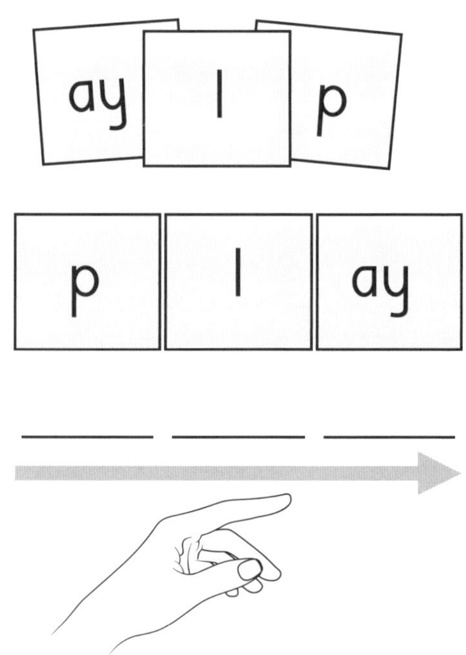

STEP 2
Application for reading

25 mins

Before reading (3 mins)

- Revisit the vocabulary taught in Step 1 (e.g. "spray"). Clearly say the word: /s/ /p/ /r/ /ae/.
- Then provide a simple definition, for example, "Spray is a liquid that is forced out in tiny drops."
- Ask questions such as "Where can we find spray?" and "Can you name some different types of spray?"
- Then write the word on the whiteboard and refer back to it throughout the week for reinforcement.

Vocabulary (2 mins)

- Pre-teach the words in the **Vocabulary** list in Book 1: Wet Day in Spain (page iv).
- Ensure students understand each word's pronunciation, meaning, and usage.

Application (10 mins)

- The chosen text for this reading activity is Book 1: Wet Day in Spain. Briefly introduce the book to spark interest.
- Lead students through a directed reading of Book 1: Wet Day in Spain. Encourage students to sound out each word carefully and then blend the sounds together to form the word.
- Provide support by modeling the blending.
- Encourage students to sound out each word and then blend to read.

Reading fluency (10 mins)

- Following the initial reading, revisit Book 1: Wet Day in Spain with a focus on fluency.
- Reading the book again allows students to practice their newly acquired skills, this time with an emphasis on reading more smoothly and confidently.
- Create an interactive reading environment by inviting students to take turns reading aloud. Encourage them to point to each word as they read.
- As students read more fluently, support them to read with more expression and prosody, changing their pitch, pace, and emphasis according to the words and punctuation.

STEP 3
Application for spelling

20 mins

Word sorting and spelling (10 mins)

- Word sorting is a useful activity to consolidate alternative spellings.
- Assign students the **Reading and spelling** activity (Activities, page 15).
- In this activity, students are provided with a list of words they need to sort according to the spellings 'ai' and 'ay.'
- Students read through the list of words and then write them in the correct column.
- Additionally, the **Spelling by sound** sheet (Activities, page 14) can be used for additional sorting activities, or it can be retained by the students for use as a dictionary of spellings by sound.

Sentence dictation (10 mins)

- Ask students to complete the **Dictation** activity (Activities, page 20).
- Use the text at the bottom of the activity for dictation: "Matt and Sim catch a train to Spain," "Matt has to wait to pay for the eggs," and "This is the best way to spend a wet day."
- Ask students to write the spelling of each sound on the provided write-on lines.
- Remind the students that some sounds can be spelled by more than one letter.
- A longer line indicates the spelling has more than one letter.

Extension activities

- For students who finish early or need additional practice, create additional activity sheets with your own passages of text and dictate these new passages to them.

STEP 4
Comprehension and consolidation
15 mins

Book reading (5 mins)

- Reread Book 1: Wet Day in Spain.
- Revisiting the book helps to reinforce familiarity with the text and supports phonetic recognition and comprehension.

Comprehension (5 mins)

- To check students' understanding of the story, conduct a group discussion.
- Ask the five comprehension questions at the back of the story ("Where do Sim and Matt go camping?", "Why was the mud as 'thick as clay'?", "Why do you think Matt drummed his nails on tin cans?", and "How do Sim and Matt spend the wet day?")
- Divide the class into small groups and ask each group to answer a question in turn.
- Encourage groups to explain their reasoning.
- Conclude with a brief discussion summarizing the key points of the story and reinforcing vocabulary.

Sequencing (5 mins)

- For this activity, the students will retell the story in a small group.
- Divide students into pairs or small groups.
- Provide each group with a set of blank cards and pens.
- Ask each group to recall key events from the story or illustrate them on the cards.
- Once the cards are created, students will work together to arrange them in the correct sequence.
- Invite each group to retell the story using their arranged cards, encouraging them to use their own words to narrate the story.

Extension activities

These comprehension activities in the Activities book can be used for extended learning:

- **Is it true?** (Activities, page 16). Students check the sentences for accuracy.
- **Developing vocabulary** (page 19). Students begin by circling the word or phrase that can be replaced by the word "wails" in a provided passage. They then write two sentences of their own using the word "wails." Remind students to begin each sentence with a capital letter and finish it with a period.

STEP 5
Tracking progress

- Assign the **Spelling assessment** (Activities, page 21) to quickly evaluate each student's progress.
- The teacher can use words from the second list of words provided for students who are ready for that stage.
- When dictating a word, first say it on its own.
- Next, say a sentence with the word in it (to put the word in a context of a sentence) and then repeat the word.
- This ensures students have heard the word correctly.
- For example: "Fainted. The boy fainted when he saw the mouse. Fainted."
- Ask students to complete the **Timed word reading** (Activities, page 18) to assess their reading speed.
- Ask students to read the words as fast as they can and record the time in each box.
- Depending on the class's performance, revisit specific activities to address skill gaps or encourage students to play one of the games below.

Extension activities

1 Phonic patterns: Color the real words (Activities, page 17).

- Fold the sheet on the dotted line. Then distribute the activity sheet to each student.
- Read out the words in each column.
- Students listen to the sounds in each word. They then color in the boxes that contain real words with 'ai' spellings.
- Students can unfold the sheet to check that their answers.

2 4-in-a-row game (Activities, page 22).

- This game is for two players: Play with two sets of colored counters. Players take turns to read a word and put a counter on it.
- The winner is the first to get four of their counters in a row in any direction.
- The winner places a counter on a picture of Moon.
- The game is played four times until all pictures of Moon boxes are covered.
- Encourage students to say the words aloud as they land on them. For those needing more support, help them to blend the word with assistance.
- Provide positive feedback and encouragement throughout the game.

ee, ea

STEP 1 Preparation

20 mins

LESSON RESOURCES

Learning goal (2 mins)

- Explain that in English there is more than one way to spell the sound /ee/. In this lesson we will learn two ways to spell the sound /ee/: 'ee' and 'ea.'
- Introduce the book Moon Dogs Vowel Spellings Book 2: Lost in the Street.
- Inform students they will also be completing some activities from Moon Dogs Vowel Spellings Activities.

Preparation (18 mins)

- Introduce the new focus spellings 'ee' and 'ea' for the sound /ee/.
- Model the sound correctly and ask pupils to copy.
- Have students watch you as they pronounce /ee/.
- Read these lists of words: "street," "seat," "been," and "green."

1 Word building and blending

- Use the same word building procedure as in previous chapters.
- For example, first build words with the grapheme 'ee.' If the student can learn another spelling alternative, introduce 'ea' and build word with this grapheme.
- Place the words in two columns and ask the student to read the words in one column and then the next.
- For word-building instructions see page 25 of the Activities book.

2 Word reading

- Write the words you have created on the whiteboard. Then ask students to blend and read the words.
- Show how to say each sound individually and then blend them together to read the word. Model blending by pointing using a swishing motion with your finger.

3 Oral segmenting

- Say a word aloud (e.g. "teach") and count the sounds in the word (3). Write the number of lines you need for all the sounds. Now ask students to listen to the sounds in the word and write a letter for every sound in the word as you spell the word.

Extension activities

- If the student is learning one spelling at a time, use decodable passages in the Activities book on pages 27 (**Story with 'ee' words**) and 29 (**Story with 'ea' words**).

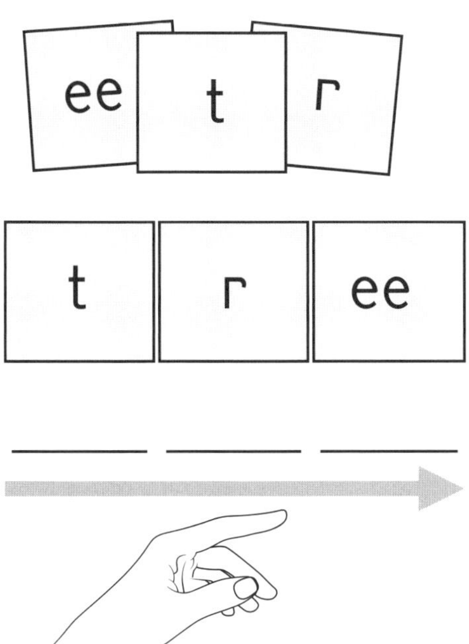

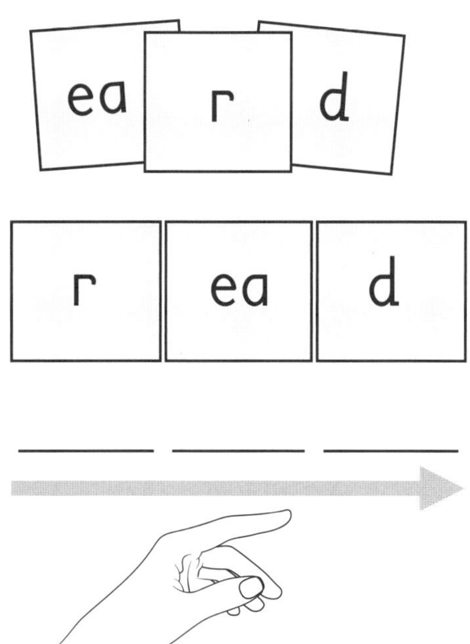

STEP 2
Application for reading

25 mins

Before reading (3 mins)

- Revisit the vocabulary taught in Step 1 (e.g. "tree"). Clearly say the word: /t/ /r/ /ee/.
- Then provide a simple definition, for example, "A tree is a plant with a trunk, branches, and leaves."
- Ask questions such as "Where might we see trees?" and "Can you name some different types of tree?"
- Then write the word on the whiteboard and refer back to it throughout the week for reinforcement.

Vocabulary (2 mins)

- Pre-teach the words in the **Vocabulary** list in Book 2: Lost in the Street (page iv).
- Ensure students understand each word's pronunciation, meaning, and usage.

Application (10 mins)

- The chosen text for this reading activity is Book 2: Lost in the Street. Briefly introduce the book to spark interest.
- Lead students through a directed reading of Book 2: Lost in the Street. Encourage students to sound out each word carefully and then blend the sounds together to form the word.
- Provide support by modeling the blending.
- Encourage students to sound out each word and then blend to read.

Reading fluency (10 mins)

- Following the initial reading, revisit Book 2: Lost in the Street with a focus on fluency.
- Reading the book again allows students to practice their newly acquired skills, this time with an emphasis on reading more smoothly and confidently.
- Create an interactive reading environment by inviting students to take turns reading aloud. Encourage them to point to each word as they read.
- As students read more fluently, support them to read with more expression and prosody, changing their pitch, pace, and emphasis according to the words and punctuation.

STEP 3
Application for spelling

20 mins

Word sorting and spelling (10 mins)

- Word sorting is a useful activity to consolidate alternative spellings.
- Assign students the **Reading and spelling** activity (Activities, page 31).
- In this activity, students are provided with a list of words they need to sort according to the spellings 'ee' and 'ea.'
- Students read through the list of words and then write them in the correct column.
- Additionally, the **Spelling by sound** sheet (Activities, page 30) can be used for additional sorting activities, or it can be retained by the students for use as a dictionary of spellings by sound.

Sentence dictation (10 mins)

- Ask students to complete the **Dictation** activity (Activities, page 36).
- Use the text at the bottom of the activity for dictation: "Tam sees a lost dog in the street," "Tam feeds him a meal. He eats and eats!" and "Next day Moon leaps up to greet Tam."
- Ask students to write the spelling of each sound on the provided write-on lines.
- Remind the students that some sounds can be spelled by more than one letter.
- A longer line indicates the spelling has more than one letter.

Extension activities

- For students who finish early or need additional practice, create additional activity sheets with your own passages of text and dictate these new passages to them.

STEP 4
Comprehension and consolidation
15 mins

Book reading (5 mins)

- Reread Book 2: Lost in the Street.
- Revisiting the book helps to reinforce familiarity with the text and supports phonetic recognition and comprehension.

Comprehension (5 mins)

- To check students' understanding of the story, conduct a group discussion.
- Ask the six comprehension questions at the back of the story. For example: "What did Tam do when she found the last dog?" and "How do you think she felt when she left the dog at the vet?"
- Divide the class into small groups and ask each group to answer a question in turn.
- Encourage groups to explain their reasoning.
- Conclude with a brief discussion summarizing the key points of the story and reinforcing vocabulary.

Sequencing (5 mins)

- For this activity, the students will retell the story in a small group.
- Divide students into pairs or small groups.
- Provide each group with a set of blank cards and pens.
- Ask each group to recall key events from the story or illustrate them on the cards.
- Once the cards are created, students will work together to arrange them in the correct sequence.
- Invite each group to retell the story using their arranged cards, encouraging them to use their own words to narrate the story.

Extension activities

These comprehension activities in the Activities book can be used for extended learning:

- **Is it true?** (Activities, page 32). Students check the sentences for accuracy.
- **Developing vocabulary** (page 35). Students begin by circling the word or phrase that can be replaced by the word "glee" in a provided passage. They then write two sentences of their own using the word "glee." Remind students to begin each sentence with a capital letter and finish it with a period.

STEP 5
Tracking progress

- Assign the **Spelling assessment** (Activities, page 37) to quickly evaluate each student's progress.
- The teacher can use words from the second list of words provided for students who are ready for that stage.
- When dictating a word, first say it on its own.
- Next, say a sentence with the word in it (to put the word in a context of a sentence) and then repeat the word.
- This ensures students have heard the word correctly.
- For example: "Meeting. Tam was meeting Jed at the shop. Meeting."
- Ask students to complete the **Timed word reading** (Activities, page 34) to assess their reading speed.
- Ask students to read the words as fast as they can and record the time in each box.
- Depending on the class's performance, revisit specific activities to address skill gaps or encourage students to play one of the games below.

Extension activities

1 Phonic patterns: Color the real words (Activities, page 33).

- Fold the sheet on the dotted line. Then distribute the activity sheet to each student.
- Read out the words in each column.
- Students listen to the sounds in each word. They then color in the boxes that contain real words with 'ee' spellings.
- Students can unfold the sheet to check that their answers.

2 4-in-a-row game (Activities, page 38).

- This game is for two players: Play with two sets of colored counters. Players take turns to read a word and put a counter on it.
- The winner is the first to get four of their counters in a row in any direction.
- The winner places a counter on picture of Moon.
- The game is played four times until all pictures of Moon are covered.
- Encourage students to say the words aloud as they land on them. For those needing more support, help them to blend the word with assistance.
- Provide positive feedback and encouragement throughout the game.

oa, ow

STEP 1
Preparation

20 mins

LESSON RESOURCES

Learning goal (2 mins)

- Explain that in English there is more than one way to spell the sound /oe/. In this lesson we will learn two ways to spell the sound /oe/: 'oa' and 'ow.'
- Introduce the book Moon Dogs Vowel Spellings Book 3: The Boat Trip.
- Inform students they will also be completing some activities from Moon Dogs Vowel Spellings Activities.

Preparation (18 mins)

- Introduce the new focus spellings 'oa' and 'ow' for the sound /oe/.
- Model the sound correctly and ask pupils to copy.
- Have students watch you as they pronounce /oe/.
- Read these lists of words: "boat," "tow," "toast," and "snow."

1 Word building and blending

- Use the same word building procedure as in previous chapters.
- For example, first build words with the grapheme 'oa.' If the student can learn another spelling alternative, introduce 'ow' and build word with this grapheme.
- Place the words in two columns and ask the student to read the words in one column and then the next.
- For word-building instructions see page 41 of the Activities book.

2 Word reading

- Write the words you have created on the whiteboard. Then ask students to blend and read the words.
- Show how to say each sound individually and then blend them together to read the word. Model blending by pointing using a swishing motion with your finger.

3 Oral segmenting

- Say a word aloud (e.g. "snow") and count the sounds in the word (3). Write the number of lines you need for all the sounds. Now ask students to listen to the sounds in the word and write a letter for every sound in the word as you spell the word.

Extension activities

- If the student is learning one spelling at a time, use decodable passages in the Activities book on pages 43 (**Story with 'oa' words**) and 45 (**Story with 'ow' words**).

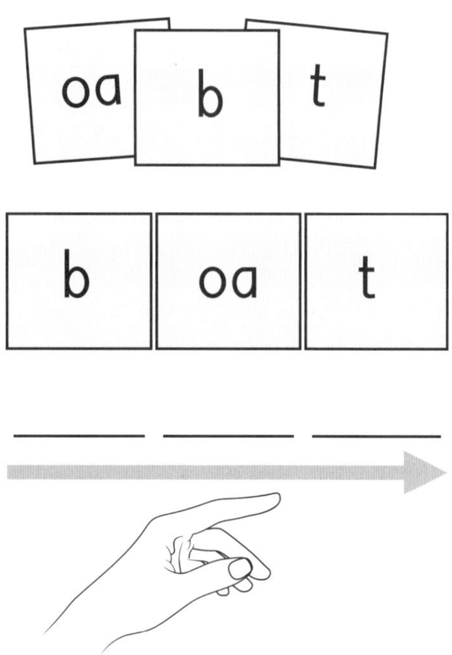

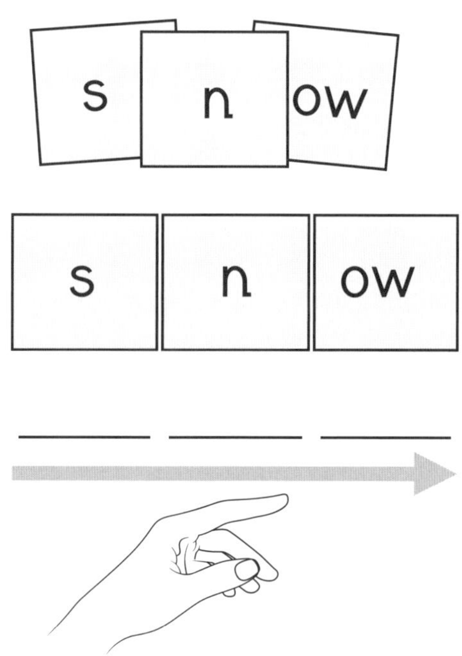

STEP 2
Application for reading

25 mins

Before reading (3 mins)

- Revisit the vocabulary taught in Step 1 (e.g. "snow"). Clearly say the word: /s/ /n/ /oe/.
- Then provide a simple definition, for example, "Snow is fallen water that falls from the sky."
- Ask questions such as "What can we do in the snow?" and "What does snow feel like to touch?"
- Then write the word on the whiteboard and refer back to it throughout the week for reinforcement.

Vocabulary (2 mins)

- Pre-teach the words in the **Vocabulary** list in Book 3: The Boat Trip (page iv).
- Ensure students understand each word's pronunciation, meaning, and usage.

Application (10 mins)

- The chosen text for this reading activity is Book 3: The Boat Trip. Briefly introduce the book to spark interest.
- Lead students through a directed reading of Book 3: The Boat Trip. Encourage students to sound out each word carefully and then blend the sounds together to form the word.
- Provide support by modeling the blending.
- Encourage students to sound out each word and then blend to read.

Reading fluency (10 mins)

- Following the initial reading, revisit Book 3: The Boat Trip with a focus on fluency.
- Reading the book again allows students to practice their newly acquired skills, this time with an emphasis on reading more smoothly and confidently.
- Create an interactive reading environment by inviting students to take turns reading aloud. Encourage them to point to each word as they read.
- As students read more fluently, support them to read with more expression and prosody, changing their pitch, pace, and emphasis according to the words and punctuation.

STEP 3
Application for spelling

20 mins

Word sorting and spelling (10 mins)

- Word sorting is a useful activity to consolidate alternative spellings.
- Assign students the **Reading and spelling** activity (Activities, page 47).
- In this activity, students are provided with a list of words they need to sort according to the spellings 'oa' and 'ow.'
- Students read through the list of words and then write them in the correct column.
- Additionally, the **Spelling by sound** sheet (Activities, page 46) can be used for additional sorting activities, or it can be retained by the students for use as a dictionary of spellings by sound.

Sentence dictation (10 mins)

- Ask students to complete the **Dictation** activity (Activities, page 52).
- Use the text at the bottom of the activity for dictation: "'That coat smells like a goat!' moans Tam," "Sim throws himself in next to Moon," and "Tam wraps Moon up in her yellow hat and black coat."
- Ask students to write the spelling of each sound on the provided write-on lines.
- Remind the students that some sounds can be spelled by more than one letter.
- A longer line indicates the spelling has more than one letter.

Extension activities

- For students who finish early or need additional practice, create additional activity sheets with your own passages of text and dictate these new passages to them.

STEP 4
Comprehension and consolidation

15 mins

Book reading (5 mins)

- Reread Book 3: The Boat Trip.
- Revisiting the book helps to reinforce familiarity with the text and supports phonetic recognition and comprehension.

Comprehension (5 mins)

- To check students' understanding of the story, conduct a group discussion.
- Ask the five comprehension questions at the back of the story ("Why is Tam cold?", "What does Moon spot in the sky?", "What happens when Moon tries to catch the crow?" "How does Sim rescue Moon?", and "Why do you think Sim wraps the coat around Moon?")
- Divide the class into small groups and ask each group to answer a question in turn.
- Encourage groups to explain their reasoning.
- Conclude with a brief discussion summarizing the key points of the story and reinforcing vocabulary.

Sequencing (5 mins)

- For this activity, the students will retell the story in a small group.
- Divide students into pairs or small groups.
- Provide each group with a set of blank cards and pens.
- Ask each group to recall key events from the story or illustrate them on the cards.
- Once the cards are created, students will work together to arrange them in the correct sequence.
- Invite each group to retell the story using their arranged cards, encouraging them to use their own words to narrate the story.

Extension activities

These comprehension activities in the Activities book can be used for extended learning:

- **Is it true?** (Activities, page 48). Students check the sentences for accuracy.
- **Developing vocabulary** (page 51). Students begin by circling the word or phrase that can be replaced by the word "moans" in a provided passage. They then write two sentences of their own using the word "moans." Remind students to begin each sentence with a capital letter and finish it with a period.

STEP 5
Tracking progress

- Assign the **Spelling assessment** (Activities, page 53) to quickly evaluate each student's progress.
- The teacher can use words from the second list of words provided for students who are ready for that stage.
- When dictating a word, first say it on its own.
- Next, say a sentence with the word in it (to put the word in a context of a sentence) and then repeat the word.
- This ensures students have heard the word correctly.
- For example: "Road. It was a long road. Road."
- Ask students to complete the **Timed word reading** (Activities, page 50) to assess their reading speed.
- Ask students to read the words as fast as they can and record the time in each box.
- Depending on the class's performance, revisit specific activities to address skill gaps or encourage students to play one of the games below.

Extension activities

1 Phonic patterns: Color the real words (Activities, page 49).

- Fold the sheet on the dotted line. Then distribute the activity sheet to each student.
- Read out the words in each column.
- Students listen to the sounds in each word. They then color in the boxes that contain real words with 'oa' spellings.
- Students can unfold the sheet to check that their answers.

2 4-in-a-row game (Activities, page 54).

- This game is for two players: Play with two sets of colored counters. Players take turns to read a word and put a counter on it.
- The winner is the first to get four of their counters in a row in any direction.
- The winner places a counter on a picture of Moon.
- The game is played four times until all pictures of Moon boxes are covered.
- Encourage students to say the words aloud as they land on them. For those needing more support, help them to blend the word with assistance.
- Provide positive feedback and encouragement throughout the game.

LESSON PLANS: Moon Dogs Vowel Spellings

ur, ir

STEP 1
Preparation

20 mins

LESSON RESOURCES

Learning goal (2 mins)

- Explain that in English there is more than one than way to spell the sound /er/. In this lesson we will learn two ways to spell the sound /er/: 'ur' and 'ir.'
- Introduce the book Moon Dogs Vowel Spellings Book 4: Birthday Lunch.
- Inform students they will also be completing some activities from Moon Dogs Vowel Spellings Activities.

Preparation (18 mins)

- Introduce the new focus spellings 'ur' and 'ir' for the sound /er/.
- Model the sound correctly and ask pupils to copy.
- Have students watch you as they pronounce /er/.
- Read these lists of words: "fur," "sir," "hurt," and "girl."

1 Word building and blending

- Use the same word building procedure as in previous chapters.
- For example, first build words with the grapheme 'ur.' If the student can learn another spelling alternative, introduce 'ir' and build word with this grapheme.
- Place the words in two columns and ask the student to read the words in one column and then the next.
- For word-building instructions see page 57 of the Activities book.

2 Word reading

- Write the words you have created on the whiteboard. Then ask students to blend and read the words.
- Show how to say each sound individually and then blend them together to read the word. Model blending by pointing using a swishing motion with your finger.

3 Oral segmenting

- Say a word aloud (e.g. "curl") and count the sounds in the word (3). Write the number of lines you need for all the sounds. Now ask students to listen to the sounds in the word and write a letter for every sound in the word as you spell the word.

Extension activities

- If the student is learning one spelling at a time, use decodable passages in the Activities book on pages 59 (**Story with 'ur' words**) and 61 (**Story with'ir' words**).

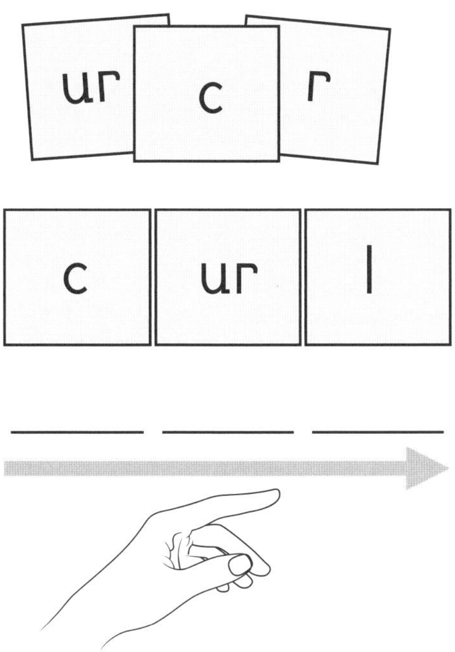

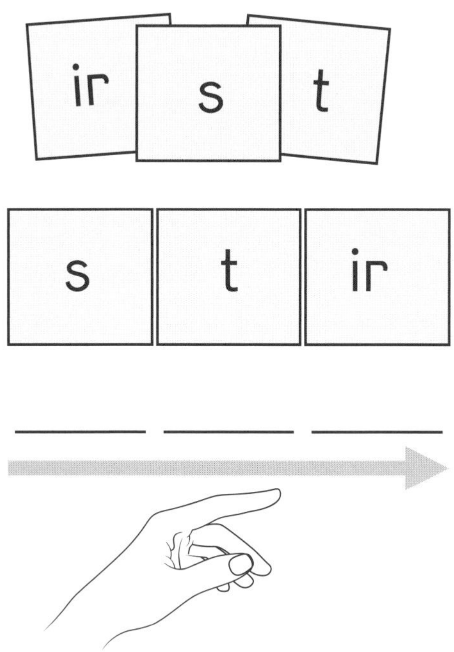

STEP 2
Application for reading
25 mins

Before reading (3 mins)

- Revisit the vocabulary taught in Step 1 (e.g. "curl"). Clearly say the word: /c/ /er/ /l/.
- Then provide a simple definition, for example, "A curl means to form into a curved or spiral shape."
- Ask questions such as "What things can curl?" and "Why would someone curl up in front of a fire?"
- Then write the word on the whiteboard and refer back to it throughout the week for reinforcement.

Vocabulary (2 mins)

- Pre-teach the words in the **Vocabulary** list in Book 4: Birthday Lunch (page iv).
- Ensure students understand each word's pronunciation, meaning, and usage.

Application (10 mins)

- The chosen text for this reading activity is Book 4: Birthday Lunch. Briefly introduce the book to spark interest.
- Lead students through a directed reading of Book 4: Birthday Lunch. Encourage students to sound out each word carefully and then blend the sounds together to form the word.
- Provide support by modeling the blending.
- Encourage students to sound out each word and then blend to read.

Reading fluency (10 mins)

- Following the initial reading, revisit Book 4: Birthday Lunch with a focus on fluency.
- Reading the book again allows students to practice their newly acquired skills, this time with an emphasis on reading more smoothly and confidently.
- Create an interactive reading environment by inviting students to take turns reading aloud. Encourage them to point to each word as they read.
- As students read more fluently, support them to read with more expression and prosody, changing their pitch, pace, and emphasis according to the words and punctuation.

STEP 3
Application for spelling
20 mins

Word sorting and spelling (10 mins)

- Word sorting is a useful activity to consolidate alternative spellings.
- Assign students the **Reading and spelling** activity (Activities, page 63).
- In this activity, students are provided with a list of words they need to sort according to the spellings 'ur' and 'ir.'
- Students read through the list of words and then write them in the correct column.
- Additionally, the **Spelling by sound** sheet (Activities, page 62) can be used for additional sorting activities, or it can be retained by the students for use as a dictionary of spellings by sound.

Sentence dictation (10 mins)

- Ask students to complete the **Dictation** activity (Activities, page 68).
- Use the text at the bottom of the activity for dictation: "Dan is making lunch for Liz's birthday," "The box crashes and bursts open" and "A bird with a hurt wing pecks at the lunch."
- Ask students to write the spelling of each sound on the provided write-on lines.
- Remind the students that some sounds can be spelled by more than one letter.
- A longer line indicates the spelling has more than one letter.

Extension activities

- For students who finish early or need additional practice, create additional activity sheets with your own passages of text and dictate these new passages to them.

STEP 4
Comprehension and consolidation
15 mins

Book reading (5 mins)
- Reread Book 4: Birthday Lunch.
- Revisiting the book helps to reinforce familiarity with the text and supports phonetic recognition and comprehension.

Comprehension (5 mins)
- To check students' understanding of the story, conduct a group discussion.
- Ask the six comprehension questions at the back of the story. For example: "Why is Dan making lunch for Liz?" and "What does Dan make for lunch?"
- Divide the class into small groups and ask each group to answer a question in turn.
- Encourage groups to explain their reasoning.
- Conclude with a brief discussion summarizing the key points of the story and reinforcing vocabulary.

Sequencing (5 mins)
- For this activity, the students will retell the story in a small group.
- Divide students into pairs or small groups.
- Provide each group with a set of blank cards and pens.
- Ask each group to recall key events from the story or illustrate them on the cards.
- Once the cards are created, students will work together to arrange them in the correct sequence.
- Invite each group to retell the story using their arranged cards, encouraging them to use their own words to narrate the story.

Extension activities

These comprehension activities in the Activities book can be used for extended learning:
- **Is it true?** (Activities, page 64). Students check the sentences for accuracy.
- **Developing vocabulary** (page 67). Students begin by circling the word or phrase that can be replaced by the word "murmurs" in a provided passage. They then write two sentences of their own using the word "murmurs." Remind students to begin each sentence with a capital letter and finish it with a period.

STEP 5
Tracking progress

- Assign the **Spelling assessment** (Activities, page 69) to quickly evaluate each student's progress.
- The teacher can use words from the second list of words provided for students who are ready for that stage.
- When dictating a word, first say it on its own.
- Next, say a sentence with the word in it (to put the word in a context of a sentence) and then repeat the word.
- This ensures students have heard the word correctly.
- For example: "Bird. The bird splashed in the pond. Bird."
- Ask students to complete the **Timed word reading** (Activities, page 66) to assess their reading speed.
- Ask students to read the words as fast as they can and record the time in each box.
- Depending on the class's performance, revisit specific activities to address skill gaps or encourage students to play one of the games below.

Extension activities

1. **Phonic patterns: Color the real words (Activities, page 65).**

- Fold the sheet on the dotted line. Then distribute the activity sheet to each student.
- Read out the words in each column.
- Students listen to the sounds in each word. They then color in the boxes that contain real words with 'ur' spellings.
- Students can unfold the sheet to check that their answers.

2. **4-in-a-row game (Activities, page 70).**

- This game is for two players: Play with two sets of colored counters. Players take turns to read a word and put a counter on it.
- The winner is the first to get four of their counters in a row in any direction.
- The winner places a counter on picture of Moon.
- The game is played four times until all pictures of Moon are covered.
- Encourage students to say the words aloud as they land on them. For those needing more support, help them to blend the word with assistance.
- Provide positive feedback and encouragement throughout the game.

e, ea

STEP 1
Preparation

20 mins

Learning goal (2 mins)

- Explain that in English there is more than one way to spell the sound /e/. In this lesson we will learn two ways to spell the sound /oe/: 'e' and 'ea.'
- Introduce the book Moon Dogs Vowel Spellings Book 5: Matt's Bad Head.
- Inform students they will also be completing some activities from Moon Dogs Vowel Spellings Activities.

Preparation (18 mins)

- Introduce the new focus spellings 'e' and 'ea' for the sound /e/.
- Model the sound correctly and ask pupils to copy.
- Have students watch you as they pronounce /e/.
- Read these lists of words: "end," "went," "head," and "bread."

1 Word building and blending

- Use the same word building procedure as in previous chapters.
- For example, first build words with the grapheme 'e.' If the student can learn another spelling alternative, introduce 'ea' and build word with this grapheme.
- Place the words in two columns and ask the student to read the words in one column and then the next.
- For word-building instructions see page 73 of the Activities book.

LESSON RESOURCES

2 Word reading

- Write the words you have created on the whiteboard. Then ask students to blend and read the words.
- Show how to say each sound individually and then blend them together to read the word. Model blending by pointing using a swishing motion with your finger.

3 Oral segmenting

- Say a word aloud (e.g. "bread") and count the sounds in the word (4). Write the number of lines you need for all the sounds. Now ask students to listen to the sounds in the word and write a letter for every sound in the word as you spell the word.

Extension activities

- If the student is learning one spelling at a time, use decodable passages in the Activities book on pages 75 (**Story with 'e' words**) and 77 (**Story with 'ea' words**).

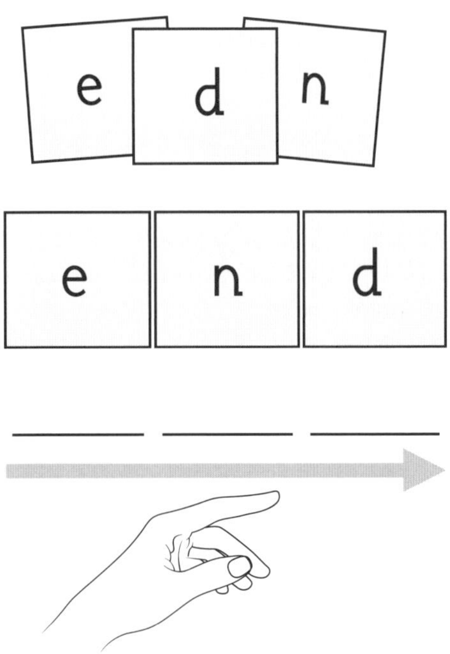

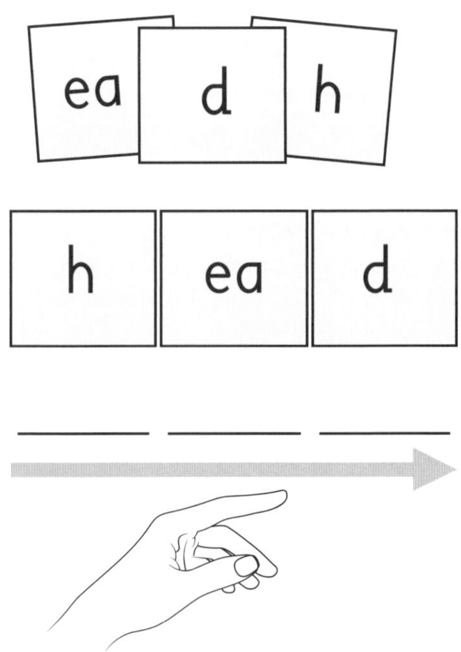

STEP 2
Application for reading

25 mins

Before reading (3 mins)

- Revisit the vocabulary taught in Step 1 (e.g. "bread"). Clearly say the word: /b/ /r/ /e/ /d/.
- Then provide a simple definition, for example, "Bread is a food made from flour, water, and yeast."
- Ask questions such as "What is your favorite spread to have with bread?" and "Can you name some different types of bread?"
- Then write the word on the whiteboard and refer back to it throughout the week for reinforcement.

Vocabulary (2 mins)

- Pre-teach the words in the **Vocabulary** list in Book 5: Matt's Bad Head (page iv).
- Ensure students understand each word's pronunciation, meaning, and usage.

Application (10 mins)

- The chosen text for this reading activity is Book 5: Matt's Bad Head. Briefly introduce the book to spark interest.
- Lead students through a directed reading of Book 5: Matt's Bad Head. Encourage students to sound out each word carefully and then blend the sounds together to form the word.
- Provide support by modeling the blending.
- Encourage students to sound out each word and then blend to read.

Reading fluency (10 mins)

- Following the initial reading, revisit Book 5: Matt's Bad Head with a focus on fluency.
- Reading the book again allows students to practice their newly acquired skills, this time with an emphasis on reading more smoothly and confidently.
- Create an interactive reading environment by inviting students to take turns reading aloud. Encourage them to point to each word as they read.
- As students read more fluently, support them to read with more expression and prosody, changing their pitch, pace, and emphasis according to the words and punctuation.

STEP 3
Application for spelling

20 mins

Word sorting and spelling (10 mins)

- Word sorting is a useful activity to consolidate alternative spellings.
- Assign students the **Reading and spelling** activity (Activities, page 79).
- In this activity, students are provided with a list of words they need to sort according to the spellings 'e' and 'ea.'
- Students read through the list of words and then write them in the correct column.
- Additionally, the **Spelling by sound** sheet (Activities, page 78) can be used for additional sorting activities, or it can be retained by the students for use as a dictionary of spellings by sound.

Sentence dictation (10 mins)

- Ask students to complete the **Dictation** activity (Activities, page 84).
- Use the text at the bottom of the activity for dictation: "Matt's head hurts and he feels dreadful," "Matt yells in his sleep. He is dripping with sweat," and "Tam hands him bread spread with cheese."
- Ask students to write the spelling of each sound on the provided write-on lines.
- Remind the students that some sounds can be spelled by more than one letter.
- A longer line indicates the spelling has more than one letter.

Extension activities

- For students who finish early or need additional practice, create additional activity sheets with your own passages of text and dictate these new passages to them.

STEP 4
Comprehension and consolidation

15 mins

Book reading (5 mins)

- Reread Book 5: Matt's Bad Head.
- Revisiting the book helps to reinforce familiarity with the text and supports phonetic recognition and comprehension.

Comprehension (5 mins)

- To check students' understanding of the story, conduct a group discussion.
- Ask the five comprehension questions at the back of the story ("Why is Matt in bed?", "What is Matt thinking about when he is stuck in bed?", "What does Matt dream about?", "Why do you think Matt dreamed about cheese?", and "What does Matt say when Liz starts to sing?")
- Divide the class into small groups and ask each group to answer a question in turn.
- Encourage groups to explain their reasoning.
- Conclude with a brief discussion summarizing the key points of the story and reinforcing vocabulary.

Sequencing (5 mins)

- For this activity, the students will retell the story in a small group.
- Divide students into pairs or small groups.
- Provide each group with a set of blank cards and pens.
- Ask each group to recall key events from the story or illustrate them on the cards.
- Once the cards are created, students will work together to arrange them in the correct sequence.
- Invite each group to retell the story using their arranged cards, encouraging them to use their own words to narrate the story.

Extension activities

These comprehension activities in the Activities book can be used for extended learning:

- **Is it true?** (Activities, page 80). Students check the sentences for accuracy.
- **Developing vocabulary** (page 83). Students begin by circling the word or phrase that can be replaced by the word "dreadful" in a provided passage. They then write two sentences of their own using the word "dreadful." Remind students to begin each sentence with a capital letter and finish it with a period.

STEP 5
Tracking progress

- Assign the **Spelling assessment** (Activities, page 85) to quickly evaluate each student's progress.
- The teacher can use words from the second list of words provided for students who are ready for that stage.
- When dictating a word, first say it on its own.
- Next, say a sentence with the word in it (to put the word in a context of a sentence) and then repeat the word.
- This ensures students have heard the word correctly.
- For example: "Bread. He had jam on the bread. Bread.."
- Ask students to complete the **Timed word reading** (Activities, page 82) to assess their reading speed.
- Ask students to read the words as fast as they can and record the time in each box.
- Depending on the class's performance, revisit specific activities to address skill gaps or encourage students to play one of the games below.

Extension activities

1 Phonic patterns: Color the real words (Activities, page 81).

- Fold the sheet on the dotted line. Then distribute the activity sheet to each student.
- Read out the words in each column.
- Students listen to the sounds in each word. They then color in the boxes that contain real words with 'ea' spellings.
- Students can unfold the sheet to check that their answers.

2 4-in-a-row game (Activities, page 86).

- This game is for two players: Play with two sets of colored counters. Players take turns to read a word and put a counter on it.
- The winner is the first to get four of their counters in a row in any direction.
- The winner places a counter on a picture of Moon.
- The game is played four times until all pictures of Moon boxes are covered.
- Encourage students to say the words aloud as they land on them. For those needing more support, help them to blend the word with assistance.
- Provide positive feedback and encouragement throughout the game.

ow, ou

STEP 1
Preparation

20 mins

Learning goal (2 mins)

- Explain that in English there is more than one way to spell the sound /ow/. In this lesson we will learn two ways to spell the sound /ow/: 'ow' and 'ou.'
- Introduce the book Moon Dogs Vowel Spellings Book 6: Mouse in the House.
- Inform students they will also be completing some activities from Moon Dogs Vowel Spellings Activities.

Preparation (18 mins)

- Introduce the new focus spellings 'ow' and 'ou' for the sound /ow/.
- Model the sound correctly and ask pupils to copy.
- Have students watch you as they pronounce /ow/.
- Read these lists of words: "now," "out," "how," and "our."

1 Word building and blending

- Use the same word building procedure as in previous chapters.
- For example, first build words with the grapheme 'ow.' If the student can learn another spelling alternative, introduce 'ou' and build word with this grapheme.
- Place the words in two columns and ask the student to read the words in one column and then the next.
- For word-building instructions see page 89 of the Activities book.

LESSON RESOURCES

2 Word reading

- Write the words you have created on the whiteboard. Then ask students to blend and read the words.
- Show how to say each sound individually and then blend them together to read the word. Model blending by pointing using a swishing motion with your finger.

3 Oral segmenting

- Say a word aloud (e.g. "round") and count the sounds in the word (4). Write the number of lines you need for all the sounds. Now ask students to listen to the sounds in the word and write a letter for every sound in the word as you spell the word.

Extension activities

- If the student is learning one spelling at a time, use decodable passages in the Activities book on pages 91 (**Story with 'ow' words**) and 93 (**Story with 'ou' words**).

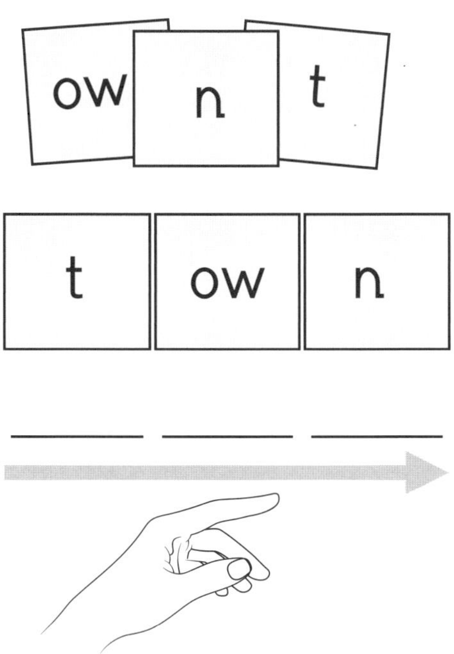

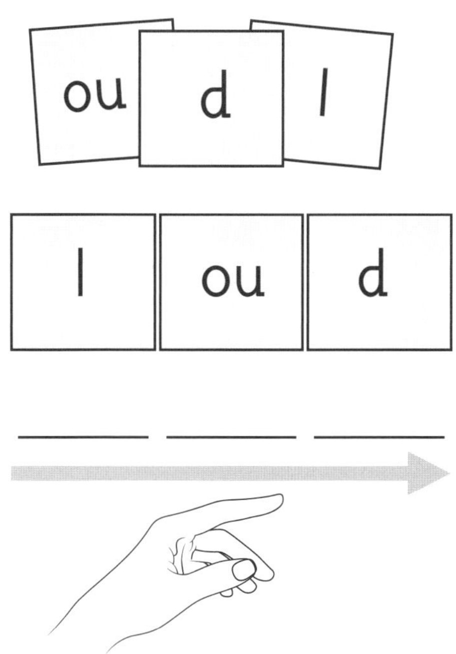

STEP 2
Application for reading
25 mins

Before reading (3 mins)

- Revisit the vocabulary taught in Step 1 (e.g. "round"). Clearly say the word: /r/ /ow/ /n/ /d/.
- Then provide a simple definition, for example, "Round means shaped like a circle or a ball."
- Ask questions such as "Can you name some sports that use a round ball?"
- Then write the word on the whiteboard and refer back to it throughout the week for reinforcement.

Vocabulary (2 mins)

- Pre-teach the words in the **Vocabulary** list in Book 6: Mouse in the House (page iv).
- Ensure students understand each word's pronunciation, meaning, and usage.

Application (10 mins)

- The chosen text for this reading activity is Book 6: Mouse in the House. Briefly introduce the book to spark interest.
- Lead students through a directed reading of Book 6: Mouse in the House. Encourage students to sound out each word carefully and then blend the sounds together to form the word.
- Provide support by modeling the blending.
- Encourage students to sound out each word and then blend to read.

Reading fluency (10 mins)

- Following the initial reading, revisit Book 6: Mouse in the House with a focus on fluency.
- Reading the book again allows students to practice their newly acquired skills, this time with an emphasis on reading more smoothly and confidently.
- Create an interactive reading environment by inviting students to take turns reading aloud. Encourage them to point to each word as they read.
- As students read more fluently, support them to read with more expression and prosody, changing their pitch, pace, and emphasis according to the words and punctuation.

STEP 3
Application for spelling
20 mins

Word sorting and spelling (10 mins)

- Word sorting is a useful activity to consolidate alternative spellings.
- Assign students the **Reading and spelling** activity (Activities, page 95).
- In this activity, students are provided with a list of words they need to sort according to the spellings 'ow' and 'ou.'
- Students read through the list of words and then write them in the correct column.
- Additionally, the **Spelling by sound** sheet (Activities, page 94) can be used for additional sorting activities, or it can be retained by the students for use as a dictionary of spellings by sound.

Sentence dictation (10 mins)

- Ask students to complete the **Dictation** activity (Activities, page 100).
- Use the text at the bottom of the activity for dictation: "'A monster!' shouts Tam loudly," "'How can we get it out?' thinks Sim with a frown," and "Wow! You have got a loud mouth, Tam!"
- Ask students to write the spelling of each sound on the provided write-on lines.
- Remind the students that some sounds can be spelled by more than one letter.
- A longer line indicates the spelling has more than one letter.

Extension activities

- For students who finish early or need additional practice, create additional activity sheets with your own passages of text and dictate these new passages to them.

STEP 4
Comprehension and consolidation
15 mins

Book reading (5 mins)

- Reread Book 6: Mouse in the House.
- Revisiting the book helps to reinforce familiarity with the text and supports phonetic recognition and comprehension.

Comprehension (5 mins)

- To check students' understanding of the story, conduct a group discussion.
- Ask the six comprehension questions at the back of the story: "Where does the mouse hide?", "How does Tam try to tempt the mouse out?", "'Sim prowls around.' What does the word 'prowl' mean?", "How does Tam get the mouse out the house?", and "How would you get a mouse out of your house?"
- Divide the class into small groups and ask each group to answer a question in turn.
- Encourage groups to explain their reasoning.
- Conclude with a brief discussion summarizing the key points of the story and reinforcing vocabulary.

Sequencing (5 mins)

- For this activity, the students will retell the story in a small group.
- Divide students into pairs or small groups.
- Provide each group with a set of blank cards and pens.
- Ask each group to recall key events from the story or illustrate them on the cards.
- Once the cards are created, students will work together to arrange them in the correct sequence.
- Invite each group to retell the story using their arranged cards, encouraging them to use their own words to narrate the story.

Extension activities

These comprehension activities in the Activities book can be used for extended learning:

- **Is it true?** (Activities, page 96). Students check the sentences for accuracy.
- **Developing vocabulary** (page 99). Students begin by circling the word or phrase that can be replaced by the word "dashes" in a provided passage. They then write two sentences of their own using the word "dashes." Remind students to begin each sentence with a capital letter and finish it with a period.

STEP 5
Tracking progress

- Assign the **Spelling assessment** (Activities, page 101) to quickly evaluate each student's progress.
- The teacher can use words from the second list of words provided for students who are ready for that stage.
- When dictating a word, first say it on its own.
- Next, say a sentence with the word in it (to put the word in a context of a sentence) and then repeat the word.
- This ensures students have heard the word correctly.
- For example: "Mouse. A mouse ran out. Mouse."
- Ask students to complete the **Timed word reading** (Activities, page 98) to assess their reading speed.
- Ask students to read the words as fast as they can and record the time in each box.
- Depending on the class's performance, revisit specific activities to address skill gaps or encourage students to play one of the games below.

Extension activities

1 Phonic patterns: Color the real words (Activities, page 97).

- Fold the sheet on the dotted line. Then distribute the activity sheet to each student.
- Read out the words in each column.
- Students listen to the sounds in each word. They then color in the boxes that contain real words with 'ou' spellings.
- Students can unfold the sheet to check that their answers.

2 4-in-a-row game (Activities, page 102).

- This game is for two players: Play with two sets of colored counters. Players take turns to read a word and put a counter on it.
- The winner is the first to get four of their counters in a row in any direction.
- The winner places a counter on picture of Moon.
- The game is played four times until all pictures of Moon are covered.
- Encourage students to say the words aloud as they land on them. For those needing more support, help them to blend the word with assistance.
- Provide positive feedback and encouragement throughout the game.

oo, ue

STEP 1
Preparation

20 mins

LESSON RESOURCES

Learning goal (2 mins)

- Explain that in English there is more than one way to spell the sound /oo/ (as in "moon"). In this lesson we will learn two ways to spell the sound /oo/: 'oo' and 'ue.'
- Introduce the book Moon Dogs Vowel Spellings Book 7: A Gloomy Room.
- Inform students they will also be completing some activities from Moon Dogs Vowel Spellings Activities.

Preparation (18 mins)

- Introduce the new focus spellings 'oo' and 'ue' for the sound /oo/.
- Model the sound correctly and ask pupils to copy.
- Have students watch you as they pronounce /oo/.
- Read these lists of words: "too," "blue," "food," and "true."

1 Word building and blending

- Use the same word building procedure as in previous chapters.
- For example, first build words with the grapheme 'oo.' If the student can learn another spelling alternative, introduce 'ue' and build word with this grapheme.
- Place the words in two columns and ask the student to read the words in one column and then the next.
- For word-building instructions see page 105 of the Activities book.

2 Word reading

- Write the words you have created on the whiteboard. Then ask students to blend and read the words.
- Show how to say each sound individually and then blend them together to read the word. Model blending by pointing using a swishing motion with your finger.

3 Oral segmenting

- Say a word aloud (e.g. "moon") and count the sounds in the word (3). Write the number of lines you need for all the sounds. Now ask students to listen to the sounds in the word and write a letter for every sound in the word as you spell the word.

Extension activities

- If the student is learning one spelling at a time, use decodable passages in the Activities book on pages 107 (**Story with 'oo' words**) and 108 (**Story with 'ue' words**).

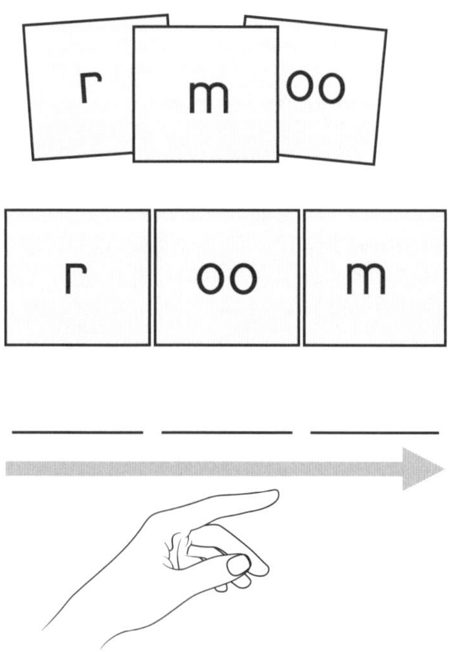

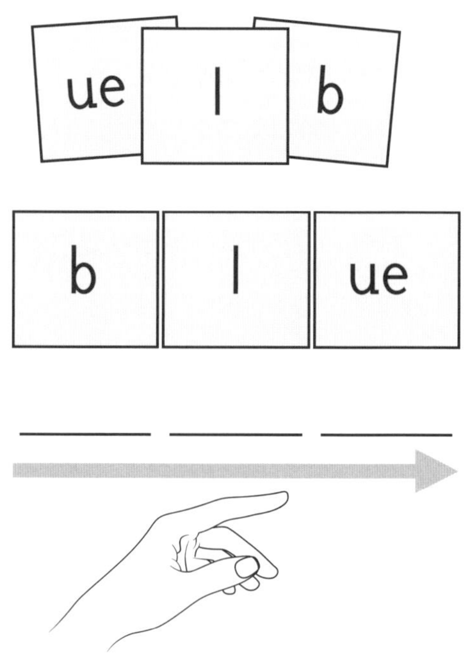

STEP 2
Application for reading

25 mins

Before reading (3 mins)

- Revisit the vocabulary taught in Step 1 (e.g. "moon"). Clearly say the word: /m/ /oo/ /n/.
- Then provide a simple definition, for example, "A moon is a large round object that orbits a planet."
- Ask questions such as "Can you name some different phases of the Earth's moon?" and "Can you name some other planets that have moons?"
- Then write the word on the whiteboard and refer back to it throughout the week for reinforcement.

Vocabulary (2 mins)

- Pre-teach the words in the **Vocabulary** list in Book 7: A Gloomy Room (page iv).
- Ensure students understand each word's pronunciation, meaning, and usage.

Application (10 mins)

- The chosen text for this reading activity is Book 7: A Gloomy Room. Briefly introduce the book to spark interest.
- Lead students through a directed reading of Book 7: A Gloomy Room. Encourage students to sound out each word carefully and then blend the sounds together to form the word.
- Provide support by modeling the blending.
- Encourage students to sound out each word and then blend to read.

Reading fluency (10 mins)

- Following the initial reading, revisit Book 7: A Gloomy Room with a focus on fluency.
- Reading the book again allows students to practice their newly acquired skills, this time with an emphasis on reading more smoothly and confidently.
- Create an interactive reading environment by inviting students to take turns reading aloud. Encourage them to point to each word as they read.
- As students read more fluently, support them to read with more expression and prosody, changing their pitch, pace, and emphasis according to the words and punctuation.

STEP 3
Application for spelling

20 mins

Word sorting and spelling (10 mins)

- Word sorting is a useful activity to consolidate alternative spellings.
- Assign students the **Reading and spelling** activity (Activities, page 111).
- In this activity, students are provided with a list of words they need to sort according to the spellings 'oo' and 'ue.'
- Students read through the list of words and then write them in the correct column.
- Additionally, the **Spelling by sound** sheet (Activities, page 110) can be used for additional sorting activities, or it can be retained by the students for use as a dictionary of spellings by sound.

Sentence dictation (10 mins)

- Ask students to complete the **Dictation** activity (Activities, page 116).
- Use the text at the bottom of the activity for dictation: "Liz gets a broom to sweep up the mess," "'The broom is not the best tool for the job!' she grumbles," and "Liz sweeps an old blue rug."
- Ask students to write the spelling of each sound on the provided write-on lines.
- Remind the students that some sounds can be spelled by more than one letter.
- A longer line indicates the spelling has more than one letter.

Extension activities

- For students who finish early or need additional practice, create additional activity sheets with your own passages of text and dictate these new passages to them.

STEP 4
Comprehension and consolidation

15 mins

Book reading (5 mins)

- Reread Book 7: A Gloomy Room.
- Revisiting the book helps to reinforce familiarity with the text and supports phonetic recognition and comprehension.

Comprehension (5 mins)

- To check students' understanding of the story, conduct a group discussion.
- Ask the five comprehension questions at the back of the story ("The room for the gig is gloomy. How does the band feel about that?", "How does Sim catch the beetle?", "Why is Liz in a bad mood?", "What does the band need to clean up the room?", and "How does the school cook thank the band?")
- Divide the class into small groups and ask each group to answer a question in turn.
- Encourage groups to explain their reasoning.
- Conclude with a brief discussion summarizing the key points of the story and reinforcing vocabulary.

Sequencing (5 mins)

- For this activity, the students will retell the story in a small group.
- Divide students into pairs or small groups.
- Provide each group with a set of blank cards and pens.
- Ask each group to recall key events from the story or illustrate them on the cards.
- Once the cards are created, students will work together to arrange them in the correct sequence.
- Invite each group to retell the story using their arranged cards, encouraging them to use their own words to narrate the story.

Extension activities

These comprehension activities in the Activities book that can be used for extended learning:

- **Is it true?** (Activities, page 112). Students check the sentences for accuracy.
- **Developing vocabulary** (page 115). Students begin by circling the word or phrase that can be replaced by the word "grumbles" in a provided passage. They then write two sentences of their own using the word "grumbles." Remind students to begin each sentence with a capital letter and finish it with a period.

STEP 5
Tracking progress

- Assign the **Spelling assessment** (Activities, page 117) to quickly evaluate each student's progress.
- The teacher can use words from the second list of words provided for students who are ready for that stage.
- When dictating a word, first say it on its own.
- Next, say a sentence with the word in it (to put the word in a context of a sentence) and then repeat the word.
- This ensures students have heard the word correctly.
- For example: "Food. There was plenty of food for lunch. Food."
- Ask students to complete the **Timed word reading** (Activities, page 114) to assess their reading speed.
- Ask students to read the words as fast as they can and record the time in each box.
- Depending on the class's performance, revisit specific activities to address skill gaps or encourage students to play one of the games below.

Extension activities

1 Phonic patterns: Color the real words (Activities, page 113).

- Fold the sheet on the dotted line. Then distribute the activity sheet to each student.
- Read out the words in each column.
- Students listen to the sounds in each word. They then color in the boxes that contain real words with 'oo' spellings.
- Students can unfold the sheet to check that their answers.

2 4-in-a-row game (Activities, page 118).

- This game is for two players: Play with two sets of colored counters. Players take turns to read a word and put a counter on it.
- The winner is the first to get four of their counters in a row in any direction.
- The winner places a counter on a picture of Moon.
- The game is played four times until all pictures of Moon boxes are covered.
- Encourage students to say the words aloud as they land on them. For those needing more support, help them to blend the word with assistance.
- Provide positive feedback and encouragement throughout the game.

LESSON PLANS: Moon Dogs Vowel Spellings

igh, i

STEP 1
Preparation

20 mins

LESSON RESOURCES

Learning goal (2 mins)

- Explain that in English there is more than one way to spell the sound /ie/. In this lesson we will learn two ways to spell the sound /ie/: 'igh' and 'i.'
- Introduce the book Moon Dogs Vowel Spellings Book 8: A Wild Night.
- Inform students they will also be completing some activities from Moon Dogs Vowel Spellings Activities.

Preparation (18 mins)

- Introduce the new focus spellings 'igh' and 'i' for the sound /ie/.
- Model the sound correctly and ask pupils to copy.
- Have students watch you as they pronounce /ie/.
- Read these lists of words: "high," "find," "light," and "wild."

1 Word building and blending

- Use the same word building procedure as in previous chapters.
- For example, first build words with the grapheme 'igh.' If the student can learn another spelling alternative, introduce 'i' and build word with this grapheme.
- Place the words in two columns and ask the student to read the words in one column and then the next.
- For word-building instructions see page 121 of the Activities book.

2 Word reading

- Write the words you have created on the whiteboard. Then ask students to blend and read the words.
- Show how to say each sound individually and then blend them together to read the word. Model blending by pointing using a swishing motion with your finger.

3 Oral segmenting

- Say a word aloud (e.g. "wild") and count the sounds in the word (4). Write the number of lines you need for all the sounds. Now ask students to listen to the sounds in the word and write a letter for every sound in the word as you spell the word.

Extension activities

- If the student is learning one spelling at a time, use decodable passages in the Activities book on pages 123 (**Story with 'igh' words**) and 125 (**Story with 'i' words**).

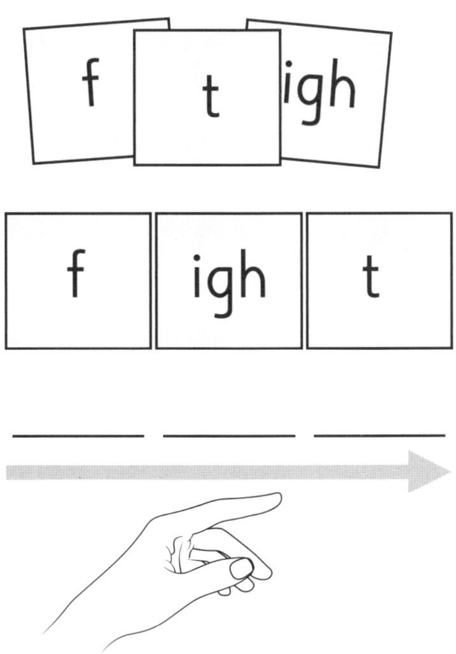

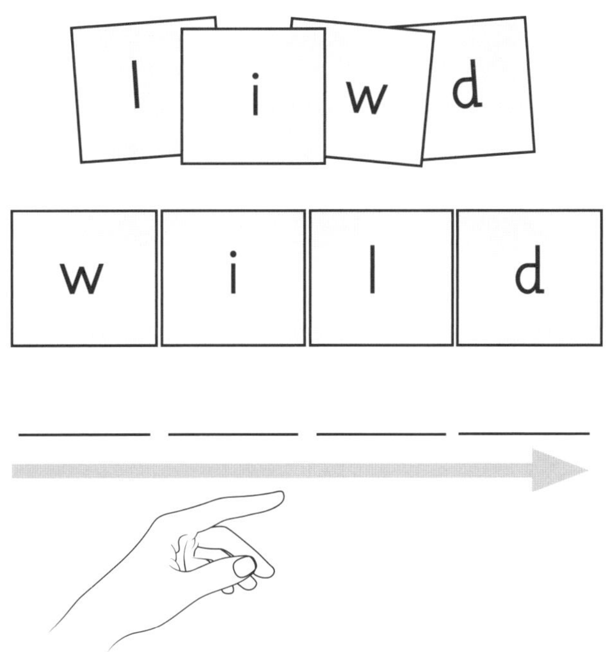

STEP 2
Application for reading
25 mins

Before reading (3 mins)

- Revisit the vocabulary taught in Step 1 (e.g. "wild"). Clearly say the word: /w/ /ie/ /l/ /d/.
- Then provide a simple definition, for example, "Wild means living or growing in the natural world."
- Ask questions such as "Where might you find wild animals?"
- Then write the word on the whiteboard and refer back to it throughout the week for reinforcement.

Vocabulary (2 mins)

- Pre-teach the words in the **Vocabulary** list in Book 8: A Wild Night (page iv).
- Ensure students understand each word's pronunciation, meaning, and usage.

Application (10 mins)

- The chosen text for this reading activity is Book 8: A Wild Night. Briefly introduce the book to spark interest.
- Lead students through a directed reading of Book 8: A Wild Night. Encourage students to sound out each word carefully and then blend the sounds together to form the word.
- Provide support by modeling the blending.
- Encourage students to sound out each word and then blend to read.

Reading fluency (10 mins)

- Following the initial reading, revisit Book 8: A Wild Night with a focus on fluency.
- Reading the book again allows students to practice their newly acquired skills, this time with an emphasis on reading more smoothly and confidently.
- Create an interactive reading environment by inviting students to take turns reading aloud. Encourage them to point to each word as they read.
- As students read more fluently, support them to read with more expression and prosody, changing their pitch, pace, and emphasis according to the words and punctuation.

STEP 3
Application for spelling
20 mins

Word sorting and spelling (10 mins)

- Word sorting is a useful activity to consolidate alternative spellings.
- Assign students the **Reading and spelling** activity (Activities, page 127).
- In this activity, students are provided with a list of words they need to sort according to the spellings 'igh' and 'i.'
- Students read through the list of words and then write them in the correct column.
- Additionally, the **Spelling by sound** sheet (Activities, page 126) can be used for additional sorting activities, or it can be retained by the students for use as a dictionary of spellings by sound.

Sentence dictation (10 mins)

- Ask students to complete the **Dictation** activity (Activities, page 132).
- Use the text at the bottom of the activity for dictation: "'It might be a lost child,' says Dan kindly," "Dan aims a bright light behind them," and "Dan finds a cat high up in a tree."
- Ask students to write the spelling of each sound on the provided write-on lines.
- Remind the students that some sounds can be spelled by more than one letter.
- A longer line indicates the spelling has more than one letter.

Extension activities

- For students who finish early or need additional practice, create additional activity sheets with your own passages of text and dictate these new passages to them.

STEP 4
Comprehension and consolidation

15 mins

Book reading (5 mins)

- Reread Book 8: A Wild Night.
- Revisiting the book helps to reinforce familiarity with the text and supports phonetic recognition and comprehension.

Comprehension (5 mins)

- To check students' understanding of the story, conduct a group discussion.
- Ask the five comprehension questions at the back of the story ("Why is Jed cold?", "What gives Jed and Dan a fright?", "What do Jed and Dan think the sound is?", "How did Jed and Dan rescue the cat?", and "What happens when the cat gets down from the tree?")
- Divide the class into small groups and ask each group to answer a question in turn.
- Encourage groups to explain their reasoning.
- Conclude with a brief discussion summarizing the key points of the story and reinforcing vocabulary.

Sequencing (5 mins)

- For this activity, the students will retell the story in a small group.
- Divide students into pairs or small groups.
- Provide each group with a set of blank cards and pens.
- Ask each group to recall key events from the story or illustrate them on the cards.
- Once the cards are created, students will work together to arrange them in the correct sequence.
- Invite each group to retell the story using their arranged cards, encouraging them to use their own words to narrate the story.

Extension activities

These comprehension activities in the Activities book can be used for extended learning:

- **Is it true?** (Activities, page 128). Students check the sentences for accuracy.
- **Developing vocabulary** (page 131). Students begin by circling the word or phrase that can be replaced by the word "sighs" in a provided passage. They then write two sentences of their own using the word "sighs." Remind students to begin each sentence with a capital letter and finish it with a period.

STEP 5
Tracking progress

- Assign the **Spelling assessment** (Activities, page 133) to quickly evaluate each student's progress.
- The teacher can use words from the second list of words provided for students who are ready for that stage.
- When dictating a word, first say it on its own.
- Next, say a sentence with the word in it (to put the word in a context of a sentence) and then repeat the word.
- This ensures students have heard the word correctly.
- For example: "Tight. The jumper was a tight fit. Tight."
- Ask students to complete the **Timed word reading** (Activities, page 130) to assess their reading speed.
- Ask students to read the words as fast as they can and record the time in each box.
- Depending on the class's performance, revisit specific activities to address skill gaps or encourage students to play one of the games below.

Extension activities

1 Phonic patterns: Color the real words (Activities, page 129).

- Fold the sheet on the dotted line. Then distribute the activity sheet to each student.
- Read out the words in each column.
- Students listen to the sounds in each word. They then color in the boxes that contain real words with 'igh' spellings.
- Students can unfold the sheet to check that their answers.

2 4-in-a-row game (Activities, page 134).

- This game is for two players: Play with two sets of colored counters. Players take turns to read a word and put a counter on it.
- The winner is the first to get four of their counters in a row in any direction.
- The winner places a counter on picture of Moon.
- The game is played four times until all pictures of Moon are covered.
- Encourage students to say the words aloud as they land on them. For those needing more support, help them to blend the word with assistance.
- Provide positive feedback and encouragement throughout the game.

oo, oul

STEP 1
Preparation

20 mins

Learning goal (2 mins)

- Explain that in English there is more than one way to spell the sound /oo/ (as in "look"). In this lesson we will learn two ways to spell the sound /oo/: 'oo' and 'oul.'
- Introduce the book Moon Dogs Vowel Spellings Book 9: A Jog in the Woods.
- Inform students they will also be completing some activities from Moon Dogs Vowel Spellings Activities.

Preparation (18 mins)

- Introduce the new focus spellings 'oo' and 'oul' for the sound /oo/.
- Model the sound correctly and ask pupils to copy.
- Have students watch you as they pronounce /oo/.
- Read these lists of words: "look," "could," "would," and "hood."

1 Word building and blending

- Use the same word building procedure as in previous chapters.
- For example, first build words with the grapheme 'oo.' If the student can learn another spelling alternative, introduce 'oul' and build word with this grapheme.
- Place the words in two columns and ask the student to read the words in one column and then the next.
- For word-building instructions see page 137 of the Activities book.

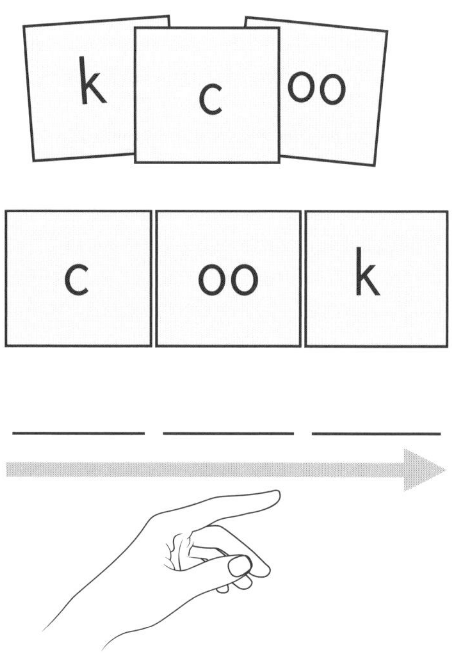

LESSON RESOURCES

2 Word reading

- Write the words you have created on the whiteboard. Then ask students to blend and read the words.
- Show how to say each sound individually and then blend them together to read the word. Model blending by pointing using a swishing motion with your finger.

3 Oral segmenting

- Say a word aloud (e.g. "wood") and count the sounds in the word (3). Write the number of lines you need for all the sounds. Now ask students to listen to the sounds in the word and write a letter for every sound in the word as you spell the word.

Extension activities

- If the student is learning one spelling at a time, use decodable passages in the Activities book on pages 139 (**Story with 'oo' words**) and 141 (**Story with 'oul' words**).

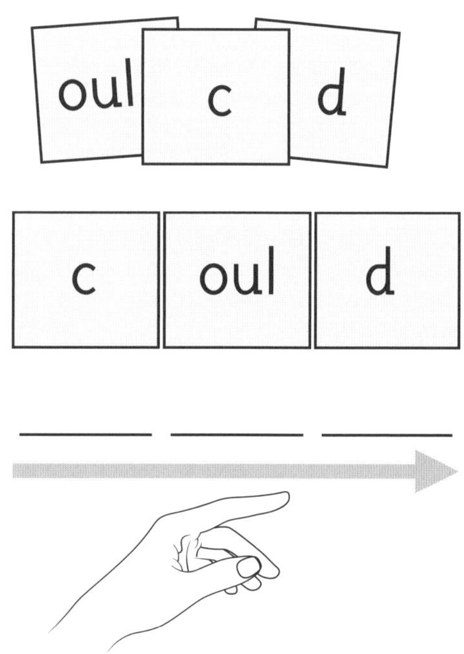

STEP 2
Application for reading

25 mins

Before reading (3 mins)

- Revisit the vocabulary taught in Step 1 (e.g. "wood"). Clearly say the word: /w/ /oo/ /d/.
- Then provide a simple definition, for example, "Wood is the hard material that comes from trees and is used for building and making furniture."
- Ask questions such as "What can we make from wood?" and "Where do we get wood from?"
- Then write the word on the whiteboard and refer back to it throughout the week for reinforcement.

Vocabulary (2 mins)

- Pre-teach the words in the **Vocabulary** list in Book 9: A Jog in the Woods (page iv).
- Ensure students understand each word's pronunciation, meaning, and usage.

Application (10 mins)

- The chosen text for this reading activity is Book 9: A Jog in the Woods. Briefly introduce the book to spark interest.
- Lead students through a directed reading of Book 9: A Jog in the Woods. Encourage students to sound out each word carefully and then blend the sounds together to form the word.
- Provide support by modeling the blending.
- Encourage students to sound out each word and then blend to read.

Reading fluency (10 mins)

- Following the initial reading, revisit Book 9: A Jog in the Woods with a focus on fluency.
- Reading the book again allows students to practice their newly acquired skills, this time with an emphasis on reading more smoothly and confidently.
- Create an interactive reading environment by inviting students to take turns reading aloud. Encourage them to point to each word as they read.
- As students read more fluently, support them to read with more expression and prosody, changing their pitch, pace, and emphasis according to the words and punctuation.

STEP 3
Application for spelling

20 mins

Word sorting and spelling (10 mins)

- Word sorting is a useful activity to consolidate alternative spellings.
- Assign students the **Reading and spelling** activity (Activities, page 143).
- In this activity, students are provided with a list of words they need to sort according to the spellings 'oo' and 'oul.'
- Students read through the list of words and then write them in the correct column.
- Additionally, the **Spelling by sound** sheet (Activities, page 142) can be used for additional sorting activities, or it can be retained by the students for use as a dictionary of spellings by sound.

Sentence dictation (10 mins)

- Ask students to complete the **Dictation** activity (Activities, page 148).
- Use the text at the bottom of the activity for dictation: "'This should keep us fit!' panted Tam," "Tam took the can out and shook it," and "'Good dog! I should bring a leash when we jog again.'"
- Ask students to write the spelling of each sound on the provided write-on lines.
- Remind the students that some sounds can be spelled by more than one letter.
- A longer line indicates the spelling has more than one letter.

Extension activities

- For students who finish early or need additional practice, create additional activity sheets with your own passages of text and dictate these new passages to them.

STEP 4
Comprehension and consolidation
15 mins

Book reading (5 mins)

- Reread Book 9: A Jog in the Woods.
- Revisiting the book helps to reinforce familiarity with the text and supports phonetic recognition and comprehension.

Comprehension (5 mins)

- To check students' understanding of the story, conduct a group discussion.
- Ask the six comprehension questions at the back of the story. For example: "Why was Tam jogging in the woods?" and "What did Moon spot in the woods?"
- Divide the class into small groups and ask each group to answer a question in turn.
- Encourage groups to explain their reasoning.
- Conclude with a brief discussion summarizing the key points of the story and reinforcing vocabulary.

Sequencing (5 mins)

- For this activity, the students will retell the story in a small group.
- Divide students into pairs or small groups.
- Provide each group with a set of blank cards and pens.
- Ask each group to recall key events from the story or illustrate them on the cards.
- Once the cards are created, students will work together to arrange them in the correct sequence.
- Invite each group to retell the story using their arranged cards, encouraging them to use their own words to narrate the story.

Extension activities

These comprehension activities in the Activities book that can be used for extended learning:

- **Is it true?** (Activities, page 144). Students check the sentences for accuracy.
- **Developing vocabulary** (page 147). Students begin by circling the word or phrase that can be replaced by the word "keen" in a provided passage. They then write two sentences of their own using the word "keen." Remind students to begin each sentence with a capital letter and finish it with a period.

STEP 5
Tracking progress

- Assign the **Spelling assessment** (Activities, page 149) to quickly evaluate each student's progress.
- The teacher can use words from the second list of words provided for students who are ready for that stage.
- When dictating a word, first say it on its own.
- Next, say a sentence with the word in it (to put the word in a context of a sentence) and then repeat the word.
- This ensures students have heard the word correctly.
- For example: "Wood. The dog ran into the wood. Wppd"
- Ask students to complete the **Timed word reading** (Activities, page 146) to assess their reading speed.
- Ask students to read the words as fast as they can and record the time in each box.
- Depending on the class's performance, revisit specific activities to address skill gaps or encourage students to play one of the games below.

Extension activities

1 Phonic patterns: Color the real words (Activities, page 145).

- Fold the sheet on the dotted line. Then distribute the activity sheet to each student.
- Read out the words in each column.
- Students listen to the sounds in each word. They then color in the boxes that contain real words with 'oo' spellings.
- Students can unfold the sheet to check that their answers.

2 4-in-a-row game (Activities, page 150).

- This game is for two players: Play with two sets of colored counters. Players take turns to read a word and put a counter on it.
- The winner is the first to get four of their counters in a row in any direction.
- The winner places a counter on a picture of Moon.
- The game is played four times until all pictures of Moon boxes are covered.
- Encourage students to say the words aloud as they land on them. For those needing more support, help them to blend the word with assistance.
- Provide positive feedback and encouragement throughout the game.

a, aw

STEP 1
Preparation

20 mins

LESSON RESOURCES

Learning goal (2 mins)

- Explain that in English there is more than one way to spell the sound /aw/. In this lesson we will learn two ways to spell the sound /aw/: 'a' and 'aw.'
- Introduce the book Moon Dogs Vowel Spellings Book 10: An Awful Day.
- Inform students they will also be completing some activities from Moon Dogs Vowel Spellings Activities.

Preparation (18 mins)

- Introduce the new focus spellings 'a' and 'aw' for the sound /aw/.
- Model the sound correctly and ask pupils to copy.
- Have students watch you as they pronounce /aw/.
- Read these lists of words: "all," "saw," "ball," and "tall."

1 Word building and blending

- Use the same word building procedure as in previous chapters.
- For example, first build words with the grapheme 'a.' If the student can learn another spelling alternative, introduce 'aw' and build word with this grapheme.
- Place the words in two columns and ask the student to read the words in one column and then the next.
- For word-building instructions see page 153 of the Activities book.

2 Word reading

- Write the words you have created on the whiteboard. Then ask students to blend and read the words.
- Show how to say each sound individually and then blend them together to read the word. Model blending by pointing using a swishing motion with your finger.

3 Oral segmenting

- Say a word aloud (e.g. "straw") and count the sounds in the word (4). Write the number of lines you need for all the sounds. Now ask students to listen to the sounds in the word and write a letter for every sound in the word as you spell the word.

Extension activities

- If the student is learning one spelling at a time, use decodable passages in the Activities book on pages 155 (**Story with 'a' words**) and 157 (**Story with 'aw' words**).

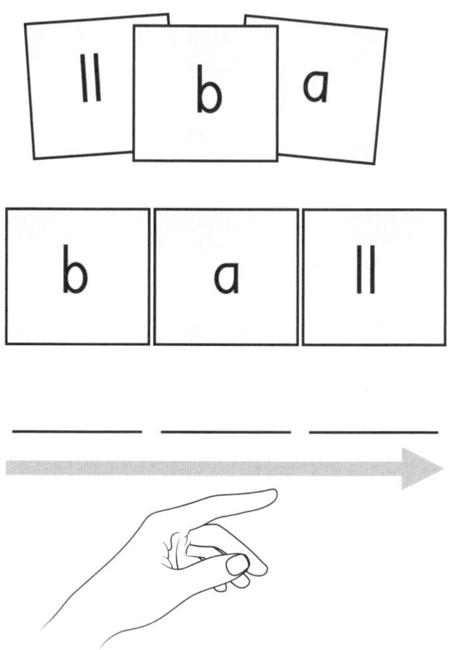

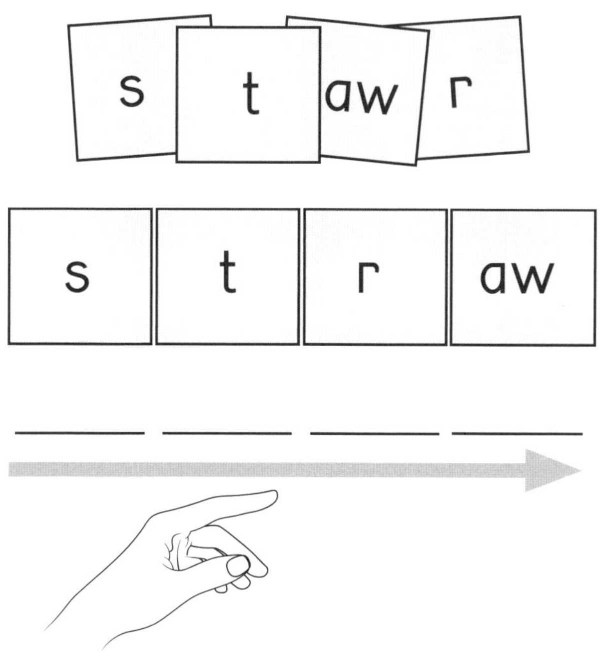

STEP 2
Application for reading
25 mins

Before reading (3 mins)

- Revisit the vocabulary taught in Step 1 (e.g. "straw"). Clearly say the word: /s/ /t/ /r/ /aw/.
- Explore different meanings of the word "straw," such as a thin dry material made from plants, or a thin tube used to drink fluids.
- Ask questions such as "What can we make with straw?"
- Then write the word on the whiteboard and refer back to it throughout the week for reinforcement.

Vocabulary (2 mins)

- Pre-teach the words in the **Vocabulary** list in Book 10: An Awful Day (page iv).
- Ensure students understand each word's pronunciation, meaning, and usage.

Application (10 mins)

- The chosen text for this reading activity is Book 10: An Awful Day. Briefly introduce the book to spark interest.
- Lead students through a directed reading of Book 10: An Awful Day. Encourage students to sound out each word carefully and then blend the sounds together to form the word.
- Provide support by modeling the blending.
- Encourage students to sound out each word and then blend to read.

Reading fluency (10 mins)

- Following the initial reading, revisit Book 10: An Awful Day with a focus on fluency.
- Reading the book again allows students to practice their newly acquired skills, this time with an emphasis on reading more smoothly and confidently.
- Create an interactive reading environment by inviting students to take turns reading aloud. Encourage them to point to each word as they read.
- As students read more fluently, support them to read with more expression and prosody, changing their pitch, pace, and emphasis according to the words and punctuation.

STEP 3
Application for spelling
20 mins

Word sorting and spelling (10 mins)

- Word sorting is a useful activity to consolidate alternative spellings.
- Assign students the **Reading and spelling** activity (Activities, page 159).
- In this activity, students are provided with a list of words they need to sort according to the spellings 'a' and 'aw.'
- Students read through the list of words and then write them in the correct column.
- Additionally, the **Spelling by sound** sheet (Activities, page 158) can be used for additional sorting activities, or it can be retained by the students for use as a dictionary of spellings by sound.

Sentence dictation (10 mins)

- Ask students to complete the **Dictation** activity (Activities, page 164).
- Use the text at the bottom of the activity for dictation: "'Awful!' says Jed. 'His legs are too small'," "'He is just jaws and claws!' moans Jed," and "There is a short rainfall. They wait in the hall."
- Ask students to write the spelling of each sound on the provided write-on lines.
- Remind the students that some sounds can be spelled by more than one letter.
- A longer line indicates the spelling has more than one letter.

Extension activities

- For students who finish early or need additional practice, create additional activity sheets with your own passages of text and dictate these new passages to them.

STEP 4
Comprehension and consolidation
15 mins

Book reading (5 mins)
- Reread Book 10: An Awful Day.
- Revisiting the book helps to reinforce familiarity with the text and supports phonetic recognition and comprehension.

Comprehension (5 mins)
- To check students' understanding of the story, conduct a group discussion.
- Ask the five comprehension questions at the back of the story ("Where are Jed and Liz visiting?", "What does Jed say about the pictures?", "What did Jed really want for his lunch?", "Jed says, 'That's the best thing we have seen today!' What was it?", and "Do you like visiting art galleries?")
- Divide the class into small groups and ask each group to answer a question in turn.
- Encourage groups to explain their reasoning.
- Conclude with a brief discussion summarizing the key points of the story and reinforcing vocabulary.

Sequencing (5 mins)
- For this activity, the students will retell the story in a small group.
- Divide students into pairs or small groups.
- Provide each group with a set of blank cards and pens.
- Ask each group to recall key events from the story or illustrate them on the cards.
- Once the cards are created, students will work together to arrange them in the correct sequence.
- Invite each group to retell the story using their arranged cards, encouraging them to use their own words to narrate the story.

Extension activities

These comprehension activities in the Activities book can be used for extended learning:
- **Is it true?** (Activities, page 160). Students check the sentences for accuracy.
- **Developing vocabulary** (page 163). Students begin by circling the word or phrase that can be replaced by the word "jabs" in a provided passage. They then write two sentences of their own using the word "jabs." Remind students to begin each sentence with a capital letter and finish it with a period.

STEP 5
Tracking progress

- Assign the **Spelling assessment** (Activities, page 165) to quickly evaluate each student's progress.
- The teacher can use words from the second list of words provided for students who are ready for that stage.
- When dictating a word, first say it on its own.
- Next, say a sentence with the word in it (to put the word in a context of a sentence) and then repeat the word.
- This ensures students have heard the word correctly.
- For example: "Lawn. The lawn was wet from the rain. Lawn."
- Ask students to complete the **Timed word reading** (Activities, page 162) to assess their reading speed.
- Ask students to read the words as fast as they can and record the time in each box.
- Depending on the class's performance, revisit specific activities to address skill gaps or encourage students to play one of the games below.

Extension activities

1 Phonic patterns: Color the real words (Activities, page 161).
- Fold the sheet on the dotted line. Then distribute the activity sheet to each student.
- Read out the words in each column.
- Students listen to the sounds in each word. They then color in the boxes that contain real words with 'aw' spellings.
- Students can unfold the sheet to check that their answers.

2 4-in-a-row game (Activities, page 166).
- This game is for two players: Play with two sets of colored counters. Players take turns to read a word and put a counter on it.
- The winner is the first to get four of their counters in a row in any direction.
- The winner places a counter on picture of Moon.
- The game is played four times until all pictures of Moon are covered.
- Encourage students to say the words aloud as they land on them. For those needing more support, help them to blend the word with assistance.
- Provide positive feedback and encouragement throughout the game.

LESSON PLANS: Moon Dogs Vowel Spellings

oy, oi

STEP 1
Preparation

20 mins

LESSON RESOURCES

Learning goal (2 mins)

- Explain that in English there is more than one way to spell the sound /oi/. In this lesson we will learn two ways to spell the sound /oi/: 'oy' and 'oi.'
- Introduce the book Moon Dogs Vowel Spellings Book 11: Out of Oil.
- Inform students they will also be completing some activities from Moon Dogs Vowel Spellings Activities.

Preparation (18 mins)

- Introduce the new focus spellings 'oy' and 'oi' for the sound /oi/.
- Model the sound correctly and ask pupils to copy.
- Have students watch you as they pronounce /oi/.
- Read these lists of words: "boy," "oil," "toy," and "boil."

1 Word building and blending

- Use the same word building procedure as in previous chapters.
- For example, first build words with the grapheme 'oy.' If the student can learn another spelling alternative, introduce 'oi' and build word with this grapheme.
- Place the words in two columns and ask the student to read the words in one column and then the next.
- For word-building instructions see page 169 of the Activities book.

2 Word reading

- Write the words you have created on the whiteboard. Then ask students to blend and read the words.
- Show how to say each sound individually and then blend them together to read the word. Model blending by pointing using a swishing motion with your finger.

3 Oral segmenting

- Say a word aloud (e.g. "coin") and count the sounds in the word (3). Write the number of lines you need for all the sounds. Now ask students to listen to the sounds in the word and write a letter for every sound in the word as you spell the word.

Extension activities

- If the student is learning one spelling at a time, use decodable passages in the Activities book on pages 171 (**Story with 'oy' words**) and 173 (**Story with 'oi' words**).

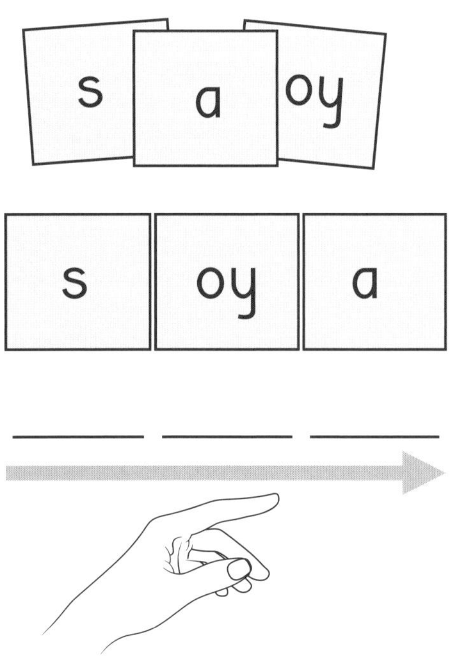

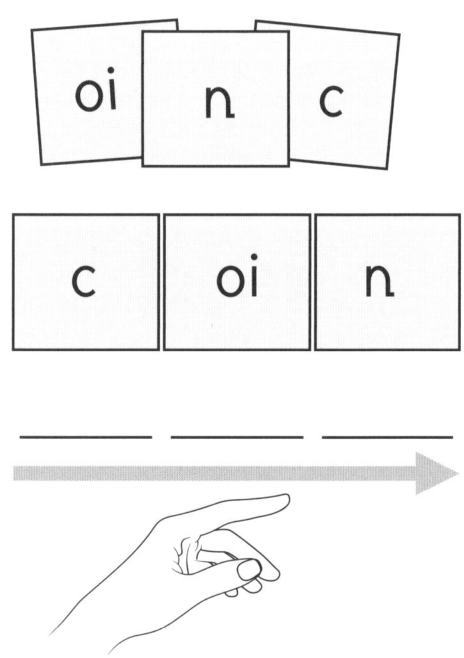

STEP 2
Application for reading
25 mins

Before reading (3 mins)

- Revisit the vocabulary taught in Step 1 (e.g. "coin"). Clearly say the word: /c/ /oi/ /n/.
- Then provide a simple definition, for example, "A coin is a flat piece of metal used as money."
- Ask questions such as "What are some different coins you know?"
- Then write the word on the whiteboard and refer back to it throughout the week for reinforcement.

Vocabulary (2 mins)

- Pre-teach the words in the **Vocabulary** list in Book 11: Out of Oil (page iv).
- Ensure students understand each word's pronunciation, meaning, and usage.

Application (10 mins)

- The chosen text for this reading activity is Book 11: Out of Oil. Briefly introduce the book to spark interest.
- Lead students through a directed reading of Book 11: Out of Oil. Encourage students to sound out each word carefully and then blend the sounds together to form the word.
- Provide support by modeling the blending.
- Encourage students to sound out each word and then blend to read.

Reading fluency (10 mins)

- Following the initial reading, revisit Book 11: Out of Oil with a focus on fluency.
- Reading the book again allows students to practice their newly acquired skills, this time with an emphasis on reading more smoothly and confidently.
- Create an interactive reading environment by inviting students to take turns reading aloud. Encourage them to point to each word as they read.
- As students read more fluently, support them to read with more expression and prosody, changing their pitch, pace, and emphasis according to the words and punctuation.

STEP 3
Application for spelling
20 mins

Word sorting and spelling (10 mins)

- Word sorting is a useful activity to consolidate alternative spellings.
- Assign students the **Reading and spelling** activity (Activities, page 175).
- In this activity, students are provided with a list of words they need to sort according to the spellings 'oy' and 'oi.'
- Students read through the list of words and then write them in the correct column.
- Additionally, the **Spelling by sound** sheet (Activities, page 174) can be used for additional sorting activities, or it can be retained by the students for use as a dictionary of spellings by sound.

Sentence dictation (10 mins)

- Ask students to complete the **Dictation** activity (Activities, page 180).
- Use the text at the bottom of the activity for dictation: "Matt points at a red light. 'We are low on oil!'", "The boys are annoyed. The day is spoiled," and "Grandpa joins his truck to the van."
- Ask students to write the spelling of each sound on the provided write-on lines.
- Remind the students that some sounds can be spelled by more than one letter.
- A longer line indicates the spelling has more than one letter.

Extension activities

- For students who finish early or need additional practice, create additional activity sheets with your own passages of text and dictate these new passages to them.

STEP 4
Comprehension and consolidation
15 mins

Book reading (5 mins)
- Reread Book 11: Out of Oil.
- Revisiting the book helps to reinforce familiarity with the text and supports phonetic recognition and comprehension.

Comprehension (5 mins)
- To check students' understanding of the story, conduct a group discussion.
- Ask the five comprehension questions at the back of the story ("What are Matt and Sim loading in the van?", "Why do they have to stop the van?", "The van is stuck. How do the boys react?", "How does Grandpa help them?", and "How do you think Matt and Sim feel when Grandpa tows them to the gig?")
- Divide the class into small groups and ask each group to answer a question in turn.
- Encourage groups to explain their reasoning.
- Conclude with a brief discussion summarizing the key points of the story and reinforcing vocabulary.

Sequencing (5 mins)
- For this activity, the students will retell the story in a small group.
- Divide students into pairs or small groups.
- Provide each group with a set of blank cards and pens.
- Ask each group to recall key events from the story or illustrate them on the cards.
- Once the cards are created, students will work together to arrange them in the correct sequence.
- Invite each group to retell the story using their arranged cards, encouraging them to use their own words to narrate the story.

Extension activities

These comprehension activities in the Activities book can be used for extended learning:
- **Is it true?** (Activities, page 176). Students check the sentences for accuracy.
- **Developing vocabulary** (page 179). Students begin by circling the word or phrase that can be replaced by the word "load" in a provided passage. They then write two sentences of their own using the word "load." Remind students to begin each sentence with a capital letter and finish it with a period.

STEP 5
Tracking progress

- Assign the **Spelling assessment** (Activities, page 181) to quickly evaluate each student's progress.
- The teacher can use words from the second list of words provided for students who are ready for that stage.
- When dictating a word, first say it on its own.
- Next, say a sentence with the word in it (to put the word in a context of a sentence) and then repeat the word.
- This ensures students have heard the word correctly.
- For example: "Toy. The train set was the best toy he had ever seen. Toy."
- Ask students to complete the **Timed word reading** (Activities, page 178) to assess their reading speed.
- Ask students to read the words as fast as they can and record the time in each box.
- Depending on the class's performance, revisit specific activities to address skill gaps or encourage students to play one of the games below.

Extension activities

1 Phonic patterns: Color the real words (Activities, page 177).
- Fold the sheet on the dotted line. Then distribute the activity sheet to each student.
- Read out the words in each column.
- Students listen to the sounds in each word. They then color in the boxes that contain real words with 'oi' spellings.
- Students can unfold the sheet to check that their answers.

2 4-in-a-row game (Activities, page 182).
- This game is for two players: Play with two sets of colored counters. Players take turns to read a word and put a counter on it.
- The winner is the first to get four of their counters in a row in any direction.
- The winner places a counter on a picture of Moon.
- The game is played four times until all pictures of Moon boxes are covered.
- Encourage students to say the words aloud as they land on them. For those needing more support, help them to blend the word with assistance.
- Provide positive feedback and encouragement throughout the game.

ar

STEP 1
Preparation

20 mins

LESSON RESOURCES

Learning goal (2 mins)

- Explain that in this lesson, students will lbe introduced to the spelling 'ar' for the sound /ar/.
- Introduce the book Moon Dogs Vowel Spellings Book 12: Beach Party.
- Inform students they will also be completing some activities from Moon Dogs Vowel Spellings Activities.

Preparation (18 mins)

- Introduce the new focus spelling 'ar' for the sound /ar/.
- Model the sound correctly and ask pupils to copy.
- Have students watch you as they pronounce /ar/.
- Read these lists of words: "park," "car," "farm," and "party."

1 Word building and blending

- Use the same word building procedure as in previous chapters.
- First, demonstrate by building the word 'farm' with the grapheme 'ar.'
- As you say the word slowly, move your finger under the lines.
- Then sound all three sounds and blend them into a word, moving your finger under the word: /f/ /ar/ /m/ → "farm."
- For word-building instructions see page 185 of the Activities book.

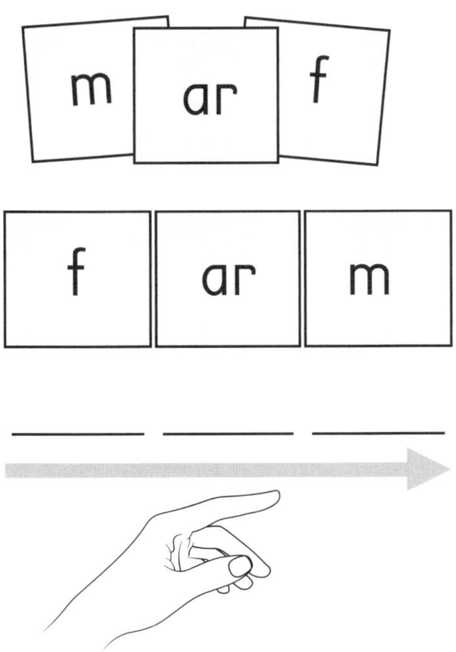

2 Word reading

- Write the words you have created on the whiteboard. Then ask students to blend and read the words.
- Show how to say each sound individually and then blend them together to read the word. Model blending by pointing using a swishing motion with your finger.

3 Oral segmenting

- Say a word aloud (e.g. "park") and count the sounds in the word (3). Write the number of lines you need for all the sounds. Now ask students to listen to the sounds in the word and write a letter for every sound in the word as you spell the word.

Extension activities

- Assign the decodable passage in the Activities book on page 187 (**Story with 'ar' words**).
- For further extension or additional practice, you can also assign the decodable passage on page 189 (**Story with longer 'ar' words**).
- Play the **Jumping Jack game** in Book 12: Beach Party. This is a game for two players. Each player has three counters, and each set should be a different color. The players take turns to move a counter by sliding it into an adjacent space or by jumping over their opponent's counter into an empty space. When a player lands on a word, they should be encouraged to read the word aloud. The winner is the first player to get all of their three counters in a straight line.
- Use the **Reading practice** cards on pages 186 or 188 to play a simple bingo game. The second set of words has longer spellings.

STEP 2
Application for reading
25 mins

Before reading (3 mins)
- Revisit the vocabulary taught in Step 1 (e.g. "park"). Clearly say the word: /p/ /ar/ /k/.
- Explore different meanings of the word "park," such as a public green space or leaving a vehicle in a particular place.
- Ask questions such as "What might you find at a park?"
- Then write the word on the whiteboard and refer back to it throughout the week for reinforcement.

Vocabulary (2 mins)
- Pre-teach the words in the **Vocabulary** list in Book 12: Beach Party (page iv).
- Ensure students understand each word's pronunciation, meaning, and usage.

Application (10 mins)
- The chosen text for this reading activity is Book 12: Beach Party. Briefly introduce the book to spark interest.
- Lead students through a directed reading of Book 12: Beach Party. Encourage students to sound out each word carefully and then blend the sounds together to form the word.
- Provide support by modeling the blending.
- Encourage students to sound out each word and then blend to read.

Reading fluency (10 mins)
- Following the initial reading, revisit Book 12: Beach Party with a focus on fluency.
- Reading the book again allows students to practice their newly acquired skills, this time with an emphasis on reading more smoothly and confidently.
- Create an interactive reading environment by inviting students to take turns reading aloud. Encourage them to point to each word as they read.
- As students read more fluently, support them to read with more expression and prosody, changing their pitch, pace, and emphasis according to the words and punctuation.

STEP 3
Application for spelling
20 mins

Spelling (10 mins)
- Assign students the **Reading and spelling** activity (Activities, page 191).
- In this activity, students are provided with a list of words that they need to write on the activity page.
- Students read through the list of words and then write them in the 'ar' column.
- Additionally, the **Spelling by sound** sheet (Activities, page 190) can be used for additional spelling activities, or it can be retained by the students for use as a dictionary of spellings by sound.

Sentence dictation (10 mins)
- Ask students to complete the **Dictation** activity (Activities, page 196).
- Use the text at the bottom of the activity for dictation: "The paint leaves marks on the carpet," "Matt parks his car on the grass by the beach," and "'At last, art with no mess!' grins Matt."
- Ask students to write the spelling of each sound on the provided write-on lines.
- Remind the students that some sounds can be spelled by more than one letter.
- A longer line indicates the spelling has more than one letter.

Extension activities
- For students who finish early or need additional practice, create additional activity sheets with your own passages of text and dictate these new passages to them.

STEP 4
Comprehension and consolidation

15 mins

Book reading (5 mins)

- Reread Book 12: Beach Party.
- Revisiting the book helps to reinforce familiarity with the text and supports phonetic recognition and comprehension.

Comprehension (5 mins)

- To check students' understanding of the story, conduct a group discussion.
- Ask the five comprehension questions at the back of the story ("What are the Moon Dogs planning?", "Why is there paint on the carpet?", "Why is the glue spilled on the table?", "What does Matt think is in the box that Jed unloads from the car?")
- Divide the class into small groups and ask each group to answer a question in turn.
- Encourage groups to explain their reasoning.
- Conclude with a brief discussion summarizing the key points of the story and reinforcing vocabulary.

Sequencing (5 mins)

- For this activity, the students will retell the story in a small group.
- Divide students into pairs or small groups.
- Provide each group with a set of blank cards and pens.
- Ask each group to recall key events from the story or illustrate them on the cards.
- Once the cards are created, students will work together to arrange them in the correct sequence.
- Invite each group to retell the story using their arranged cards, encouraging them to use their own words to narrate the story.

Extension activities

These comprehension activities in the Activities book can be used for extended learning:

- **Is it true?** (Activities, page 192). Students check the sentences for accuracy.
- **Developing vocabulary** (page 195). Students begin by circling the word or phrase that can be replaced by the word "groans" in a provided passage. They then write two sentences of their own using the word "groans." Remind students to begin each sentence with a capital letter and finish it with a period.

STEP 5
Tracking progress

- Assign the **Spelling assessment** (Activities, page 197) to quickly evaluate each student's progress.
- The teacher can use words from the second list of words provided for students who are ready for that stage.
- When dictating a word, first say it on its own.
- Next, say a sentence with the word in it (to put the word in a context of a sentence) and then repeat the word.
- This ensures students have heard the word correctly.
- For example: "Barn. The cows slept in a barn. Barn."
- Ask students to complete the **Timed word reading** (Activities, page 194) to assess their reading speed.
- Ask students to read the words as fast as they can and record the time in each box.
- Depending on the class's performance, revisit specific activities to address skill gaps or encourage students to play one of the games below.

Extension activities

1 Phonic patterns: Color the real words (Activities, page 193).

- Fold the sheet on the dotted line. Then distribute the activity sheet to each student.
- Read out the words in each column.
- Students listen to the sounds in each word. They then color in the boxes that contain real words with 'ar' spellings.
- Students can unfold the sheet to check that their answers.

2 4-in-a-row game (Activities, page 198).

- This game is for two players: Play with two sets of colored counters. Players take turns to read a word and put a counter on it.
- The winner is the first to get four of their counters in a row in any direction.
- The winner places a counter on picture of Moon.
- The game is played four times until all pictures of Moon are covered.
- Encourage students to say the words aloud as they land on them. For those needing more support, help them to blend the word with assistance.
- Provide positive feedback and encouragement throughout the game.

LESSON PLANS: Moon Dogs Vowel Spellings

air, are

STEP 1 Preparation

20 mins

Learning goal (2 mins)

- Explain that in English there is more than one way to spell the sound /air/. In this lesson we will learn two ways to spell the sound /air/: 'air' and 'are.'
- Introduce the book Moon Dogs Vowel Spellings Book 13: A Scary Haircut.
- Inform students they will also be completing some activities from Moon Dogs Vowel Spellings Activities.

Preparation (18 mins)

- Introduce the new focus spellings 'air' and 'are' for the sound /air/.
- Model the sound correctly and ask pupils to copy.
- Have students watch you as they pronounce /air/.
- Read these lists of words: "hair," "fare," "pair," and "dare."

1 Word building and blending

- Use the same word building procedure as in previous chapters.
- For example, first build words with the grapheme 'air.' If the student can learn another spelling alternative, introduce 'are' and build word with this grapheme.
- Place the words in two columns and ask the student to read the words in one column and then the next.
- For word-building instructions see page 201 of the Activities book.

LESSON RESOURCES

2 Word reading

- Write the words you have created on the whiteboard. Then ask students to blend and read the words.
- Show how to say each sound individually and then blend them together to read the word. Model blending by pointing using a swishing motion with your finger.

3 Oral segmenting

- Say a word aloud (e.g. "stare") and count the sounds in the word (3). Write the number of lines you need for all the sounds. Now ask students to listen to the sounds in the word and write a letter for every sound in the word as you spell the word.

Extension activities

- If the student is learning one spelling at a time, use decodable passages in the Activities book on pages 203 (**Story with 'air' words**) and 205 (**Story with 'are' words**).

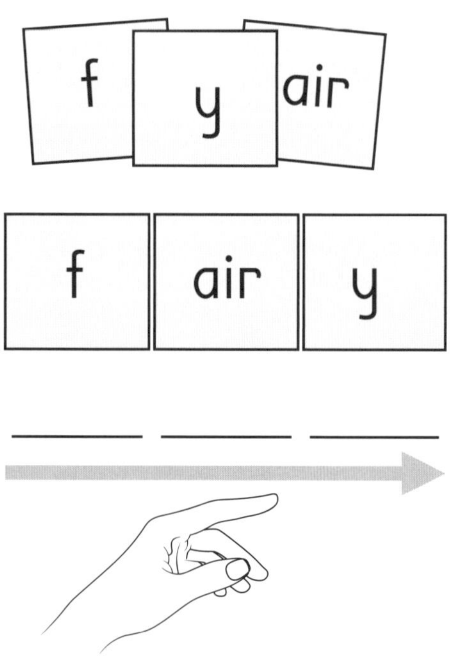

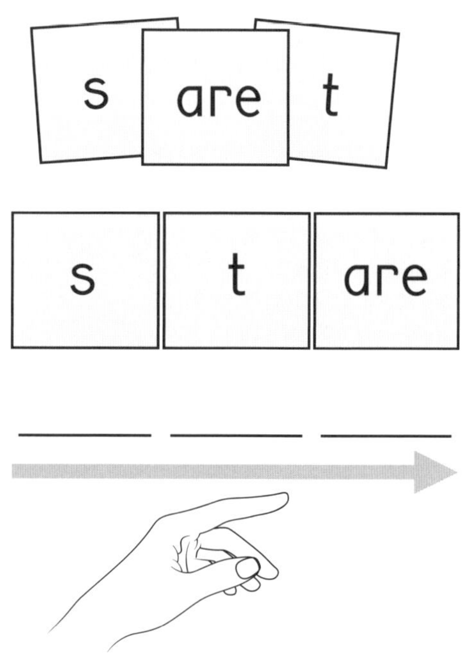

STEP 2 Application for reading

25 mins

Before reading (3 mins)

- Revisit the vocabulary taught in Step 1 (e.g. "stare"). Clearly say the word: /s/ /t/ /air/.
- Explore the homonyms "stare" and "stair."
- Ask questions such as "Have you ever stared at someone in amazement?" and "Why do you think it's often considered rude to stare?"
- Then write the word on the whiteboard and refer back to it throughout the week for reinforcement.

Vocabulary (2 mins)

- Pre-teach the words in the **Vocabulary** list in Book 13: A Scary Haircut (page iv).
- Ensure students understand each word's pronunciation, meaning, and usage.

Application (10 mins)

- The chosen text for this reading activity is Book 13: A Scary Haircut. Briefly introduce the book to spark interest.
- Lead students through a directed reading of A Scary Haircut. Encourage students to sound out each word carefully and then blend the sounds together to form the word.
- Provide support by modeling the blending.
- Encourage students to sound out each word and then blend to read.

Reading fluency (10 mins)

- Following the initial reading, revisit Book 13: A Scary Haircut with a focus on fluency.
- Reading the book again allows students to practice their newly acquired skills, this time with an emphasis on reading more smoothly and confidently.
- Create an interactive reading environment by inviting students to take turns reading aloud. Encourage them to point to each word as they read.
- As students read more fluently, support them to read with more expression and prosody, changing their pitch, pace, and emphasis according to the words and punctuation.

STEP 3 Application for spelling

20 mins

Word sorting and spelling (10 mins)

- Word sorting is a useful activity to consolidate alternative spellings.
- Assign students the **Reading and spelling** activity (Activities, page 207).
- In this activity, students are provided with a list of words they need to sort according to the spellings 'air' and 'are.'
- Students read through the list of words and then write them in the correct column.
- Additionally, the **Spelling by sound** sheet (Activities, page 206) can be used for additional sorting activities, or it can be retained by the students for use as a dictionary of spellings by sound.

Sentence dictation (10 mins)

- Ask students to complete the **Dictation** activity (Activities, page 212).
- Use the text at the bottom of the activity for dictation: "'I can cut hair!' says Matt. 'I will be careful,'" "'Rainbow hair is for the tooth fairy!' glares Tam," and "Matt runs upstairs to fetch hats."
- Ask students to write the spelling of each sound on the provided write-on lines.
- Remind the students that some sounds can be spelled by more than one letter.
- A longer line indicates the spelling has more than one letter.

Extension activities

- For students who finish early or need additional practice, create additional activity sheets with your own passages of text and dictate these new passages to them.

STEP 4
Comprehension and consolidation

15 mins

Book reading (5 mins)

- Reread Book 13: A Scary Haircut.
- Revisiting the book helps to reinforce familiarity with the text and supports phonetic recognition and comprehension.

Comprehension (5 mins)

- To check students' understanding of the story, conduct a group discussion.
- Ask the five comprehension questions at the back of the story ("Why does Matt offer to cut Tam's hair?", "What does Matt do to Tam's hair?", "How does Tam react?", "How does Matt save the day?", "Have you ever had a terrible haircut? What happened?")
- Divide the class into small groups and ask each group to answer a question in turn.
- Encourage groups to explain their reasoning.
- Conclude with a brief discussion summarizing the key points of the story and reinforcing vocabulary.

Sequencing (5 mins)

- For this activity, the students will retell the story in a small group.
- Divide students into pairs or small groups.
- Provide each group with a set of blank cards and pens.
- Ask each group to recall key events from the story or illustrate them on the cards.
- Once the cards are created, students will work together to arrange them in the correct sequence.
- Invite each group to retell the story using their arranged cards, encouraging them to use their own words to narrate the story.

Extension activities

These comprehension activities in the Activities book can be used for extended learning:

- **Is it true?** (Activities, page 208). Students check the sentences for accuracy.
- **Developing vocabulary** (page 211). Students begin by circling the word or phrase that can be replaced by the word "glares" in a provided passage. They then write two sentences of their own using the word "glares." Remind students to begin each sentence with a capital letter and finish it with a period.

STEP 5
Tracking progress

- Assign the **Spelling assessment** (Activities, page 213) to quickly evaluate each student's progress.
- The teacher can use words from the second list of words provided for students who are ready for that stage.
- When dictating a word, first say it on its own.
- Next, say a sentence with the word in it (to put the word in a context of a sentence) and then repeat the word.
- This ensures students have heard the word correctly.
- For example: "Repair. It is better to try and repair things than just thrown them away. Repair."
- Ask students to complete the **Timed word reading** (Activities, page 210) to assess their reading speed.
- Ask students to read the words as fast as they can and record the time in each box.
- Depending on the class's performance, revisit specific activities to address skill gaps or encourage students to play one of the games below.

Extension activities

1 Phonic patterns: Color the real words (Activities, page 209).

- Fold the sheet on the dotted line. Then distribute the activity sheet to each student.
- Read out the words in each column.
- Students listen to the sounds in each word. They then color in the boxes that contain real words with 'air' spellings.
- Students can unfold the sheet to check that their answers.

2 4-in-a-row game (Activities, page 214).

- This game is for two players: Play with two sets of colored counters. Players take turns to read a word and put a counter on it.
- The winner is the first to get four of their counters in a row in any direction.
- The winner places a counter on a picture of Moon.
- The game is played four times until all pictures of Moon boxes are covered.
- Encourage students to say the words aloud as they land on them. For those needing more support, help them to blend the word with assistance.
- Provide positive feedback and encouragement throughout the game.

LESSON PLANS: Moon Dogs Vowel Spellings

ear, eer

STEP 1
Preparation

20 mins

LESSON RESOURCES

Learning goal (2 mins)

- Explain that in English there is more than one way to spell the sound /ear/. In this lesson we will learn two ways to spell the sound /ear/: 'ear' and 'eer.'
- Introduce the book Moon Dogs Vowel Spellings Book 14: Steer Clear.
- Inform students they will also be completing some activities from Moon Dogs Vowel Spellings Activities.

Preparation (18 mins)

- Introduce the new focus spellings 'ear' and 'eer' for the sound /ear/.
- Model the sound correctly and ask pupils to copy.
- Have students watch you as they pronounce /ear/.
- Read these lists of words: "gear," "deer," "clear," and "jeer."

1 Word building and blending

- Use the same word building procedure as in previous chapters.
- For example, first build words with the grapheme 'ee.' If the student can learn another spelling alternative, introduce 'ea' and build word with this grapheme.
- Place the words in two columns and ask the student to read the words in one column and then the next.
- For word-building instructions see page 217 of the Activities book.

2 Word reading

- Write the words you have created on the whiteboard. Then ask students to blend and read the words.
- Show how to say each sound individually and then blend them together to read the word. Model blending by pointing using a swishing motion with your finger.

3 Oral segmenting

- Say a word aloud (e.g. "sneer") and count the sounds in the word (3). Write the number of lines you need for all the sounds. Now ask students to listen to the sounds in the word and write a letter for every sound in the word as you spell the word.

Extension activities

- If the student is learning one spelling at a time, use decodable passages in the Activities book on pages 219 (**Story with 'ear' words**) and 221 (**Story with 'eer' words**).

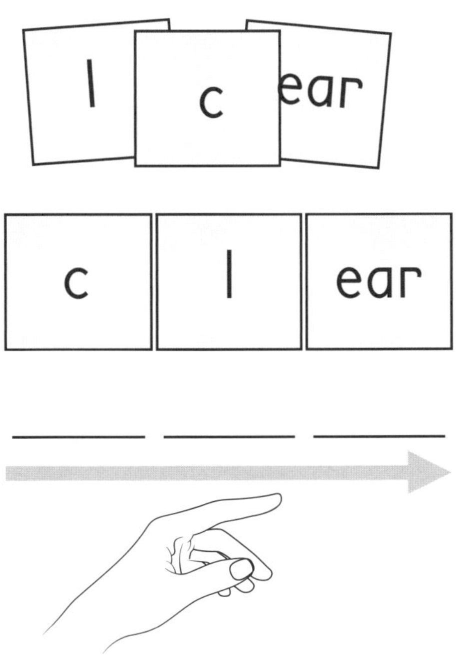

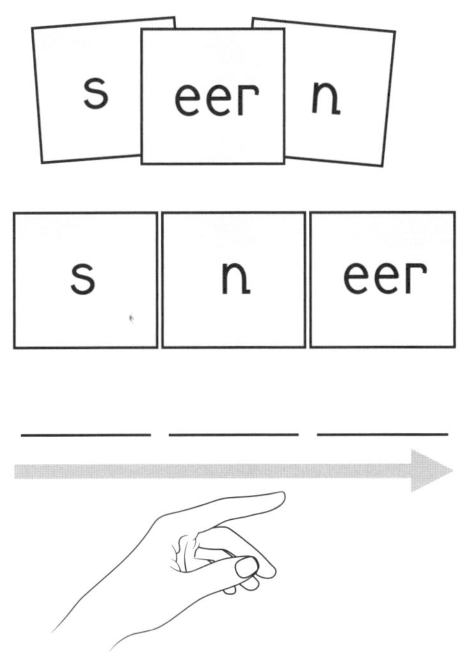

STEP 2
Application for reading
25 mins

Before reading (3 mins)

- Revisit the vocabulary taught in Step 1 (e.g. "deer"). Clearly say the word: /d/ /ee/ /r/.
- Explore the homonyms "deer" and "dear" and explain their different meanings.
- Ask questions such as "Where might you find a deer?" and "When might you use the word "dear" in a piece of writing?"
- Then write the words on the whiteboard and refer back to it throughout the week for reinforcement.

Vocabulary (2 mins)

- Pre-teach the words in the **Vocabulary** list in Book 14: Steer Clear (page iv).
- Ensure students understand each word's pronunciation, meaning, and usage.

Application (10 mins)

- The chosen text for this reading activity is Book 14: Steer Clear. Briefly introduce the book to spark interest.
- Lead students through a directed reading of Book 14: Steer Clear. Encourage students to sound out each word carefully and then blend the sounds together to form the word.
- Provide support by modeling the blending.
- Encourage students to sound out each word and then blend to read.

Reading fluency (10 mins)

- Following the initial reading, revisit Book 14: Steer Clear with a focus on fluency.
- Reading the book again allows students to practice their newly acquired skills, this time with an emphasis on reading more smoothly and confidently.
- Create an interactive reading environment by inviting students to take turns reading aloud. Encourage them to point to each word as they read.
- As students read more fluently, support them to read with more expression and prosody, changing their pitch, pace, and emphasis according to the words and punctuation.

STEP 3
Application for spelling
20 mins

Word sorting and spelling (10 mins)

- Word sorting is a useful activity to consolidate alternative spellings.
- Assign students the **Reading and spelling** activity (Activities, page 223).
- In this activity, students are provided with a list of words they need to sort according to the spellings 'ear' and 'eer.'
- Students read through the list of words and then write them in the correct column.
- Additionally, the **Spelling by sound** sheet (Activities, page 222) can be used for additional sorting activities, or it can be retained by the students for use as a dictionary of spellings by sound.

Sentence dictation (10 mins)

- Ask students to complete the **Dictation** activity (Activities, page 228).
- Use the text at the bottom of the activity for dictation: "'Oh dear!' gasps Liz. 'His teeth are as sharp as spears!'", "'Let's steer clear of them!' says Liz in fear," and "The meerkats bob up cheerfully."
- Ask students to write the spelling of each sound on the provided write-on lines.
- Remind the students that some sounds can be spelled by more than one letter.
- A longer line indicates the spelling has more than one letter.

Extension activities

- For students who finish early or need additional practice, create additional activity sheets with your own passages of text and dictate these new passages to them.

STEP 4
Comprehension and consolidation 15 mins

Book reading (5 mins)

- Reread Book 14: Steer Clear.
- Revisiting the book helps to reinforce familiarity with the text and supports phonetic recognition and comprehension.

Comprehension (5 mins)

- To check students' understanding of the story, conduct a group discussion.
- Ask the six comprehension questions at the back of the story. For example: "Liz and Jed have different feelings about visiting the zoo. What are they?" and "Jed peers into the shark tank. What does 'peers' mean?"
- Divide the class into small groups and ask each group to answer a question in turn.
- Encourage groups to explain their reasoning.
- Conclude with a brief discussion summarizing the key points of the story and reinforcing vocabulary.

Sequencing (5 mins)

- For this activity, the students will retell the story in a small group.
- Divide students into pairs or small groups.
- Provide each group with a set of blank cards and pens.
- Ask each group to recall key events from the story or illustrate them on the cards.
- Once the cards are created, students will work together to arrange them in the correct sequence.
- Invite each group to retell the story using their arranged cards, encouraging them to use their own words to narrate the story.

Extension activities

These comprehension activities in the Activities book can be used for extended learning:

- **Is it true?** (Activities, page 224). Students check the sentences for accuracy.
- **Developing vocabulary** (page 227). Students begin by circling the word or phrase that can be replaced by the word "peers" in a provided passage. They then write two sentences of their own using the word "peers." Remind students to begin each sentence with a capital letter and finish it with a period.

STEP 5
Tracking progress

- Assign the **Spelling assessment** (Activities, page 229) to quickly evaluate each student's progress.
- The teacher can use words from the second list of words provided for students who are ready for that stage.
- When dictating a word, first say it on its own.
- Next, say a sentence with the word in it (to put the word in a context of a sentence) and then repeat the word.
- This ensures students have heard the word correctly.
- For example: "Hear. He did not hear the parrots in the garden. Hear."
- Ask students to complete the **Timed word reading** (Activities, page 226) to assess their reading speed.
- Ask students to read the words as fast as they can and record the time in each box.
- Depending on the class's performance, revisit specific activities to address skill gaps or encourage students to play one of the games below.

Extension activities

1 Phonic patterns: Color the real words (Activities, page 225).

- Fold the sheet on the dotted line. Then distribute the activity sheet to each student.
- Read out the words in each column.
- Students listen to the sounds in each word. They then color in the boxes that contain real words with 'ear' spellings.
- Students can unfold the sheet to check that their answers.

2 4-in-a-row game (Activities, page 230).

- This game is for two players: Play with two sets of colored counters. Players take turns to read a word and put a counter on it.
- The winner is the first to get four of their counters in a row in any direction.
- The winner places a counter on picture of Moon.
- The game is played four times until all pictures of Moon are covered.
- Encourage students to say the words aloud as they land on them. For those needing more support, help them to blend the word with assistance.
- Provide positive feedback and encouragement throughout the game.

ay, ai, a, a–e, ea, ey

STEP 1
Preparation
20 mins

Learning goal (2 mins)

- Explain that in English there is more than one way to spell the sound /ae/. In this lesson we will learn six ways to spell the sound /ae/: 'ay,' 'ai,' 'a,' 'a–e,' 'ea,' and 'ey.'
- Introduce the book Island Adventure Book 1: Saving the Day.
- Inform students they will also be completing some activities from Island Adventure Activities.

Preparation (18 mins)

- Introduce the new focus spellings 'ay,' 'ai,' 'a,' 'a–e,' 'ea,' and 'ey' for the sound /ae/.
- Model the sound correctly and ask students to copy.
- Have students watch you as they say /ae/.

1 Word building and blending

- Using sound cards or magnetic letters, start with a word building activity for each of the graphemes: 'ay,' 'ai,' 'a,' 'a–e,' 'ea,' and 'ey.'
- Assign the **Blending and segmenting /ae/** activity (Activities, page 9).
- Students segment each word into sounds by writing one sound in each square.
- VCe spellings (a–e) are represented by half squares linked together by a curved line that runs underneath the squares.
- Students may need reminding how to blend a–e spellings. Emphasize how the pair of vowel letters are connected to form a single long vowel sound.

2 Word sorting

- Now write the graphemes at the top of six columns.
- Use the words on page 10 of the Activities book to sort the words into "teams."

LESSON RESOURCES

Extension activities

1 Word reading

- Show how to say each sound individually and then blend them together to read the word. Model blending by pointing using a swishing motion with your finger.

2 Oral segmenting

- Say a word aloud (e.g. "train") and count the sounds in the word (4). Write the number of lines you need for all the sounds. Now ask students to listen to the sounds in the word and write a letter for every sound in the word as you spell the word.

3 Phonic patterns

- Assign the **Phonic patterns** activity (Activities, page 14).
- Fold the sheet on the dotted line.
- Students then read the words in the column on the left.
- They then listen to the sounds in the words.
- Next, they color in the boxes with words that have /ae/ spellings.
- Students repeat this in the other columns.
- Unfold the sheet and check that the correct words have been colored in.
- If students require assistance, provide verbal cues or offer examples to help them identify words with /ae/ spellings.

ay	ai	a	a–e	ea	ey
day	train	able	late	break	they
stay	faint	lazy	blame	great	prey

STEP 2
Application for reading

25 mins

Before reading (3 mins)

- Revisit the vocabulary taught in Step 1 (e.g. "rain"). Clearly say the word: /r/ /ai/ /n/.
- Then provide a simple definition, for example, "Rain is water droplets falling from the sky."
- Ask questions such as "How does rain benefit plants and animals?"
- Then write the word on the whiteboard and refer back to it throughout the week for reinforcement.

Vocabulary (7 mins)

- Pre-teach the words in the **Vocabulary** list in Book 1: Saving the Day (page iv).
- Ensure students understand each word's pronunciation, meaning, and usage.

Application (10 mins)

- The chosen text for this reading activity is Book 1: Saving the Day. Briefly introduce the book to spark interest.
- Lead students through a directed reading of Book 1: Saving the Day. Encourage students to sound out each word carefully and then blend the sounds together to form the word.
- Provide support by modeling the blending.
- Encourage students to sound out each word and then blend to read.

Reading fluency (10 mins)

- Following the initial reading, revisit Book 1: Saving the Day with a focus on fluency.
- Reading the book again allows students to practice their newly acquired skills, this time with an emphasis on reading more smoothly and confidently.
- Create an interactive reading environment by inviting students to take turns reading aloud. Encourage them to point to each word as they read.
- As students read more fluently, support them to read with more expression and prosody, changing their pitch, pace, and emphasis according to the words and punctuation.

STEP 3
Application for spelling

20 mins

Segmenting and spelling (10 mins)

- Invite students to complete the **Reading and spelling words with 'ae' spellings** activity (Activities, page 11).
- In this activity, the student writes the missing words into each spelling category.
- After students complete the activity, model the formation of each letter that was written during the activity on the whiteboard.
- Focus on the starting point, stroke direction, and completion of each letter to ensure proper handwriting techniques.
- Demonstrating proper letter formation is crucial for developing legible handwriting and building foundational writing skills.

Sentence dictation (10 mins)

- Ask students to complete the **Dictation** activity (Activities, page 17).
- Use the text at the bottom of the activity for dictation.
- Cut and fold along the dotted line before giving it to the students.
- Ask students to write the spelling of each sound on the provided write-on lines.
- Remind the students that some sounds can be spelled by more than one letter.
- A longer line indicates the spelling has more than one letter.
- The curved lines running underneath the write-on lines indicate a VCe spelling.
- For students who finish early or need additional practice, create additional activity sheets with your own passages of text and dictate these new passages to them.

Extension

- Ask students to complete the **Chunking two-syllable words with 'ae'** activity for additional spelling practice (Activities, page 13).
- Students split each word into two syllables.
- They then write each syllable in a box.
- Encourage the students to write the whole word while saying the syllables.
- For students who finish early or need additional practice, create additional activity sheets with your own words for them to split into two-syllables.

STEP 4
Comprehension and consolidation
15 mins

Book reading (5 mins)

- Reread Book 1: Saving the Day.
- Revisiting the book helps to reinforce familiarity with the text and supports phonetic recognition and comprehension.

Comprehension (5 mins)

- To check students' understanding of the story, conduct a group discussion.
- Ask some comprehension questions, for example, "How did Jack and Gran initially spend their time before Snub went missing?" and "What event in Gran's past does Grandpa recall while rescuing Snub?"
- Divide the class into small groups and ask each group to answer a question in turn.
- Encourage groups to explain their reasoning.
- Conclude with a brief discussion summarizing the key points of the story and reinforcing vocabulary.

Sequencing (5 mins)

- For this activity, the students will retell the story in a small group.
- Divide students into pairs or small groups.
- Provide each group with a set of blank cards and pens.
- Ask each group to recall key events from the story or illustrate them on the cards.
- Once the cards are created, students will work together to arrange them in the correct sequence.
- Invite each group to retell the story using their arranged cards, encouraging them to use their own words to narrate the story.

Extension activities

There are a range of activities in the Activities book that can be used for extended learning:

- **Is it true?** (page 15) Students check the sentences for accuracy.
- **Picture the scene** (page 16) Students draw the details of the picture as described in the text.
- **Developing vocabulary** (page 19) Students circle the word or phrase that can be replaced with the word "scanned" ("looked").
- **Character profile** (page 20) Students use prompts from the word bank to help them create a character profile for Snub.
- **Nonfiction: Blanket bogs** (page 22) Students draw on the information given in the text to create a safety flyer.

STEP 5
Tracking progress

- Assign the **Spelling assessment** (Activities, page 24) to quickly evaluate each student's progress.
- Depending on the class's performance, revisit specific activities to address skill gaps or encourage students to play one of the games below.

Extension activities

1 Stepping stones game (Activities, page 21).

- This game is suitable for 1–4 players and requires counters and a die.
- Provide positive feedback and encouragement throughout the game.
- For those needing more support, help them to blend the letter sound or word with assistance.

2 Dice game (Activities, page 23).

- This game is for two players.
- Each player needs a batch of counters of one color.
- The players take turns to throw the die.
- They read a word in the column that corresponds to the number on the die and place their counter on that word or letter.
- The first to have three of their counters in a row in any direction is the winner.

PARALLEL BOOKS

In addition to Book 1: Saving the Day, the following books also cover alternative vowel spellings for the sound /ae/ and can be used for more practice of decoding, for book bags to take home.

Talisman 1
Book 1: The Talisman

Rescue
Book 1: A Great Break

Alba
Book 6: A Brave Escape

Totem
Book 6: Dangers on the Plain

Pet Sitters
Book 6: The Waiting Game

ee, ea, y, e, ie, e–e, ei

STEP 1
Preparation

20 mins

Learning goal (2 mins)

- Explain that in English there is more than one way to spell the sound /ee/. In this lesson we will learn seven ways to spell the sound /ee/: 'ee,' 'ea,' 'y,' 'e,' 'ie,' 'e–e,' and 'ei.'
- Introduce the book Island Adventure Book 2: Sea Change.
- Inform students they will also be completing some activities from Island Adventure Activities.

Preparation (18 mins)

- Introduce the new focus spellings 'ee,' 'ea,' 'y,' 'e,' 'ie,' 'e–e,' and 'ei' for the sound /ee/.
- Model the sound correctly and ask students to copy.
- Have students watch you as they say /ee/.

1 Word building and blending

- Using sound cards or magnetic letters, start with a word building activity for each of the graphemes: 'ee,' 'ea,' 'y,' 'e,' 'ie,' 'e–e,' and 'ei.'
- Assign the **Blending and segmenting /ee/** activity (Activities, page 27).
- Students segment each word into sounds by writing one sound in each square.
- VCe spellings (e–e) are represented by half squares linked together by a curved line that runs underneath the squares.
- Students may need reminding how to blend e–e spellings. Emphasize how the pair of vowel letters are connected to form a single long vowel sound.

2 Word reading

- Now write the graphemes at the top of seven columns.
- Use the words on page 28 of the Activities book to sort the words into "teams."

LESSON RESOURCES

Extension activities

1 Word reading

- Write the words you have created on the whiteboard. Then ask students to blend and read the words. Model blending by pointing using a swishing motion with your finger.

2 Oral segmenting

- Say a word aloud (e.g. "brief") and count the sounds in the word (4). Write the number of lines you need for all the sounds. Now ask students to listen to the sounds in the word and write a letter for every sound in the word as you spell the word.

3 Phonic patterns

- Assign the **Phonic patterns** activity (Activities, page 32).
- Fold the sheet on the dotted line.
- Students then read the words in the column on the left.
- They then listen to the sounds in the words.
- Next, they color in the boxes with words that have /ee/ spellings.
- Students repeat this in the other columns.
- Unfold the sheet and check that the correct words have been colored in.
- If students require assistance, provide verbal cues or offer examples to help them identify words with /ee/ spellings.

ee	ea	y	e	ie	e–e	ei
reed	sneak	messy	she	field	delete	receive
seem	steal	frilly	begin	grief	Pete	ceiling

STEP 2
Application for reading
25 mins

Before reading (3 mins)

- Revisit the vocabulary taught in Step 1 (e.g. "sneak"). Clearly say the word: /s/ /n/ /ea/ /k/.
- Then provide a simple definition, for example, "To sneak means to move quietly to avoid being noticed."
- Ask questions such as "What are some reasons why someone might want to sneak?"
- Then write the word on the whiteboard and refer back to it throughout the week for reinforcement.

Vocabulary (7 mins)

- Pre-teach the words in the **Vocabulary** list in Book 2: Sea Change (page iv).
- Ensure students understand each word's pronunciation, meaning, and usage.

Application (10 mins)

- The chosen text for this reading activity is Book 2: Sea Change. Briefly introduce the book to spark interest.
- Lead students through a directed reading of Book 2: Sea Change. Encourage students to sound out each word carefully and then blend the sounds together to form the word.
- Provide support by modeling the blending.
- Encourage students to sound out each word and then blend to read.

Reading fluency (10 mins)

- Following the initial reading, revisit Book 2: Sea Change with a focus on fluency.
- Reading the book again allows students to practice their newly acquired skills, this time with an emphasis on reading more smoothly and confidently.
- Create an interactive reading environment by inviting students to take turns reading aloud. Encourage them to point to each word as they read.
- As students read more fluently, support them to read with more expression and prosody, changing their pitch, pace, and emphasis according to the words and punctuation.

STEP 3
Application for spelling
20 mins

Segmenting and spelling (10 mins)

- Invite students to complete the **Reading and spelling words with 'ee' spellings** activity (Activities, page 29).
- In this activity, the student writes the missing words into each spelling category.
- After students complete the activity, model the formation of each letter that was written during the activity on the whiteboard.
- Focus on the starting point, stroke direction, and completion of each letter to ensure proper handwriting techniques.
- Demonstrating proper letter formation is crucial for developing legible handwriting and building foundational writing skills.

Sentence dictation (10 mins)

- Ask students to complete the **Dictation** activity (Activities, page 35).
- Use the text at the bottom of the activity for dictation.
- Cut and fold along the dotted line before giving it to the students.
- Ask students to write the spelling of each sound on the provided write-on lines.
- Remind the students that some sounds can be spelled by more than one letter.
- A longer line indicates the spelling has more than one letter.
- The curved lines running underneath the write-on lines indicate a VCe spelling.
- For students who finish early or need additional practice, create additional activity sheets with your own passages of text and dictate these new passages to them.

Extension

- Ask students to complete the **Chunking two-syllable words with 'ee'** activity for additional spelling practice (Activities, page 31).
- Students split each word into two syllables.
- They then write each syllable in a box.
- Encourage the students to write the whole word while saying the syllables.
- For students who finish early or need additional practice, create additional activity sheets with your own words for them to split into two-syllables.

STEP 4
Comprehension and consolidation

15 mins

Book reading (5 mins)

- Reread Book 2: Sea Change.
- Revisiting the book helps to reinforce familiarity with the text and supports phonetic recognition and comprehension.

Comprehension (5 mins)

- To check students' understanding of the story, conduct a group discussion.
- Ask some comprehension questions, for example, "How did Gran react when she realized the workshop was crashing into the sea?" and "What unexpected discovery did they make when attempting to salvage some of Gran's belongings?"
- Divide the class into small groups and ask each group to answer a question in turn.
- Encourage groups to explain their reasoning.
- Conclude with a brief discussion summarizing the key points of the story and reinforcing vocabulary.

Sequencing (5 mins)

- For this activity, the students will retell the story in a small group.
- Divide students into pairs or small groups.
- Provide each group with a set of blank cards and pens.
- Ask each group to recall key events from the story or illustrate them on the cards.
- Once the cards are created, students will work together to arrange them in the correct sequence.
- Invite each group to retell the story using their arranged cards, encouraging them to use their own words to narrate the story.

Extension activities

There are a range of activities in the Activities book that can be used for extended learning:

- **Is it true?** (page 33) Students check the sentences for accuracy.
- **Picture the scene** (page 34) Students draw the details of the picture as described in the text.
- **Developing vocabulary** (page 37) Students circle the word or phrase that can be replaced with the word "frantic" ("very upset").
- **Character profile** (page 38) Students use prompts from the word bank to help them create a character profile for Jack.
- **Nonfiction: Snub-nosed monkeys** (page 40) Students draw on the information given in the text to create a fact card

STEP 5
Tracking progress

- Assign the **Spelling assessment** (Activities, page 42) to quickly evaluate each student's progress.
- Depending on the class's performance, revisit specific activities to address skill gaps or encourage students to play one of the games below.

Extension activities

1 Stepping stones game (Activities, page 39)

- This game is suitable for 1–4 players and requires counters and a die.
- Provide positive feedback and encouragement throughout the game.
- For those needing more support, help them to blend the letter sound or word with assistance.

2 Dice game (Activities, page 41)

- This game is for two players.
- Each player needs a batch of counters of one color.
- The players take turns to throw the die.
- They read a word in the column that corresponds to the number on the die and place their counter on that word or letter.
- The first to have three of their counters in a row in any direction is the winner.

PARALLEL BOOKS

In addition to Book 2: Sea Change, the following books also cover alternative vowel spellings for the sound /ee/ and can be used for more practice of decoding, for book bags to take home.

Talisman 1
Book 2: The Talisman

Rescue
Book 2: A Great Break

Alba
Book 7: Apple Trees

Totem
Book 7: Valley of Dreams

LESSON PLANS: Island Adventure

ow, oa, oe, o–e, o

STEP 1
Preparation

20 mins

LESSON RESOURCES

Learning goal (2 mins)

- Explain that in English there is more than one way to spell the sound /oe/. In this lesson we will learn five ways to spell the sound /oe/: 'ow,' 'oa,' 'oe,' 'o–e,' and 'o.'
- Introduce the book Island Adventure Book 3: Coast to Coast.
- Inform students they will also be completing some activities from Island Adventure Activities.

Preparation (18 mins)

- Introduce the new focus spellings 'ow,' 'oa,' 'oe,' 'o–e,' and 'o' for the sound /oe/.
- Model the sound correctly and ask students to copy.
- Have students watch you as they say /oe/.

1 Word building and blending

- Using sound cards or magnetic letters, start with a word building activity for each of the graphemes: 'ow,' 'oa,' 'oe,' 'o–e,' and 'o.'
- Assign the **Blending and segmenting /oe/** activity (Activities, page 45).
- Students segment each word into sounds by writing one sound in each square.
- VCe spellings (o–e) are represented by half squares linked together by a curved line that runs underneath the squares.
- Students may need reminding how to blend o–e spellings. Emphasize how the pair of vowel letters are connected to form a single long vowel sound.

2 Word sorting

- Now write the graphemes at the top of five columns.
- Use the words on page 46 of the Activities book to sort the words into "teams."

Extension activities

1 Word reading

- Show how to say each sound individually and then blend them together to read the word. Model blending by pointing using a swishing motion with your finger.

2 Oral segmenting

- Say a word aloud (e.g. "rope") and count the sounds in the word (3). Write the number of lines you need for all the sounds. Now ask students to listen to the sounds in the word and write a letter for every sound in the word as you spell the word.

3 Phonic patterns

- Assign the **Phonic patterns** activity (Activities, page 50).
- Fold the sheet on the dotted line.
- Students then read the words in the column on the left.
- They then listen to the sounds in the words.
- Next, they color in the boxes with words that have /oe/ spellings.
- Students repeat this in the other columns.
- Unfold the sheet and check that the correct words have been colored in.
- If students require assistance, provide verbal cues or offer examples to help them identify words with /oe/ spellings.

ow	oa	oe	o–e	o
bow	load	toe	rope	go
flow	float	goes	note	most

STEP 2
Application for reading
25 mins

Before reading (3 mins)

- Revisit the vocabulary taught in Step 1 (e.g. "boat"). Clearly say the word: /b/ /oe/ /t/.
- Then provide a simple definition, for example, "A boat is a small vessel used for traveling on water."
- Ask questions such as "What are some different types of boats?"
- Then write the word on the whiteboard and refer back to it throughout the week for reinforcement.

Vocabulary (7 mins)

- Pre-teach the words in the **Vocabulary** list in Book 3: Coast to Coast (page iv).
- Ensure students understand each word's pronunciation, meaning, and usage.

Application (10 mins)

- The chosen text for this reading activity is Book 3: Coast to Coast. Briefly introduce the book to spark interest.
- Lead students through a directed reading of Book 3: Coast to Coast. Encourage students to sound out each word carefully and then blend the sounds together to form the word.
- Provide support by modeling the blending.
- Encourage students to sound out each word and then blend to read.

Reading fluency (10 mins)

- Following the initial reading, revisit Book 3: Coast to Coast with a focus on fluency.
- Reading the book again allows students to practice their newly acquired skills, this time with an emphasis on reading more smoothly and confidently.
- Create an interactive reading environment by inviting students to take turns reading aloud. Encourage them to point to each word as they read.
- As students read more fluently, support them to read with more expression and prosody, changing their pitch, pace, and emphasis according to the words and punctuation.

STEP 3
Application for spelling
20 mins

Segmenting and spelling (10 mins)

- Invite students to complete the **Reading and spelling words with 'oe' spellings** activity (Activities, page 47).
- In this activity, the student writes the missing words into each spelling category.
- After students complete the activity, model the formation of each letter that was written during the activity on the whiteboard.
- Focus on the starting point, stroke direction, and completion of each letter to ensure proper handwriting techniques.
- Demonstrating proper letter formation is crucial for developing legible handwriting and building foundational writing skills.

Sentence dictation (10 mins)

- Ask students to complete the **Dictation** activity (Activities, page 53).
- Use the text at the bottom of the activity for dictation.
- Cut and fold along the dotted line before giving it to the students.
- Ask students to write the spelling of each sound on the provided write-on lines.
- Remind the students that some sounds can be spelled by more than one letter.
- A longer line indicates the spelling has more than one letter.
- The curved lines running underneath the write-on lines indicate a VCe spelling.
- For students who finish early or need additional practice, create additional activity sheets with your own passages of text and dictate these new passages to them.

Extension

- Ask students to complete the **Chunking two-syllable words with 'oe'** activity for additional spelling practice (Activities, page 49).
- Students split each word into two syllables.
- They then write each syllable in a box.
- Encourage the students to write the whole word while saying the syllables.
- For students who finish early or need additional practice, create additional activity sheets with your own words for them to split into two-syllables.

STEP 4
Comprehension and consolidation
15 mins

Book reading (5 mins)

- Reread Book 3: Coast to Coast.
- Revisiting the book helps to reinforce familiarity with the text and supports phonetic recognition and comprehension.

Comprehension (5 mins)

- To check students' understanding of the story, conduct a group discussion.
- Ask some comprehension questions, for example, "Why did Grandpa need to yell to Jack that his mom was on the phone?" and "What crashed into the truck?"
- Divide the class into small groups and ask each group to answer a question in turn.
- Encourage groups to explain their reasoning.
- Conclude with a brief discussion summarizing the key points of the story and reinforcing vocabulary.

Sequencing (5 mins)

- For this activity, the students will retell the story in a small group.
- Divide students into pairs or small groups.
- Provide each group with a set of blank cards and pens.
- Ask each group to recall key events from the story or illustrate them on the cards.
- Once the cards are created, students will work together to arrange them in the correct sequence.
- Invite each group to retell the story using their arranged cards, encouraging them to use their own words to narrate the story.

Extension activities

There are a range of activities in the Activities book that can be used for extended learning:

- **Is it true?** (page 51) Students check the sentences for accuracy.
- **Picture the scene** (page 52) Students draw the details of the picture as described in the text.
- **Developing vocabulary** (page 55) Students circle the word or phrase that can be replaced with the word "nipped" ("nibbled").
- **Character profile** (page 56) Students use prompts from the word bank to help them create a character profile for Grandpa.
- **Nonfiction: Sea stacks** (page 58) Students draw on the information given in the text to create a factual postcard.

STEP 5
Tracking progress

- Assign the **Spelling assessment** (Activities, page 60) to quickly evaluate each student's progress.
- Depending on the class's performance, revisit specific activities to address skill gaps or encourage students to play one of the games below.

Extension activities

1 Stepping stones game (Activities, page 57)

- This game is suitable for 1–4 players and requires counters and a die.
- Provide positive feedback and encouragement throughout the game.
- For those needing more support, help them to blend the letter sound or word with assistance.

2 Dice game (Activities, page 59)

- This game is for two players.
- Each player needs a batch of counters of one color.
- The players take turns to throw the die.
- They read a word in the column that corresponds to the number on the die and place their counter on that word or letter.
- The first to have three of their counters in a row in any direction is the winner.

PARALLEL BOOKS

In addition to Book 3: Coast to Coast, the following books also cover alternative vowel spellings for the sound /oe/ and can be used for more practice of decoding, for book bags to take home.

Talisman 1
Book 3: Shadow in the River

Rescue
Book 3: Rainbow Fish

Alba
Book 8: The Long Road Home

Totem
Book 8: The Monster Below

Pet Sitters
Book 8: Get in the Boat!

LESSON PLANS: Island Adventure

er, ir, ur, or, ear

STEP 1 Preparation

20 mins

Learning goal (2 mins)

- Explain that in English there is more than one way to spell the sound /er/. In this lesson we will learn five ways to spell the sound /er/: 'er,' 'ir,' 'ur,' 'or,' and 'ear.'
- Introduce the book Island Adventure Book 4: A World Away.
- Inform students they will also be completing some activities from Island Adventure Activities.

Preparation (18 mins)

- Introduce the new focus spellings 'er,' 'ir,' 'ur,' 'or,' and 'ear' for the sound /er/.
- Model the sound correctly and ask students to copy.
- Have students watch you as they say /er/.

1 Word building and blending

- Using sound cards or magnetic letters, start with a word building activity for each of the graphemes: 'er,' 'ir,' 'ur,' 'or,' and 'ear.'
- Assign the **Blending and segmenting /er/** activity (Activities, page 63).
- Students segment each word into sounds by writing one sound in each square.

2 Word reading

- Now write the graphemes at the top of five columns.
- Use the words on page 64 of the Activities book to sort the words into "teams."

LESSON RESOURCES

Extension activities

1 Word reading

- Write the words you have created on the whiteboard. Then ask students to blend and read the words. Model blending by pointing using a swishing motion with your finger.

2 Oral segmenting

- Say a word aloud (e.g. "first") and count the sounds in the word (4). Write the number of lines you need for all the sounds. Now ask students to listen to the sounds in the word and write a letter for every sound in the word as you spell the word.

3 Phonic patterns

- Assign the **Phonic patterns** activity (Activities, page 68).
- Fold the sheet on the dotted line.
- Students then read the words in the column on the left.
- They then listen to the sounds in the words.
- Next, they color in the boxes with words that have /er/ spellings.
- Students repeat this in the other columns.
- Unfold the sheet and check that the correct words have been colored in.
- If students require assistance, provide verbal cues or offer examples to help them identify words with /er/ spellings.

er	ir	ur	or	ear
her	first	burp	worth	earn
jerk	stir	curl	worm	heard

STEP 2
Application for reading
25 mins

Before reading (3 mins)

- Revisit the vocabulary taught in Step 1 (e.g. "turn"). Clearly say the word: /t/ /er/ /n/.
- Then provide a simple definition, for example, "To turn means to change direction or move around a point."
- Ask questions such as "What are some examples of things that turn?"
- Then write the word on the whiteboard and refer back to it throughout the week for reinforcement.

Vocabulary (7 mins)

- Pre-teach the words in the **Vocabulary** list in Book 4: A World Away (page iv).
- Ensure students understand each word's pronunciation, meaning, and usage.

Application (10 mins)

- The chosen text for this reading activity is Book 4: A World Away. Briefly introduce the book to spark interest.
- Lead students through a directed reading of Book 4: A World Away. Encourage students to sound out each word carefully and then blend the sounds together to form the word.
- Provide support by modeling the blending.
- Encourage students to sound out each word and then blend to read.

Reading fluency (10 mins)

- Following the initial reading, revisit Book 4: A World Away with a focus on fluency.
- Reading the book again allows students to practice their newly acquired skills, this time with an emphasis on reading more smoothly and confidently.
- Create an interactive reading environment by inviting students to take turns reading aloud. Encourage them to point to each word as they read.
- As students read more fluently, support them to read with more expression and prosody, changing their pitch, pace, and emphasis according to the words and punctuation.

STEP 3
Application for spelling
20 mins

Segmenting and spelling (10 mins)

- Invite students to complete the **Reading and spelling words with 'er' spellings** activity (Activities, page 65).
- In this activity, the student writes the missing words into each spelling category.
- After students complete the activity, model the formation of each letter that was written during the activity on the whiteboard.
- Focus on the starting point, stroke direction, and completion of each letter to ensure proper handwriting techniques.
- Demonstrating proper letter formation is crucial for developing legible handwriting and building foundational writing skills.

Sentence dictation (10 mins)

- Ask students to complete the **Dictation** activity (Activities, page 71).
- Use the text at the bottom of the activity for dictation.
- Cut and fold along the dotted line before giving it to the students.
- Ask students to write the spelling of each sound on the provided write-on lines.
- Remind the students that some sounds can be spelled by more than one letter.
- A longer line indicates the spelling has more than one letter.
- For students who finish early or need additional practice, create additional activity sheets with your own passages of text and dictate these new passages to them.

Extension

- Ask students to complete the **Chunking two-syllable words with 'er'** activity for additional spelling practice (Activities, page 67).
- Students split each word into two syllables.
- They then write each syllable in a box.
- Encourage the students to write the whole word while saying the syllables.
- For students who finish early or need additional practice, create additional activity sheets with your own words for them to split into two-syllables.

STEP 4
Comprehension and consolidation
15 mins

Book reading (5 mins)

- Reread Book 4: A World Away.
- Revisiting the book helps to reinforce familiarity with the text and supports phonetic recognition and comprehension.

Comprehension (5 mins)

- To check students' understanding of the story, conduct a group discussion.
- Ask some comprehension questions, for example, "Why is the girl sobbing?" and "What did they make with the bottles?"
- Divide the class into small groups and ask each group to answer a question in turn.
- Encourage groups to explain their reasoning.
- Conclude with a brief discussion summarizing the key points of the story and reinforcing vocabulary.

Sequencing (5 mins)

- For this activity, the students will retell the story in a small group.
- Divide students into pairs or small groups.
- Provide each group with a set of blank cards and pens.
- Ask each group to recall key events from the story or illustrate them on the cards.
- Once the cards are created, students will work together to arrange them in the correct sequence.
- Invite each group to retell the story using their arranged cards, encouraging them to use their own words to narrate the story.

Extension activities

There are a range of activities in the Activities book that can be used for extended learning:

- **Is it true?** (page 69) Students check the sentences for accuracy.
- **Picture the scene** (page 70) Students draw the details of the picture as described in the text.
- **Developing vocabulary** (page 73) Students circle the word or phrase that can be replaced with the word "clusters" ("Grops of").
- **Character profile** (page 74) Students use prompts from the word bank to help them create a character profile for Gran.
- **Nonfiction: Marine plastic pollution** (page 76) Students draw on the information given in the text to create a poster.

STEP 5
Tracking progress

- Assign the **Spelling assessment** (Activities, page 78) to quickly evaluate each student's progress.
- Depending on the class's performance, revisit specific activities to address skill gaps or encourage students to play one of the games below.

Extension activities

1 Stepping stones game (Activities, page 75)

- This game is suitable for 1–4 players and requires counters and a die.
- Provide positive feedback and encouragement throughout the game.
- For those needing more support, help them to blend the letter sound or word with assistance.

2 Dice game (Activities, page 77)

- This game is for two players.
- Each player needs a batch of counters of one color.
- The players take turns to throw the die.
- They read a word in the column that corresponds to the number on the die and place their counter on that word or letter.
- The first to have three of their counters in a row in any direction is the winner.

PARALLEL BOOKS

In addition to Book 4: A World Away, the following books also cover alternative vowel spellings for the sound /er/ and can be used for more practice of decoding, for book bags to take home.

Talisman 1
Book 4: Deep Sea Danger

Rescue
Book 4: On with the Search

Alba
Book 9: Supper

Pet Sitters
Book 9: Murky Waters

Pet Sitters
Book 9: Turtle Alert!

ow, ou, and oi, oy

STEP 1 Preparation

20 mins

Learning goal (2 mins)

- Explain that in English there is more than one way to spell sounds. In this lesson we will learn the spellings 'ow' and 'ou' for the sound /ow/ and 'oi' and 'oy' for the sound /oi/
- Introduce the book Island Adventure Book 5: Sounds and Shadows
- Inform students they will also be completing some activities from Island Adventure Activities.

Preparation (18 mins)

- Introduce the new focus spellings 'ow' and 'ou' for the sound /ow/ and 'oi' and 'oy' for the sound /oi/.
- Model the sounds correctly and ask students to copy.
- Have students watch you as they say each sound.

1 Word building and blending

- Assign the **Blending and segmenting 'ow'** activity (Activities, page 81).
- Follow this up with the **Blending and segmenting 'oi'** activity (Activities, page 82).
- Students segment each word into sounds by writing one sound in each square.

Extension activities

1 Word sorting

- Now write the graphemes at the top of four columns.
- Use the words on page 83 the Activities book to sort the words into "teams" for the /ow/ and /oi/ sounds, respectively.

LESSON RESOURCES

1 Word reading

- Show how to say each sound individually and then blend them together to read the word. Model blending by pointing using a swishing motion with your finger.

2 Oral segmenting

- Say a word aloud (e.g. "howl") and count the sounds in the word (3). Write the number of lines you need for all the sounds. Now ask students to listen to the sounds in the word and write a letter for every sound in the word as you spell the word.

3 Phonic patterns

- Assign the **Phonic patterns** activity (Activities, page 90).
- Fold the sheet on the dotted line.
- Students then read the words in the column on the left.
- They then listen to the sounds in the words.
- Next, they color in the boxes with words that have /ow/ spellings where the /ow/ is pronounced as in 'clown.'
- Students repeat this in the other columns.
- Unfold the sheet and check that the correct words have been colored in.
- If students require assistance, provide verbal cues or offer examples to help them identify words with /ow/ ('clown') spellings.

ow	ou	oi	oy
howl	aloud	soil	toy
allow	bound	point	annoy

STEP 2 Application for reading

25 mins

Before reading (3 mins)

- Revisit the vocabulary taught in Step 1 (e.g. "sound"). Clearly say the word: /s/ /ou/ /n/ /d/.
- Then provide a simple definition, for example, "sound is a vibration that travels through the air and can be heard when it reaches a person's ear."
- Ask questions such as "What are some examples of sounds you hear every day?"
- Then write the word on the whiteboard and refer back to it throughout the week for reinforcement.

Vocabulary (7 mins)

- Pre-teach the words in the **Vocabulary** list in Book 5: Sounds and Shadows (page iv).
- Ensure students understand each word's pronunciation, meaning, and usage.

Application (10 mins)

- The chosen text for this reading activity is Book 5: Sounds and Shadows. Briefly introduce the book to spark interest.
- Lead students through a directed reading of Book 5: Sounds and Shadows. Encourage students to sound out each word carefully and then blend the sounds together to form the word.
- Provide support by modeling the blending.
- Encourage students to sound out each word and then blend to read.

Reading fluency (10 mins)

- Following the initial reading, revisit Book 5: Sounds and Shadows with a focus on fluency.
- Reading the book again allows students to practice their newly acquired skills, this time with an emphasis on reading more smoothly and confidently.
- Create an interactive reading environment by inviting students to take turns reading aloud. Encourage them to point to each word as they read.
- As students read more fluently, support them to read with more expression and prosody, changing their pitch, pace, and emphasis according to the words and punctuation.

STEP 3 Application for spelling

20 mins

Segmenting and spelling (10 mins)

- Invite students to complete the **Reading and spelling words with 'ow' and 'oi' spellings** activity (Activities, page 84).
- In this activity, the student writes the missing words into each spelling category.
- After students complete the activity, model the formation of each letter that was written during the activity on the whiteboard.
- Focus on the starting point, stroke direction, and completion of each letter to ensure proper handwriting techniques.
- Demonstrating proper letter formation is crucial for developing legible handwriting and building foundational writing skills.

Sentence dictation (10 mins)

- Ask students to complete the **Dictation** activity (Activities, page 93).
- Use the text at the bottom of the activity for dictation.
- Cut and fold along the dotted line before giving it to the students.
- Ask students to write the spelling of each sound on the provided write-on lines.
- Remind the students that some sounds can be spelled by more than one letter.
- A longer line indicates the spelling has more than one letter.
- For students who finish early or need additional practice, create additional activity sheets with your own passages of text and dictate these new passages to them.

Extension

- Ask students to complete the two **Chunking two-syllable words** activities for additional spelling practice (Activities, pages 87–88).
- Students split each word into two syllables.
- They then write each syllable in a box.
- Encourage the students to write the whole word while saying the syllables.
- For students who finish early or need additional practice, create additional activity sheets with your own words for them to split into two-syllables.

STEP 4
Comprehension and consolidation

15 mins

Book reading (5 mins)

- Reread Book 5: Sounds and Shadows.
- Revisiting the book helps to reinforce familiarity with the text and supports phonetic recognition and comprehension.

Comprehension (5 mins)

- To check students' understanding of the story, conduct a group discussion.
- Ask some comprehension questions, for example, "Why is the girl sobbing?" and "What did they make with the bottles?"
- Divide the class into small groups and ask each group to answer a question in turn.
- Encourage groups to explain their reasoning.
- Conclude with a brief discussion summarizing the key points of the story and reinforcing vocabulary.

Sequencing (5 mins)

- For this activity, the students will retell the story in a small group.
- Divide students into pairs or small groups.
- Provide each group with a set of blank cards and pens.
- Ask each group to recall key events from the story or illustrate them on the cards.
- Once the cards are created, students will work together to arrange them in the correct sequence.
- Invite each group to retell the story using their arranged cards, encouraging them to use their own words to narrate the story.

Extension activities

There are a range of activities in the Activities book that can be used for extended learning:

- **Is it true?** (page 91) Students check the sentences for accuracy.
- **Picture the scene** (page 92) Students draw the details of the picture as described in the text.
- **Developing vocabulary** (page 95) Students circle the word or phrase that can be replaced with the word "tucked" ("placed it").
- **Character profile** (page 96) Students use prompts from the word bank to help them create a character profile for Ash.
- **Nonfiction: Plastic bottle greenhouses** (page 98) Students draw on the information given in the text to create a factual postcard.

STEP 5
Tracking progress

- Assign the **Spelling assessment** (Activities, page 100) to quickly evaluate each student's progress.
- Depending on the class's performance, revisit specific activities to address skill gaps or encourage students to play one of the games below.

Extension activities

1 Stepping stones game (Activities, page 97)

- This game is suitable for 1–4 players and requires counters and a die.
- Provide positive feedback and encouragement throughout the game.
- For those needing more support, help them to blend the letter sound or word with assistance.

2 Dice game (Activities, page 99)

- This game is for two players.
- Each player needs a batch of counters of one color.
- The players take turns to throw the die.
- They read a word in the column that corresponds to the number on the die and place their counter on that word or letter.
- The first to have three of their counters in a row in any direction is the winner.

PARALLEL BOOKS

In addition to Book 5: Sounds and Shadows, the following books also cover alternative vowel spellings for the sounds /ow/ or /oi/ and can be used for more practice of decoding, for book bags to take home.

Talisman 1
Book 5: Hounded in the Snow

Rescue
Book 5: A Long Way Down

Alba
Book 10: Howling Wind

Totem
Book 10: Danger All Around

Pet Sitters
Book 10: Round Them U

oo, ue, u–e, ew, ou, u

STEP 1 Preparation

20 mins

LESSON RESOURCES

Learning goal (2 mins)

- Explain that in English there is more than one way to spell the sound /oo/ (as in 'boot'). In this lesson we will learn six ways to spell /oo/: 'oo,' 'ue,' 'u–e,' 'ew,' 'ou,' and 'u.'
- Introduce the book Island Adventure Book 6: A Shrewd Route.
- Inform students they will also be completing some activities from Island Adventure Activities.

Preparation (18 mins)

- Introduce the new focus spellings 'oo,' 'ue,' 'u–e,' 'ew,' 'ou,' and 'u' for the sound /oo/ (as in 'boot').
- Model the sound correctly and ask students to copy.
- Have students watch you as they say /oo/.

1 Word building and blending

- Using sound cards or magnetic letters, start with a word building activity for each of the graphemes: oo,' 'ue,' 'u–e,' 'ew,' 'ou,' and 'u.'
- Assign the **Blending and segmenting /oo/** activity (Activities, page 103).
- Students segment each word into sounds by writing one sound in each square.
- VCe spellings (u–e) are represented by half squares linked together by a curved line that runs underneath the squares.
- Students may need reminding how to blend u–e spellings. Emphasize how the pair of vowel letters are connected to form a single long vowel sound.

2 Word reading

- Now write the graphemes at the top of six columns.
- Use the words on page 104 of the Activities book to sort the words into "teams."

Extension activities

1 Word reading

- Write the words you have created on the whiteboard. Then ask students to blend and read the words. Model blending by pointing using a swishing motion with your finger.

2 Oral segmenting

- Say a word aloud (e.g. "plume") and count the sounds in the word (4). Write the number of lines you need for all the sounds. Now ask students to listen to the sounds in the word and write a letter for every sound in the word as you spell the word.

3 Phonic patterns

- Assign the **Phonic patterns** activity (Activities, page 108).
- Fold the sheet on the dotted line.
- Students then read the words in the column on the left.
- They then listen to the sounds in the words.
- Next, they color in the boxes with words that have /oo/ spellings.
- Students repeat this in the other columns.
- Unfold the sheet and check that the correct words have been colored in.
- If students require assistance, provide verbal cues or offer examples to help them identify words with /oo/ spellings.

oo	ue	u–e	ew	ou	u
proof	true	plume	drew	group	brutal
shoot	sue	crude	crew	youth	judo

STEP 2
Application for reading
25 mins

Before reading (3 mins)

- Revisit the vocabulary taught in Step 1 (e.g. "Judo"). Clearly say the word: /j/ /oo/ /d/ /oe/.
- Then provide a simple definition, for example, "Judo is a type of martial art."
- Ask questions such as "Would you like to try Judo?"
- Then write the word on the whiteboard and refer back to it throughout the week for reinforcement.

Vocabulary (7 mins)

- Pre-teach the words in the **Vocabulary** list in Book 6: A Shrewd Route (page iv).
- Ensure students understand each word's pronunciation, meaning, and usage.

Application (10 mins)

- The chosen text for this reading activity is Book 6: A Shrewd Route. Briefly introduce the book to spark interest.
- Lead students through a directed reading of Book 6: A Shrewd Route. Encourage students to sound out each word carefully and then blend the sounds together to form the word.
- Provide support by modeling the blending.
- Encourage students to sound out each word and then blend to read.

Reading fluency (10 mins)

- Following the initial reading, revisit Book 6: A Shrewd Route with a focus on fluency.
- Reading the book again allows students to practice their newly acquired skills, this time with an emphasis on reading more smoothly and confidently.
- Create an interactive reading environment by inviting students to take turns reading aloud. Encourage them to point to each word as they read.
- As students read more fluently, support them to read with more expression and prosody, changing their pitch, pace, and emphasis according to the words and punctuation.

STEP 3
Application for spelling
20 mins

Segmenting and spelling (10 mins)

- Invite students to complete the **Reading and spelling words with 'oo' spellings** activity (Activities, page 105).
- In this activity, the student writes the missing words into each spelling category.
- After students complete the activity, model the formation of each letter that was written during the activity on the whiteboard.
- Focus on the starting point, stroke direction, and completion of each letter to ensure proper handwriting techniques.
- Demonstrating proper letter formation is crucial for developing legible handwriting and building foundational writing skills.

Dictation (10 mins)

- Ask students to complete the **Dictation** activity (Activities, page 111).
- Use the text at the bottom of the activity for dictation.
- Cut and fold along the dotted line before giving it to the students.
- Ask students to write the spelling of each sound on the provided write-on lines.
- Remind the students that some sounds can be spelled by more than one letter.
- A longer line indicates the spelling has more than one letter.
- The curved lines running underneath the write-on lines indicate a VCe spelling.
- For students who finish early or need additional practice, create additional activity sheets with your own passages of text and dictate these new passages to them.

Extension

- Ask students to complete the **Chunking two-syllable words with 'oo'** activity for additional spelling practice (Activities, page 107).
- Students split each word into two syllables.
- They then write each syllable in a box.
- Encourage the students to write the whole word while saying the syllables.
- For students who finish early or need additional practice, create additional activity sheets with your own words for them to split into two-syllables.

STEP 4
Comprehension and consolidation

15 mins

Book reading (5 mins)

- Reread Book 6: A Shrewd Route.
- Revisiting the book helps to reinforce familiarity with the text and supports phonetic recognition and comprehension.

Comprehension (5 mins)

- To check students' understanding of the story, conduct a group discussion.
- Ask some comprehension questions, for example, "Why was Jack in a bad mood?" and "What was on Jack's wish list?"
- Divide the class into small groups and ask each group to answer a question in turn.
- Encourage groups to explain their reasoning.
- Conclude with a brief discussion summarizing the key points of the story and reinforcing vocabulary.

Sequencing (5 mins)

- Assign the **Retell the story** activity (Activities, page 114).
- Cut out the cards for each student.
- Then jumble them up and ask the student to sequence and number them in the correct order of the story.
- The students then retell the story in their own order.
- They then write the story on a separate sheet of paper.

Extension activities

There are a range of activities in the Activities book that can be used for extended learning:

- **Is it true?** (page 109) Students check the sentences for accuracy.
- **Picture the scene** (page 110) Students draw the details of the picture as described in the text.
- **Developing vocabulary** (page 113) Students circle the word or phrase that can be replaced with the word "snoozing" ("sleeping").
- **Nonfiction: Mountain apples** (page 116) Students draw on the information given in the text to create an information card.

STEP 5
Tracking progress

- Assign the **Spelling assessment** (Activities, page 118) to quickly evaluate each student's progress.
- Depending on the class's performance, revisit specific activities to address skill gaps or encourage students to play one of the games below.

Extension activities

1 Stepping stones game (Activities, page 115)

- This game is suitable for 1–4 players and requires counters and a die.
- Provide positive feedback and encouragement throughout the game.
- For those needing more support, help them to blend the letter sound or word with assistance.

2 Dice game (Activities, page 117)

- This game is for two players.
- Each player needs a batch of counters of one color.
- The players take turns to throw the die.
- They read a word in the column that corresponds to the number on the die and place their counter on that word or letter.
- The first to have three of their counters in a row in any direction is the winner.

PARALLEL BOOKS

In addition to Book 6: A Shrewd Route, the following books also cover alternative vowel spellings for the sound b/oo/t and can be used for more practice of decoding, for book bags to take home.

Talisman 1
Book 6: Death at Noon

Rescue
Book 6: A Gruesome Monster

Alba
Book 12: The Truth

Totem
Book 12: Hooves!

Pet Sitters
Book 12: In the Moonlight

LESSON PLANS: Island Adventure

igh, ie, i–e, i, y

STEP 1
Preparation

20 mins

Learning goal (2 mins)

- Explain that in English there is more than one way to spell the sound /ie/. In this lesson we will learn five ways to spell the sound /ie/: 'igh,' 'ie,' 'i–e,' i,' and 'y.'
- Introduce the book Island Adventure Book 7: An Amazing Find.
- Inform students they will also be completing some activities from Island Adventure Activities.

Preparation (18 mins)

- Introduce the new focus spellings 'igh,' 'ie,' 'i–e,' i,' and 'y' for the sound /ie/.
- Model the sound correctly and ask students to copy.
- Have students watch you as they say /ie/.

1 Word building and blending

- Using sound cards or magnetic letters, start with a word building activity for each of the graphemes: 'igh,' 'ie,' 'i–e,' i,' and 'y.'
- Assign the **Blending and segmenting /ie/** activity (Activities, page 121).
- Students segment each word into sounds by writing one sound in each square.
- VCe spellings (i–e) are represented by half squares linked together by a curved line that runs underneath the squares.
- Students may need reminding how to blend i–e spellings. Emphasize how the pair of vowel letters are connected to form a single long vowel sound.

2 Word sorting

- Now write the graphemes at the top of five columns.
- Use the words on page 122 of the Activities book to sort the words into "teams."

LESSON RESOURCES

Extension activities

1 Word reading

- Show how to say each sound individually and then blend them together to read the word. Model blending by pointing using a swishing motion with your finger.

2 Oral segmenting

- Say a word aloud (e.g. "shy") and count the sounds in the word (2). Write the number of lines you need for all the sounds. Now ask students to listen to the sounds in the word and write a letter for every sound in the word as you spell the word.

3 Phonic patterns

- Assign the **Phonic patterns** activity (Activities, page 126).
- Fold the sheet on the dotted line.
- Students then read the words in the column on the left.
- They then listen to the sounds in the words.
- Next, they color in the boxes with words that have /ie/ spellings.
- Students repeat this in the other columns.
- Unfold the sheet and check that the correct words have been colored in.
- If students require assistance, provide verbal cues or offer examples to help them identify words with /ie/ spellings.

igh	ie	i–e	i	y
high	flies	slime	idol	shy
thigh	spies	nice	final	try

STEP 2
Application for reading

25 mins

Before reading (3 mins)

- Revisit the vocabulary taught in Step 1 (e.g. "spies"). Clearly say the word: /s/ /p/ /ie/ /z/.
- Then provide a simple definition, for example, "spies are people who secretly obtain information."
- Ask questions such as "What might spies look for when gathering information?"
- Then write the word on the whiteboard and refer back to it throughout the week for reinforcement.

Vocabulary (7 mins)

- Pre-teach the words in the **Vocabulary** list in Book 7: An Amazing Find (page iv).
- Ensure students understand each word's pronunciation, meaning, and usage.

Application (10 mins)

- The chosen text for this reading activity is Book 7: An Amazing Find. Briefly introduce the book to spark interest.
- Lead students through a directed reading of Book 7: An Amazing Find. Encourage students to sound out each word carefully and then blend the sounds together to form the word.
- Provide support by modeling the blending.
- Encourage students to sound out each word and then blend to read.

Reading fluency (10 mins)

- Following the initial reading, revisit Book 7: An Amazing Find with a focus on fluency.
- Reading the book again allows students to practice their newly acquired skills, this time with an emphasis on reading more smoothly and confidently.
- Create an interactive reading environment by inviting students to take turns reading aloud. Encourage them to point to each word as they read.
- As students read more fluently, support them to read with more expression and prosody, changing their pitch, pace, and emphasis according to the words and punctuation.

STEP 3
Application for spelling

20 mins

Segmenting and spelling (10 mins)

- Invite students to complete the **Reading and spelling words with 'ie' spellings** activity (Activities, page 123).
- In this activity, the student writes the missing words into each spelling category.
- After students complete the activity, model the formation of each letter that was written during the activity on the whiteboard.
- Focus on the starting point, stroke direction, and completion of each letter to ensure proper handwriting techniques.
- Demonstrating proper letter formation is crucial for developing legible handwriting and building foundational writing skills.

Dictation (10 mins)

- Ask students to complete the **Dictation** activity (Activities, page 129).
- Use the text at the bottom of the activity for dictation.
- Cut and fold along the dotted line before giving it to the students.
- Ask students to write the spelling of each sound on the provided write-on lines.
- Remind the students that some sounds can be spelled by more than one letter.
- A longer line indicates the spelling has more than one letter.
- The curved lines running underneath the write-on lines indicate a VCe spelling.
- For students who finish early or need additional practice, create additional activity sheets with your own passages of text and dictate these new passages to them.

Extension

- Ask students to complete the **Chunking two-syllable words with 'ie'** activity for additional spelling practice (Activities, page 125).
- Students split each word into two syllables.
- They then write each syllable in a box.
- Encourage the students to write the whole word while saying the syllables.
- For students who finish early or need additional practice, create additional activity sheets with your own words for them to split into two-syllables.

STEP 4
Comprehension and consolidation

15 mins

Book reading (5 mins)

- Reread Book 7: An Amazing Find.
- Revisiting the book helps to reinforce familiarity with the text and supports phonetic recognition and comprehension.

Comprehension (5 mins)

- To check students' understanding of the story, conduct a group discussion.
- Ask some comprehension questions, for example, "What did they have for breakfast?" and "What does Jack hate?"
- Divide the class into small groups and ask each group to answer a question in turn.
- Encourage groups to explain their reasoning.
- Conclude with a brief discussion summarizing the key points of the story and reinforcing vocabulary.

Sequencing (5 mins)

- Assign the **Retell the story** activity (Activities, page 132).
- Cut out the cards for each student.
- Then jumble them up and ask the student to sequence and number them in the correct order of the story.
- The students then retell the story in their own order.
- They then write the story on a separate sheet of paper.

Extension activities

There are a range of activities in the Activities book that can be used for extended learning:

- **Is it true?** (page 127) Students check the sentences for accuracy.
- **Picture the scene** (page 128) Students draw the details of the picture as described in the text.
- **Developing vocabulary** (page 131) Students circle the word or phrase that can be replaced with the word "bobbed" ("jerked").
- **Nonfiction: Secret messages** (page 134) Students draw on the information given in the text to create an information card.

STEP 5
Tracking progress

- Assign the **Spelling assessment** (Activities, page 136) to quickly evaluate each student's progress.
- Depending on the class's performance, revisit specific activities to address skill gaps or encourage students to play one of the games below.

Extension activities

1 Stepping stones game (Activities, page 133)

- This game is suitable for 1–4 players and requires counters and a die.
- Provide positive feedback and encouragement throughout the game.
- For those needing more support, help them to blend the letter sound or word with assistance.

2 Dice game (Activities, page 135)

- This game is for two players.
- Each player needs a batch of counters of one color.
- The players take turns to throw the die.
- They read a word in the column that corresponds to the number on the die and place their counter on that word or letter.
- The first to have three of their counters in a row in any direction is the winner.

PARALLEL BOOKS

In addition to Book 7: An Amazing Find, the following books also cover alternative vowel spellings for the sound /ie/ and can be used for more practice of decoding, for book bags to take home.

Talisman 1
Book 7: A Cry in the Dark

Rescue
Book 7: Time is Running out

Alba
Book 11: River Flight

Totem
Book 11: Jungle Fright

Pet Sitters
Book 11: Spidery Night

LESSON PLANS: Island Adventure

a, aw, awe, au, al, ough

STEP 1
Preparation 20 mins

Learning goal (2 mins)

- Explain that in English there is more than one way to spell the sound /aw/. In this lesson we will learn six ways to spell the sound /aw/: 'a,' 'aw,' 'awe,' 'au,' 'al,' and 'ough.'
- Introduce the book Island Adventure Book 8: Awesome Morning.
- Inform students they will also be completing some activities from Island Adventure Activities.

Preparation (18 mins)

- Introduce the new focus spellings 'a,' 'aw,' 'awe,' 'au,' 'al,' and 'ough' for the sound /aw/.
- Model the sound correctly and ask students to copy.
- Have students watch you as they say /aw/.

1 Word building and blending

- Using sound cards or magnetic letters, start with a word building activity for each of the graphemes: 'a,' 'aw,' 'awe,' 'au,' 'al,' and 'ough.'
- Assign the **Blending and segmenting /aw/** activity (Activities, page 139).
- Students segment each word into sounds by writing one sound in each square.

2 Word reading

- Now write the graphemes at the top of six columns.
- Use the words on page 140 of the Activities book to sort the words into "teams."

LESSON RESOURCES

Extension activities

1 Word reading

- Write the words you have created on the whiteboard. Then ask students to blend and read the words. Model blending by pointing using a swishing motion with your finger.

2 Oral segmenting

- Say a word aloud (e.g. "hawk") and count the sounds in the word (3). Write the number of lines you need for all the sounds. Now ask students to listen to the sounds in the word and write a letter for every sound in the word as you spell the word.

3 Phonic patterns

- Assign the **Phonic patterns** activity (Activities, page 144).
- Fold the sheet on the dotted line.
- Students then read the words in the column on the left.
- They then listen to the sounds in the words.
- Next, they color in the boxes with words that have /aw/ spellings.
- Students repeat this in the other columns.
- Unfold the sheet and check that the correct words have been colored in.
- If students require assistance, provide verbal cues or offer examples to help them identify words with /aw/ spellings.

a	aw	awe	au	al	ough
hall	hawk	awe	haul	talk	bought
ball	draw		haunt	scald	fought

STEP 2
Application for reading
25 mins

Before reading (3 mins)

- Revisit the vocabulary taught in Step 1 (e.g. "hawk"). Clearly say the word: /h/ /aw/ /k/.
- Then provide a simple definition, for example, "A hawk is a bird of prey with broad wings and a long tail."
- Ask questions such as "What do you think makes a hawk a good hunter?"
- Then write the word on the whiteboard and refer back to it throughout the week for reinforcement.

Vocabulary (7 mins)

- Pre-teach the words in the **Vocabulary** list in Book 8: Awesome Morning (page iv).
- Ensure students understand each word's pronunciation, meaning, and usage.

Application (10 mins)

- The chosen text for this reading activity is Book 8: Awesome Morning. Briefly introduce the book to spark interest.
- Lead students through a directed reading of Book 8: Awesome Morning. Encourage students to sound out each word carefully and then blend the sounds together to form the word.
- Provide support by modeling the blending.
- Encourage students to sound out each word and then blend to read.

Reading fluency (10 mins)

- Following the initial reading, revisit Book 8: Awesome Morning with a focus on fluency.
- Reading the book again allows students to practice their newly acquired skills, this time with an emphasis on reading more smoothly and confidently.
- Create an interactive reading environment by inviting students to take turns reading aloud. Encourage them to point to each word as they read.
- As students read more fluently, support them to read with more expression and prosody, changing their pitch, pace, and emphasis according to the words and punctuation.

STEP 3
Application for spelling
20 mins

Segmenting and spelling (10 mins)

- Invite students to complete the **Reading and spelling words with 'aw' spellings** activity (Activities, page 140).
- In this activity, the student writes the missing words into each spelling category.
- After students complete the activity, model the formation of each letter that was written during the activity on the whiteboard.
- Focus on the starting point, stroke direction, and completion of each letter to ensure proper handwriting techniques.
- Demonstrating proper letter formation is crucial for developing legible handwriting and building foundational writing skills.

Dictation (10 mins)

- Ask students to complete the **Dictation** activity (Activities, page 147).
- Use the text at the bottom of the activity for dictation.
- Cut and fold along the dotted line before giving it to the students.
- Ask students to write the spelling of each sound on the provided write-on lines.
- Remind the students that some sounds can be spelled by more than one letter.
- A longer line indicates the spelling has more than one letter.
- For students who finish early or need additional practice, create additional activity sheets with your own passages of text and dictate these new passages to them.

Extension

- Ask students to complete the **Chunking two-syllable words with 'aw'** activity for additional spelling practice (Activities, page 143).
- Students split each word into two syllables.
- They then write each syllable in a box.
- Encourage the students to write the whole word while saying the syllables.
- For students who finish early or need additional practice, create additional activity sheets with your own words for them to split into two-syllables.

STEP 4
Comprehension and consolidation

15 mins

Book reading (5 mins)

- Reread Book 8: Awesome Morning.
- Revisiting the book helps to reinforce familiarity with the text and supports phonetic recognition and comprehension.

Comprehension (5 mins)

- To check students' understanding of the story, conduct a group discussion.
- Ask some comprehension questions, for example, "Who was waving wildly from the boat?" and "What was as small as Gran's thumbnail?"
- Divide the class into small groups and ask each group to answer a question in turn.
- Encourage groups to explain their reasoning.
- Conclude with a brief discussion summarizing the key points of the story and reinforcing vocabulary.

Sequencing (5 mins)

- Assign the **Retell the story** activity (Activities, page 150).
- Cut out the cards for each student.
- Then jumble them up and ask the student to sequence and number them in the correct order of the story.
- The students then retell the story in their own order.
- They then write the story on a separate sheet of paper.

Extension activities

There are a range of activities in the Activities book that can be used for extended learning:

- **Is it true?** (page 145) Students check the sentences for accuracy.
- **Picture the scene** (page 146) Students draw the details of the picture as described in the text.
- **Developing vocabulary** (page 149) Students circle the word or phrase that can be replaced with the word "hurling" ("throwing").
- **Nonfiction: Giant spider's web** (page 152) Students draw on the information given in the text to create an information card.

STEP 5
Tracking progress

- Assign the **Spelling assessment** (Activities, page 154) to quickly evaluate each student's progress.
- Depending on the class's performance, revisit specific activities to address skill gaps or encourage students to write a secret code.

Extension activities

1 Stepping stones game (Activities, page 151)

- This game is suitable for 1–4 players and requires counters and a die.
- Provide positive feedback and encouragement throughout the game.
- For those needing more support, help them to blend the letter sound or word with assistance.

2 Dice game (Activities, page 153)

- This game is for two players.
- Each player needs a batch of counters of one color.
- The players take turns to throw the die.
- They read a word in the column that corresponds to the number on the die and place their counter on that word or letter.
- The first to have three of their counters in a row in any direction is the winner.

PARALLEL BOOKS

In addition to Book 8: Awesome Morning, the following books also cover alternative vowel spellings for the sound /ie/ and can be used for more practice of decoding, for book bags to take home.

Talisman 1

Book 8: Attack at Nightfall

Rescue

Book 8: An Awful Planet

air, are, ear, ere, eir

STEP 1
Preparation

20 mins

LESSON RESOURCES

Learning goal (2 mins)

- Explain that in English there is more than one way to spell the sound /air/. In this lesson we will learn five ways to spell the sound /air/: 'air,' 'are,' 'ear,' 'ere,' and 'eir.'
- Introduce the book Island Adventure Book 9: Don't Be Scared.
- Inform students they will also be completing some activities from Island Adventure Activities.

Preparation (18 mins)

- Introduce the new focus spellings 'air,' 'are,' 'ear,' 'ere,' and 'eir' for the sound /air/.
- Model the sound correctly and ask students to copy.
- Have students watch you as they say /air/.

1 Word building and blending

- Using sound cards or magnetic letters, start with a word building activity for each of the graphemes: 'air,' 'are,' 'ear,' 'ere,' and 'eir.'
- Assign the **Blending and segmenting /air/** activity (Activities, page 157).
- Students segment each word into sounds by writing one sound in each square.

2 Word sorting

- Now write the graphemes at the top of five columns.
- Use the words on page 158 of the Activities book to sort the words into "teams."

Extension activities

1 Word reading

- Show how to say each sound individually and then blend them together to read the word. Model blending by pointing using a swishing motion with your finger.

2 Oral segmenting

- Say a word aloud (e.g. "train") and count the sounds in the word (4). Write the number of lines you need for all the sounds. Now ask students to listen to the sounds in the word and write a letter for every sound in the word as you spell the word.

3 Phonic patterns

- Assign the **Phonic patterns** activity (Activities, page 162).
- Fold the sheet on the dotted line.
- Students then read the words in the column on the left.
- They then listen to the sounds in the words.
- Next, they color in the boxes with words that have /air/ spellings.
- Students repeat this in the other columns.
- Unfold the sheet and check that the correct words have been colored in.
- If students require assistance, provide verbal cues or offer examples to help them identify words with /air/ spellings.

air	are	ear	ere	eir
fair	stare	wear	there	heir
stair	blare	swear	where	their

STEP 2
Application for reading
25 mins

Before reading (3 mins)

- Revisit the vocabulary taught in Step 1 (e.g. "wear"). Clearly say the word: /w/ /air/.
- Then provide a simple definition, for example, "To wear means to put on clothing."
- Ask questions such as "Apart from clothing, what else can you wear?"
- Then write the word on the whiteboard and refer back to it throughout the week for reinforcement.

Vocabulary (7 mins)

- Pre-teach the words in the **Vocabulary** list in Book 9: Don't Be Scared (page iv).
- Ensure students understand each word's pronunciation, meaning, and usage.

Application (10 mins)

- The chosen text for this reading activity is Book 9: Don't Be Scared. Briefly introduce the book to spark interest.
- Lead students through a directed reading of Book 9: Don't Be Scared. Encourage students to sound out each word carefully and then blend the sounds together to form the word.
- Provide support by modeling the blending.
- Encourage students to sound out each word and then blend to read.

Reading fluency (10 mins)

- Following the initial reading, revisit Book 9: Don't Be Scared with a focus on fluency.
- Reading the book again allows students to practice their newly acquired skills, this time with an emphasis on reading more smoothly and confidently.
- Create an interactive reading environment by inviting students to take turns reading aloud. Encourage them to point to each word as they read.
- As students read more fluently, support them to read with more expression and prosody, changing their pitch, pace, and emphasis according to the words and punctuation.

STEP 3
Application for spelling
20 mins

Segmenting and spelling (10 mins)

- Invite students to complete the **Reading and spelling words with 'air' spellings** activity (Activities, page 160).
- In this activity, the student writes the missing words into each spelling category.
- After students complete the activity, model the formation of each letter that was written during the activity on the whiteboard.
- Focus on the starting point, stroke direction, and completion of each letter to ensure proper handwriting techniques.
- Demonstrating proper letter formation is crucial for developing legible handwriting and building foundational writing skills.

Dictation (10 mins)

- Ask students to complete the **Dictation** activity (Activities, page 165).
- Use the text at the bottom of the activity for dictation.
- Cut and fold along the dotted line before giving it to the students.
- Ask students to write the spelling of each sound on the provided write-on lines.
- Remind the students that some sounds can be spelled by more than one letter.
- A longer line indicates the spelling has more than one letter.
- For students who finish early or need additional practice, create additional activity sheets with your own passages of text and dictate these new passages to them.

Extension

- Ask students to complete the **Chunking two-syllable words with 'air'** activity for additional spelling practice (Activities, page 161).
- Students split each word into two syllables.
- They then write each syllable in a box.
- Encourage the students to write the whole word while saying the syllables.
- For students who finish early or need additional practice, create additional activity sheets with your own words for them to split into two-syllables.

STEP 4
Comprehension and consolidation
15 mins

Book reading (5 mins)

- Reread Book 9: Don't Be Scared.
- Revisiting the book helps to reinforce familiarity with the text and supports phonetic recognition and comprehension.

Comprehension (5 mins)

- To check students' understanding of the story, conduct a group discussion.
- Ask some comprehension questions, for example, "Why did the hairs on Jack's neck stand up?" and "Why does Ash sob at the end of the story?"
- Divide the class into small groups and ask each group to answer a question in turn.
- Encourage groups to explain their reasoning.
- Conclude with a brief discussion summarizing the key points of the story and reinforcing vocabulary.

Sequencing (5 mins)

- Assign the **Retell the story** activity (Activities, page 168).
- Cut out the cards for each student.
- Then jumble them up and ask the student to sequence and number them in the correct order of the story.
- The students then retell the story in their own order.
- They then write the story on a separate sheet of paper.

Extension activities

There are a range of activities in the Activities book that can be used for extended learning:

- **Is it true?** (page 163) Students check the sentences for accuracy.
- **Picture the scene** (page 164) Students draw the details of the picture as described in the text.
- **Developing vocabulary** (page 167) Students circle the word or phrase that can be replaced with the word "hurling" ("throwing").
- **Nonfiction: Turtle nesting ground** (page 170) Students draw on the information given in the text to create a warning sign.

STEP 5
Tracking progress

- Assign the **Spelling assessment** (Activities, page 172) to quickly evaluate each student's progress.
- Depending on the class's performance, revisit specific activities to address skill gaps or encourage students to play one of the games below.

Extension activities

1 Stepping stones game (Activities, page 169).

- This game is suitable for 1–4 players and requires counters and a die.
- Provide positive feedback and encouragement throughout the game.
- For those needing more support, help them to blend the letter sound or word with assistance.

2 Dice game (Activities, page 171).

- This game is for two players.
- Each player needs a batch of counters of one color.
- The players take turns to throw the die.
- They read a word in the column that corresponds to the number on the die and place their counter on that word or letter.
- The first to have three of their counters in a row in any direction is the winner.

PARALLEL BOOKS

In addition to Book 9: Don't Be Scared, the following books also cover alternative vowel spellings for the sound /air/ and can be used for more practice of decoding, for book bags to take home.

Talisman 1

Book 9: Mountain Scare

Rescue

Book 9: No Time to Spare

LESSON PLANS: Island Adventure

ar

STEP 1
Preparation

20 mins

LESSON RESOURCES

Learning goal (2 mins)

- Explain the lesson intention: learning to read and spell words with the spelling 'ar.'
- Introduce the book Island Adventure Book 10: Arty Party.
- Inform students they will also be completing some activities from Island Adventure Activities.

Preparation (18 mins)

- Introduce the sounds of the 'ar' spelling ('ar' as in "art," "vary," and "warm.")
- Model how to say each sound correctly and "purely" and ask students to copy.
- Have students watch you as they pronounce each 'ar' spelling.
- Read this list of words: "army," "wary," and "warp."
- For each word, point to the letters as you slowly pronounce them, demonstrating the different ways the 'ar' spelling can be pronounced.

1 Word building and blending

- Assign the **Blending and segmenting /ar/** activity (Activities, page 175).
- In this activity, the student is given a list of words to blend and segment.
- Students segment each word into sounds by writing one sound in each square.
- For advanced students, you could provide additional words with more complex spellings or extra syllables.

2 Word sorting

- Assign the **Reading and sorting: words with 'ar' spellings** activity (Activities, page 176).
- Read and sort words according to the different sounds the spelling 'ar' makes' ('ar' as in "art," "vary," and "warm."

Extension activities

1 Word reading

- Write the words you have created on the whiteboard. Then ask students to blend and read the words. Model blending by pointing using a swishing motion with your finger.

2 Oral segmenting

- Say a word aloud (e.g. "brief") and count the sounds in the word (4). Write the number of lines you need for all the sounds. Now ask students to listen to the sounds in the word and write a letter for every sound in the word as you spell the word.

3 Phonic patterns

- Assign the **Phonic patterns** activity (Activities, page 180).
- Fold the sheet on the dotted line.
- Students then read the words in the column on the left.
- They then listen to the sounds in the words.
- Next, they color in the boxes with words that have the 'ar' spelling with the /ar/ sound as in "art."
- Students repeat this in the other columns.
- Unfold the sheet and check that the correct words have been colored in.
- If students require assistance, provide verbal cues or offer examples to help them identify words with this /ar/ sound.

ar as in "art"		'ar' as in "vary"		'ar' as in "warm"	
dart	harsh	wary	caring	warp	wart
army	shark	start	artist	warn	wharf

STEP 2
Application for reading

25 mins

Before reading (3 mins)

- Revisit the vocabulary taught in Step 1 (e.g. "art"). Clearly say the word: /ar/ /t/.
- Then provide a simple definition, for example, "Art is making things like drawings or paintings."
- Ask questions such as "What types of art do you like?"
- Then write the word on the whiteboard and refer back to it throughout the week for reinforcement.

Vocabulary (7 mins)

- Pre-teach the words in the **Vocabulary** list in Book 10: Arty Party (page iv).
- Ensure students understand each word's pronunciation, meaning, and usage.

Application (10 mins)

- The chosen text for this reading activity is Book 10: Arty Party. Briefly introduce the book to spark interest.
- Lead students through a directed reading of Book 10: Arty Party. Encourage students to sound out each word carefully and then blend the sounds together to form the word.
- Provide support by modeling the blending.
- Encourage students to sound out each word and then blend to read.

Reading fluency (10 mins)

- Following the initial reading, revisit Book 10: Arty Party with a focus on fluency.
- Reading the book again allows students to practice their newly acquired skills, this time with an emphasis on reading more smoothly and confidently.
- Create an interactive reading environment by inviting students to take turns reading aloud. Encourage them to point to each word as they read.
- As students read more fluently, support them to read with more expression and prosody, changing their pitch, pace, and emphasis according to the words and punctuation.

STEP 3
Application for spelling

20 mins

Segmenting and spelling (10 mins)

- Invite students to complete the **Spelling: ar** activity (Activities, page 177).
- In this activity, the student reads the text in Book 10: Arty Party.
- They then look for words with 'ar' spellings.
- The student then writes the words in the left column of the table and the page number they found the words on in the right column of the table.
- Focus on the starting point, stroke direction, and completion of each letter to ensure proper handwriting techniques.
- Demonstrating proper letter formation is crucial for developing legible handwriting and building foundational writing skills.

Dictation (10 mins)

- Ask students to complete the **Dictation** activity (Activities, page 183).
- Use the text at the bottom of the activity for dictation.
- Cut and fold along the dotted line before giving it to the students.
- Ask students to write the spelling of each sound on the provided write-on lines.
- Remind the students that some sounds can be spelled by more than one letter.
- A longer line indicates the spelling has more than one letter.
- For students who finish early or need additional practice, create additional activity sheets with your own passages of text and dictate these new passages to them.

Extension

- Ask students to complete the **Chunking two-syllable words with ar spellings** activity for additional spelling practice (Activities, page 179).
- Students split each word into two syllables.
- They then write each syllable in a box.
- Encourage the students to write the whole word while saying the syllables.
- For students who finish early or need additional practice, create additional activity sheets with your own words for them to split into two-syllables.

STEP 4
Comprehension and consolidation

15 mins

Book reading (5 mins)

- Reread Book 10: Arty Party.
- Revisiting the book helps to reinforce familiarity with the text and supports phonetic recognition and comprehension.

Comprehension (5 mins)

- To check students' understanding of the story, conduct a group discussion.
- Ask some comprehension questions, for example, "Why did the characters have to move fast?" and "Why does Ash take notes as the vet team work?"
- Divide the class into small groups and ask each group to answer a question in turn.
- Encourage groups to explain their reasoning.
- Conclude with a brief discussion summarizing the key points of the story and reinforcing vocabulary.

Sequencing (5 mins)

- Assign the **Retell the story** activity (Activities, page 186).
- Cut out the cards for each student.
- Then jumble them up and ask the student to sequence and number them in the correct order of the story.
- The students then retell the story in their own order.
- They then write the story on a separate sheet of paper.

Extension activities

There are a range of activities in the Activities book that can be used for extended learning:

- **Is it true?** (page 181) Students check the sentences for accuracy.
- **Picture the scene** (page 182) Students draw the details of the picture as described in the text.
- **Developing vocabulary** (page 185) Students circle the word or phrase that can be replaced with the word "lurched" ("tipped").
- **Nonfiction: Repairing turtle shells** (page 188) Students draw on the information given in the text to create a flyer.

STEP 5
Tracking progress

- Assign the **Spelling assessment** (Activities, page 190) to quickly evaluate each student's progress.
- Depending on the class's performance, revisit specific activities to address skill gaps or encourage students to play one of the games below.

Extension activities

1 Stepping stones game (Activities, page 187)

- This game is suitable for 1–4 players and requires counters and a die.
- Provide positive feedback and encouragement throughout the game.
- For those needing more support, help them to blend the letter sound or word with assistance.

2 Dice game (Activities, page 189)

- This game is for two players.
- Each player needs a batch of counters of one color.
- The players take turns to throw the die.
- They read a word in the column that corresponds to the number on the die and place their counter on that word or letter.
- The first to have three of their counters in a row in any direction is the winner.

PARALLEL BOOKS

In addition to Book 10: Arty Party, the following books also cover alternative sounds for the spelling /ar/ and can be used for more practice of decoding, for book bags to take home.

Talisman 1

Book 10: The Dark Master

Rescue

Book 10: Dark Times

GLOSSARY

Alphabetic Code The framework that shows how the 44 sounds of English are represented by letters and letter combinations.

Alphabetic Principle A fundamental concept in phonics instruction where written letters or graphemes correspond to specific sounds (phonemes) of a spoken language. These sounds come together to form words, which is crucial for learning to read as it allows students to decode written text into spoken language.

Analytic phonics A method of teaching reading that focuses on breaking the word into parts. This begins with an analysis of the whole word, which is broken into onset and rime, e.g. 'fr' + 'og' for "frog."

Blending The process where students learning to read with explicit systematic phonics are encouraged to sound out letters in words and push the sounds together into words. Each letter is sounded out separately and blended from left to right throughout the word. This is the most reliable strategy to read a new word.

Consonant blend Also called a consonant cluster, these are two or more adjacent consonants in a word that spell two or more separate sounds. For example, in the word "stop," the letters 's' and 't' spell the sounds /s/ and /t/.

Consonant digraph When two letters represent a consonant sound. For example, the letters 's' and 'h' spell the sound /sh/ in the word "ship."

Decodable text Text that students can sound out using phonics they have been taught. Decodable texts encourage students to use blending sounds into words as the first strategy when reading.

Decoding Involves translating symbols or letters into sounds and words.

Encoding The process of translating words and sounds into symbols or letters.

Fluency The ability to read text accurately and quickly, including proper expression, known as prosody.

Grapheme A written representation or spelling of a sound (phoneme) in a word.

High-frequency words Common words with "tricky spellings" that students have not yet learned. Students are encouraged to use their phonic knowledge while the teacher provides the "tricky spelling" until the students can decode these words independently.

Letter A character used for representing sounds in speech.

Morpheme A unit of meaning in a word.

Phoneme The smallest unit of sound in a word. For example, the word "cat" has three phonemes: /k/ /a/ /t/.

Phonemic awareness The ability to identify and manipulate individual sounds in words, which includes blending, segmenting, and manipulating sounds.

Phonics A method of teaching reading and writing that focuses on the relationship between sounds (phonemes) and their spellings (graphemes).

Phonological awareness The ability to break down words into smaller parts, such as syllables (e.g. mag-net), alliteration (e.g. Bobby beetle bounced), onset and rime (e.g. m-at), and phonemic awareness (e.g. m-a-t).

Phonology An area of linguistics that deals with speech sound systems and sound patterns of spoken language.

Schwa A weak vowel sounds in an unstressed syllable, e.g. the word "chicken" becoming "chickin" or "chick'n."

Science of Reading An evidence-based approach to teaching reading that emphasizes phonemic awareness, phonics, fluency, vocabulary, and comprehension.

Segmenting The ability to separate sounds in words. When spelling, students learn to isolate each sound in the word and represent it with a spelling.

Simple View of Reading A model that demonstrates reading as having two basic components: word recognition and language comprehension. This model offers a clear and effective framework for reading instruction.

Sounds-Write® Reading and Spelling Program A structured literacy program focusing on teaching reading and spelling using a systematic and explicit phonics approach.

Syllables Mouthfuls of words, typically containing a vowel sound.

Synthetic Phonics A method of teaching reading where the reader is taught to sound out individual sounds in a word and blend these sounds together to form the word. This method emphasizes the synthesis (blending) of individual sounds into a word. For example, the word "frog" is learned by sounding out each phoneme, /f/ /r/ /o/ /g/, and then blending these sounds to say "frog."

Systematic Synthetic Phonics (SSP) A method that focuses on the systematic instruction of phonics. In this approach, students are taught to sound out graphemes and blend (synthesize) them into words.

Vowel-Consonant-e (VCe) Spelling When the spelling for the vowel sounds /ae/, /ee/, /ie/, /oe/, /oo/, and /ue/ is split by a consonant. For example, /ae/ is represented as a–e in the word "gate."

Vowel team Two or more letters that represent a vowel sound. For example, the letters 'a' and 'i' spell the sound /ae/ in the word "rain."

Word chain A list of words used to develop phonemic awareness skills such as blending, segmenting, and phoneme manipulation. For example: nip—nap—tap—top—mop—map—sap—sip—tip—nip.

Word A distinct meaningful unit of speech or writing.

3-Cueing vs. Decoding Strategies While the 3-cueing approach focuses on using context and visual cues to identify words, the decoding approach emphasizes systematically breaking down words into their phonetic components. The 3-cueing approach is considered a guessing strategy that can lead the reader away from the text, whereas the decoding approach focuses on letter–sound correspondences in words.